ON LATIN ADVERBS

NORTH-HOLLAND LINGUISTIC SERIES

6

Edited by S. C. DIK and J. G. KOOIJ

ON LATIN ADVERBS

H. PINKSTER

Institute of Classical Philology
University of Amsterdam

1972

NORTH-HOLLAND PUBLISHING COMPANY
AMSTERDAM · LONDON

© NORTH-HOLLAND PUBLISHING COMPANY – 1972

Library of Congress Catalog Card Number: 70-189891

ISBN of this series: 0 7204 6180 4
ISBN of this volume: 0 7204 6186 3

Publisher:
NORTH-HOLLAND PUBLISHING COMPANY – AMSTERDAM

PRINTED IN THE NETHERLANDS

To Karri
To my parents

PREFACE

This book was submitted as a doctoral thesis to the Faculty of Arts of the University of Amsterdam under the supervision of Prof. S.C. Dik and Prof. A.D. Leeman. It owes much to the interest and criticism of a number of friends both in the Institute of Classical Philology and in the Institute of General Linguistics.

Prof. Leeman stimulated the work on this thesis by his continuous interest in both my personal and my working circumstances and greatly contributed to style and content.

Prof. Dik left no paragraph unchanged by his merciless criticism and has made it permanently impossible for me to repay to him what he has done for me in this and former studies.

Prof. Ruijgh did not confine himself to advising the Faculty on this book — actually, that would have been rather hard to imagine — but made many pertinent remarks.

Mrs. A.M. Pool-Bolkestein's critical remarks are almost the size of a book themselves. Miss E. Vester and Drs. A. Rijksbaron, too, expressed their scepticism abundantly. They all spent many hours in discussing problematic sections with me. Drs. J. J. L. Smolenaars proved not to be the layman in linguistics he would make me believe he is. Mr. N.S.H. Smith endeavoured to make the language this study is written in at least look like English.

A number of assistants in the Institute of Classical Philology as well as Mrs. A.M. Pool-Bolkestein, Miss E. Vester, Drs. A. Rijksbaron and Drs. J. J. L. Smolenaars helped in reading the proofs and so did my wife. She has for several years bravely endured the fate of being married to someone writing a thesis. More than to anyone I owe her a debt of gratitude and an apology.

H. PINKSTER

CONTENTS

Contents

INTRODUCTION

1. Intention

This study deals with a number of aspects of the words which are usually called adverbs in Latin. It contains on the one hand a critical discussion of their treatment in Latin grammatical studies — the characteristics attributed to them, their relationship to other words — and on the other hand a discussion of the conditions that have to be met in order to achieve a better (sub)classification — general problems of classification as well as criteria for effecting such classification — and a better description of the functions of adverbs in larger constructions. The study contains, therefore, both language-specific sections and more general ones. I have tried to write the passages specifically dealing with Latin in such a way that they are clear enough to the non-Latinist[1], the more general passages in such a way that they are understandable for Latinists who are not acquainted with recent developments in linguistics. I can only hope that I have avoided the risk of being either obscure or trivial to both groups of readers.

2. Survey of the content

The book consists of three parts. The first deals with general problems. The second part (ch. 3-7) contains a discussion of the class of Latin adverbs, the

---

[1] Therefore I have added English translations to the Latin examples. I have used published translations (Loeb library, Shackleton Bailey's translation of Cicero's letters) whenever possible.

1

criteria used to define them and a discussion of a new means of achieving a subclassification. In the third part (ch. 8-11) I deal with the relationship between adverbs and other so-called uninflected words with respect to syntactic behaviour. Clearly, a fourth part might have been added dealing with the syntactic characteristics of adverbs and other constituents (such as ablative case forms of nouns, prepositional phrases, subordinate clauses) which are often called 'adverbial adjuncts', 'adverbials', etc. Such a study would require to be of considerable length and exceed the bounds of a dissertation. It is my intention, however, to devote a separate monograph to this subject.

The general problems dealt with in part one concern the nature of the material we have to work with (ch. 1) and classificatory problems (ch. 2). I will expound the idea that the work of the Latin linguist is seriously hampered by the fact that it has to be based on a closed corpus, which has been selected to a large extent as a result of literary and other not primarily linguistic factors. On the other hand the linguist's work may be facilitated by his knowledge of general linguistic facts.

In ch. 2 I will point out that classification of linguistic items is useful, whatever type of grammar one has in mind, in that it forces the linguist to state explicitly the similarities and differences among these items. They may be classified on the basis of phonological, morphological, syntactic and semantic criteria, which are as a rule not directly interrelated. There is no objection to using criteria of different levels to define particular classes (as has been done for the class of adverbs) nor to the overlapping of classes. The main objection that may be raised against the traditional classification of words into the class of adverbs lies in the fact that too few criteria are given.

Most words that are now considered adverbs in Latin grammar were so considered in ancient Roman grammatical theory as well. I illustrate this by summarizing the chapters on adverbs by Priscian and to a smaller extent Charisius (ch. 3). Both the morphological criterion of 'uninflectedness' and the syntactic one of 'modification' (of a verb) underlie their class of adverbs. As in modern grammars[2] their subclassification is based on semantic considerations.

The main progress in modern grammars is that the relationship between on the one hand adverbs and on the other hand certain adverbs and adjectives is mentioned in the definition of adverbs (invariable words that modify a verb, adjective or adverb). The intuitive nature of the subclassification in

---

[2] 'Modern' as opposed to 'ancient'. They are not necessarily recent.

the grammars is demonstrated with regard to manner adverbs said to be used as intensifiers (*vehementer* − 'vehemently', 'strongly'). I observe next that the definition of adverbs is ambiguous, insufficiently specific and inadequate for describing the characteristics of words which are nonetheless regarded as adverbs (ch. 4).

Two chapters are devoted to the morphological and syntactic criteria mentioned in the definition of adverbs. As to the criterion of uninflectedness (ch. 5), I will show that recent suggestions to describe the relationship between *prudens* ('wise') and *prudenter* ('wisely') as flexional overlook a number of difficulties.

Subsequently the concept of modification will be examined (ch. 6). If modification is equated with 'optionality' − as it is − the definition of adverbs raises no difficulties at the phrase level. However, it is not unproblematic at the clause and sentence levels. Certain adverbs and other constituents likewise functioning as ADJUNCT[3] appear to be obligatory with certain verbs, just as OBJECT and SUBJECT constituents are obligatory with certain verbs. In more general terms this points to differences of degrees of closeness of constituents, with respect to the verb in particular. Once this is realized, it is clear that an adverb cannot be simply defined on the basis of its *modifying* a verb. As far as the structure of sentences is concerned, this new insight into the way constituents seem to be associated with each other should be expressed somehow. It appears, moreover, that there are also problems in recognizing different degrees of closeness of relation to the verb in the case of constituents which are optional with respect to the verb. This is illustrated in detail with regard to the so-called ablativus causae and temporal and local adverbs (or rather ADJUNCT constituents). Within this conception of various degrees of closeness of relationship the so-called modal adverbs (sentence adverbials) find almost satisfactory explanation. Actually, these words may be said to be optional expansions of the whole sentence, or rather the central part of the sentence, which is itself built up of certain peripheral constituents and a nuclear part which comprises the verb and a number of obligatory constituents that depend on the particular verb chosen. Not all adverbs occur at all these levels. This fact should, of course, be mentioned explicitly in their definition.

The discussion about the structure of sentences goes far beyond what is necessary for a description of adverbs alone. I feel fully justified in doing this since any definition of a class of words, whether ancient or modern,

---

[3] See below in section 3.

presupposes explicitly or implicitly a descriptive model. It is, to my mind, useless to discuss a class of words separately from the grammatical framework within which these words find a place.

In ch. 7 I endeavour to show that, given the fact that our study is necessarily corpus-oriented, coordination is the best heuristic means for establishing similarities and differences of linguistic items. Consequently I put forward a theory of coordination which takes into account both formal aspects (syntactic characteristics of words and their syntactic function) and semantic aspects (lexical semantic aspects of words and their semantic role[3]). This theory is subsequently applied to some Latin adverbs. A few instructive cases are discussed.

The third part of this book is devoted to the relationship between adverbs and words which are usually assigned to the classes of interjections, prepositions and conjunctions. If adverbs are regarded as words which may, but need not – in contrast with interjections – occur in one-word sentences, we may conclude as far as the material allows us to, that not only are prepositions and conjunctions excluded from independent occurrence, but that several words regarded as adverbs in traditional grammar have also then to be rejected from the class of adverbs (ch. 8).

As for prepositions (ch. 9), they differ from adverbs in their obligatorily occurring with case forms. The diachronic hypothesis of a development from adverbs to prepositions is probably too simple. It should, at any rate, not be transferred to synchronic analysis, since this creates several difficulties.

A subclass of coordinating conjunctions (e.g. *ergo* – 'so') is often regarded as, or at any rate not clearly distinguished from, adverbs. They appear to be different in a number of syntactic characteristics (ch. 10).

The last chapter deals with adverbs in their relation to subordinating conjunctions. After a discussion of hypotaxis and the role of subordinating conjunctions in this, it is observed that some or all subordinating conjunctions in so-called adverbial clauses could be described as relative adverbs (ch. 11).

3. General framework and terminology

This study is written within a functional framework. In my opinion (cf. Dik 1968; Becker 1967a,b) a grammatical description of the following sentences should at least give four types of information.

(1) pater filium laudat ('the father praises his son').
(2) filius a patre laudatur ('the son is praised by his father').
(3) pater a filio laudatur ('the father is praised by his son').

In (1), *pater* ('father') is a noun (syntactic lexical information), which refers to a human being (is human; semantic lexical information), it is SUBJECT in the sentence (syntactic function) in contradistinction to *filium* ('son'), which shares the first two characteristics, but is OBJECT and in contradistinction to *patre* in (2), which belongs to a prepositional phrase and is syntactically ADJUNCT. Moreover, *pater* in (1) is *AGENT* (semantic role) and is opposed in this respect to *pater* in (3), where *pater* is *PATIENT.*

The information about syntactic function and semantic role will be combined in the following way: SUBJECT$_{AGENT}$. Semantic roles are indicated as subscripts of functions. In the case of ADJUNCT in particular (comparable with the traditional 'adverbial adjunct'), a large number of semantic roles is assumed.

Expressions in accordance with the terminology adopted would be

(1) a constituent function as ADJUNCT$_{MOTIVE}$, or
(2) an ADJUNCT$_{MOTIVE}$ constituent, or
(3) a causal adverb functioning as ADJUNCT$_{MOTIVE}$.

On various occasions, however, I will use a less formal formulation, for the sake of simplicity. I hope that this will not have the opposite effect of confusing the reader.

One of the arguments in favour of the type of description followed in this study is presented by the behaviour of constituents in coordination patterns (cf. 7.3.). I do not believe, as Chomsky (1965: 63-74) does, that the relevant functional information can be described solely in terms of relations between constituents. In fact, constituents may stand in various relations to each other (cf. 7.1.). Nor do I think that one can fully dispense with functional information and restrict oneself to the information on semantic role (as Fillmore 1968 seems to imply). The description of Case (in the usual sense of the term) would be complicated: it is possible to account for Case on the basis of the function of the nominal constituent. The semantic role of the nominal constituent is not instructive for the assignment of Case. Finally, I do not think that one can manage with syntactic functions alone. In fact, it is remarkable that a constituent may have different functions, but remain the same from the semantic point of view, e.g. *pater* and *a patre* in (1) and (2).

As for the term 'adverb', it has been used in different ways and it will be useful to state at the outset what is meant by it. The following uses can be found

(a) Hermes (1968: 99) distinguishes 'Adjektivadverbien' like *longe* ('far'), *propius* ('nearer'), *citius* ('faster'), from 'Adverbien' like *adhuc* ('thus far'), *tamen* ('still'), *procul* ('far'), *nec* ('and not'), *quam* ('than'). This distinction is, given the heterogeneity of the latter class, not very illuminating.

(b) O'Brien (1965: 39) makes a sensible distinction between 'adverbs' and 'adverbials'. By adverbs he understands the derived words ending in *-e, -(i)ter, -ies, -tim, -tus*, by adverbials the non-derived words like *cras* ('tomorrow'), *clam* ('secretly'), *sic* ('so'), *antea* ('before') as well as the supines (p. 100).

(c) G. Lakoff (1968: 5ff.) speaks of instrumental adverbs with reference to expressions as *with a knife* in

(4) Seymour sliced the salami with a knife,

that is, he uses 'adverb' instead of the traditional term 'adverbial adjunct', or, in my own terminology, 'prepositional phrase functioning as ADJUNCT-INSTRUMENT'.

(d) Steinitz (1969: 1) understands by 'Adverbial' what has been called 'adverbial adjunct'. Moreover, words like *trotzdem* are reckoned within this group (p. 12), for which, traditionally, the term 'adverb' is used. Apart from these stand 'sogenannte reine Adverbien' like *oben, unten, rechts.*

With regard to (c) and (d) it should be realized that in transformational grammar 'adverb' is not used for the regular or adjectival adverb, since these are taken as transformationally related to adjectives. For a textbook treatment see Lyons (1968: 326-7).

I will use 'adverb' in the traditional sense, e.g. as it is used by Kühner–Stegmann[4]. For the sake of clarity I will sometimes speak of 'traditional adverb'. By this I understand: 'a word that is traditionally called an adverb'. This does not mean that I accept the traditional nomenclature and classification. My own point of view will become clear, I hope, in the following chapters. In case confusion should arise from my using the word 'adverb', I will clarify my intentions by adding epithets and the like. In order to give an impression of what I call adverbs I have collected a number of examples that will be discussed later in this book. I have indicated the adverbs by using italics. The pages refer to the future discussion.

---

[4] At I, p. 794 they use the term more loosely for 'ADJUNCT constituent'.

(5) *multum* maius (*'much* more important'; p. 14).

(6) *parve* per eos flectitur delphinus ('the dolphin moves *dimly* among them'; ch. 2, n. 17).

(7) prudens homo *prudenter* agit ('the wise man acts *wisely'*; p. 37).

(8) *insignite* improbus (*'remarkably* bad'; p. 50).

(9) hominum concordiae causa *sapienter* popularium ('men who *wisely* favoured popular measures to preserve peace'; p. 52).

(10) amore gloriae *nimis* acri *fortasse* ('a love for honour which is *over*-keen *perhaps'*; p. 58).

(11) homini *illic* nobilissimo ('to a man who was *there* in high esteem'; p. 60).

I use several terms that are probably unfamiliar to some readers. I will mention here only the terms 'phrase level' (cf. p. 3) and 'slot' (cf. 6.2.1.1. init.). I use 'phrase level' in the sense intended by Longacre (1964: 74) for a level between the word and the clause and sentence. Examples are noun phrases (*a sharp knife*). 'Slot' is a common term in tagmemic grammar. A linguistic expression could be seen as a structure of a number of open places occupied by certain constituents, such as words, phrases, clauses, in certain functions. For example, in a sentence a place is reserved for a constitutent which may function as SUBJECT in that sentence. The SUBJECT 'slot' may be 'filled' by a noun, a noun phrase, etc.

Other terms will be explained in the text and are recorded in the index[5].

---

[5] As for a number of typographical indications, by '?' I indicate questionable grammaticalness, by '*' ungrammaticalness. Double colon (::) indicates that another person begins to speak. Syntactic functions are written in capitals (SUBJECT), semantic roles in italicized capitals (*AGENT*). Abbreviations of Latin works are in accordance with the New Oxford Latin Dictionary.

1. GENERAL PROBLEMS OF STUDYING A DEAD LANGUAGE

In this chapter I will discuss a number of problems that are inherent in the study of a dead language. Next, I will expound what consequences these general problems have for the choice of the material. Finally, I will justify the use of linguistic universals in studying Latin adverbs after a brief exposition of the nature of this concept.

1.1. Problems of the use of a closed corpus

Some of the most important problems one has to face when undertaking a syntactic study of some aspect of the Latin language result from the fact that Latin is a dead language. The lack of native speakers as well as the fact that the corpus that has come down to us is almost definitely closed gives rise to certain difficulties, mainly of three types: (i) concerning productivity; (ii) concerning grammaticality; (iii) concerning the adequateness of the corpus as to variety of constructions. These factors are complicated further by the uncertainty of the manuscript tradition.

1.1.1. Productivity
It is impossible to decide which of the utterances we find exemplify productive formation types and which do not. Some of them may agree with rules that were productive in former stages of the language, others with rules that possibly had not yet come fully into use. A decision could be reached by comparing stages of the language — assuming that the construction underlying the problematic utterance is attested in other stages — and by distinguishing different social strata. There is, of course, a large number

of comparative studies, but most of them take the total system insufficiently into account and concentrate on details. The investigation of different social strata is difficult on account of the lack of material and has been carried out mainly from an aprioristic psycholinguistic point of view. Cf. Happ (1967: 64-78) on Hofmann (1963).

Since a division into productive and unproductive constructions is difficult, it is hard to decide which constructions should be described in the grammar and which should be referred to the lexicon as being idioms (De Groot 1956b: 22-4).

The problem of productivity is furthermore connected with the problem of grammaticality, which will be discussed shortly. Should we consider a construction that is not productive (assuming that we can find this out), ungrammatical or not? In case we answer this question in the affirmative, we must assume that language development takes place via ungrammatical expressions. This would be rather unattractive. A notion like 'restricted grammaticality' (i.e. 'a low degree of grammaticalness'[1]) seems necessary. Application of these remarks on productivity to a Latin example can be found below 1.2.

1.1.2. Grammaticality
It is also difficult to decide which of the utterances we find exemplify grammatical expressions, and which do not (Isenberg 1965: 160ff.; Ruwet 1968: 36ff.). Any corpus is bound to contain ungrammatical or less grammatical elements. This problem cannot be solved by extending the corpus, e.g. by taking Caesar in addition to Cicero, since the number of ungrammatical items would be extended as well. Whereas the linguist who is working on a modern language may check his corpus with the aid of informants, this is impossible in the case of a dead language. That is to say, it is not only impossible to check the rules that one sets up on the basis of the data by constructing new expressions to be tested, it is also impossible to decide whether the data on the basis of which the rules are to be set up were correct in Latin. Of course, we have a number of statements by Roman scholars on certain constructions, e.g. Quintilian's remark that *in Alexandriam* ('to Alexandria') is incorrect (*Inst.* 1,5,38), but generally speaking these statements are only of moderate value, especially for a syntactic study. Most Roman grammarians lived in a later period than that in which

---

[1] On the question of degrees of grammaticalness see Chomsky (1957: 16, n. 2; 1965: 148-53). Criticism in Jakobson (1959).

the constructions we are interested in were in use, and they were not particularly interested in syntax. Their greatest value is in their chapters on style. From the very fact that they discuss certain phenomena as stylistic we may conclude that such constructions were peculiar and try to determine why they considered them peculiar. For example, the notion 'zeugma' can be used in the description of coordination in Latin (7.3.1.5.).

The problem of grammaticality is even more serious in Latin because of the way in which the data have been handed down to us, the manuscript tradition. We cannot be sure that what we read has indeed been said or written as it stands — whether it is correct or not. The linguistic study of a dead language, consequently, must be firmly based on textual criticism.

The notion of grammaticality has evoked a lot of criticism since Chomsky (1957: 14) stressed its importance[2]. I will add a few remarks about it. Two notions are closely connected with the notion of grammaticality, viz. acceptability to a native speaker and conformance to a rule of grammar. Now, in my opinion, it should be clear that something can be considered grammatical, not because it is acceptable to a native speaker (an idealized native speaker), but because it apparently fits in with the rules that must be assumed as underlying language usage. Usage is not accidental, but shows systematic patterning. In other words, grammaticality of a construction is a relative notion: grammaticality of one construction implies ungrammaticality of other ones. Only a good survey of the network of constructions warrants a reliable decision about the grammaticality of one construction in this network. It is highly improbable that a native speaker possesses anything resembling such a survey. Moreover, there is reason enough to assume a feed-back from language teaching at school to judgment on grammaticality. Hjelmslev's remark (1935: 76) seems to be fully pertinent to this problem: 'la linguistique de nos jours a pris une forte allure de psychologisme et a institué une idolâtrie de ce sentiment linguistique des sujets parlants qui n'est en réalité que l'effet immédiat de la doctrine traditionaliste'.

Now, what the linguist is doing is setting up a system of rules that describe the utterances he finds and predict others. These rules need not be identical with the rules that have been postulated as underlying language usage, but must be expected to deliver the same results (correct language usage). Indirectly, therefore, something may be called grammatical if it conforms with the rules that are formulated by the linguist. Thus, *pater est bonus* ('father is good') is grammatical (and will probably be accepted),

---

[2] Hill (1961) observes that objective criteria are lacking.

since it is in accordance with the rules regarding Case, Number, Gender, etc., whereas *pater est bono* is not (and is probably unacceptable), because it does not conform to the rule regarding agreement of Case. Judgments of native speakers about grammaticality are, therefore, only useful if they can be shown to be related to the rules of the grammar. 'L'uniformité et la cohérence des jugements portés par un grand nombre de sujets' (Ruwet 1968: 43) in itself is no proof[3].

We have seen by now that if an utterance occurs in a given corpus, it cannot be considered a grammatical expression on that account alone. One might suggest that frequency of occurrence should tip the scale. In my opinion, Chomsky (1957: 15-6; 1965: 195, n. 5) has rightly pointed to the fact that here, too, the crucial question is whether the particular utterance agrees or disagrees with a rule of grammar. Of course, the utterance may be an idiom which stands outside the rules of the grammar, either because it is still unproductive or has become unproductive (see 1.1.1.), or because it is an isolated idiom as such.

More important is the circumstance that frequency of occurrence cannot be used in a negative sense either. The non-existence or low frequency of parallels can never prove that something has not been used (Riemann 1879: 3-4) nor that a particular utterance is incorrect. In not a few Latin studies this seems to have been forgotten, i.e. 'is not attested' is understood as 'is not correct' or even 'was avoided', e.g. on stylistic grounds. On the other hand frequency is often used as a guide for determining the correct reading of a text. Thus Nisbet (ad Cic. *Pis.* 23) reads *luce palam* ('openly in daylight') in conflict with the manuscripts (*luce et palam*), not because the manuscript reading is ungrammatical — which it is not —, but because 'the normal expression is luce palam' (see 7.3.3. below).

These reservations about attestation should not be interpreted to mean that I adhere to the view advanced by R. Lakoff (1968: 2ff.), that attestation is not necessary in order to judge the grammaticality of an utterance. Attested utterances may be seen to form some sort of network from which, with the above reservations, conclusions can be drawn about what is Latin and what not, and which types of construction words may enter into. Of course, every grammar, not only one of a dead language, is in the end based upon an inventory of attested utterances. The same holds when the linguist uses his own judgment in determining whether an utterance in a non-native, specifically a dead language, is grammatical or not.

---
[3] For general observations on acceptability and the use of informants see Quirk–Svartvik (1966).

1.1.3. Adequateness of the corpus

It is not only impossible to establish the grammatical reliability of the corpus, as was concluded in the preceding section, but is is also impossible to ascertain whether all facts which are necessary for the construction of a grammar are taken into account and, of course, the corpus was not intended to provide material for a linguistic study, but constitutes a rather accidental collection.

A considerable part consists of literary texts, which were created under stringent literary conventions. As far as poetic texts are concerned metrical considerations have been at work. For instance, quite a lot of adverbs are excluded on metrical grounds (Priess 1909). Other works are of technical character. Documents of everyday Latin are not long enough to guarantee reliable results. A representative corpus (Harris 1966: 13), if obtainable at all for living languages, can certainly not be obtained for Latin. There are too many extralinguistic factors involved.

1.2. Choice of material

In view of the difficulties mentioned in 1.1. it seemed best to base a classification of adverbs on a body of texts of considerable size, written within a fairly limited period, dealing with a range of subjects as wide as possible, and influenced as little as possible by stylistic considerations, that is to say, prose, not poetry. Consequently I was driven to Cicero, whose work, moreover, has the advantage of showing more linguistic coherence (being more 'one dialect') than would be found in a corpus selected from several different authors.[4] This implies that I do not intend to give a description of the Latin spoken in Cicero's time. On the other hand, differences between educated and everyday language are differences of 'style' only (Robins 1964: 52) and there may be a considerable parallelism between Cicero's Latin and the Latin spoken in everyday use in his time.

Though there are arguments for choosing Cicero's works as a basis, a restriction to these works only would prevent a better insight into several problems. When Cicero's works offered no examples or an insufficient number of examples, whereas good instances could be found in other authors, I have used them. For example, Plautus offers a large number of question—answer patterns. I have consulted Plautus, therefore, when

---

[4] Of course, Cicero's works are shaped by literary principles as well and are highly stylistic.

examining the usefulness of question words as a criterion for classification. However, I have not tried to use data from various authors to give a diachronic survey of a construction. For such a study, in my opinion, the necessary synchronic basis is lacking.

The choice of Cicero has not been dictated by overestimation of his prose. One may well be aware of Cicero's effort to write correct Latin, without denying that his prose yields expressions which otherwise do not occur in so-called classical Latin, or which only occur in the few documents of 'Vulgar Latin'. Too many passages in Cicero, however, are emended because a stylist like Cicero 'could not have written it'. As an instance of such an overestimation of Ciceronian prose and basing a wrong conclusion on low frequency of a construction, take the textual problem which occurs in Cic. *de Orat.* 3,92. Here the manuscripts have *multum maius* ('much more important'). There is no other example of *multum* ('much') used in this way in Cicero. *Multo* is his normal usage (so-called ablativus mensurae). Manutius acoordingly proposed *multo*. This has appeared attractive to many scholars. Szantyr (: 136) remarks that *multum* is hardly acceptable in Cicero. There are few instances in other authors (Plautus, Pliny the Elder, see Szantyr (1.c.) and Thes. VIII, 1618, 19ff.) which are accepted. I would suggest that those who retain *multum* (e.g. Kumaniecki in the Teubner edition) are right. There is reason enough to suppose that *multum* is an adverb (Woelfflin 1885: 99) and not a so-called adverbial accusative, as Szantyr has it. In Cicero's works we find *multum dormire* ('to sleep much'), *multum Athenis esse* ('to be often in Athens'), *multum praestare* ('to excel much'; cf. Lundström 1961: 73-5), *multum bonus* ('very good'), *permultum ante* ('very much before'). In this interpretation *multum* fits in with other constructions of adverb+comparative adjective, e.g. *longe melius* ('far better'). This construction competed with a construction like *multo maius,* i.e. an independent adjective in the ablative case+comparative adjective (so-called ablativus mensurae), but was not yet fully productive (Krebs–Schmalz 1905: II, 33). Parallels with words other than *multum* can be found (Kühner–Stegmann: I, 402). This particular use of *multum* is exceptional, but does agree with a rule of grammar.

1.3.   Universals and related problems

In studying an unknown language the linguist may find support for his analysis in knowledge about other languages known to him, and especially in knowledge of so-called universals of language. This observation, of course, reflects current practice in linguistics. The value of such knowledge is mainly heuristic. The linguist should not be tempted, of course, to project phenomena from one language to another automatically (Jespersen 1933: 46 — 'squinting grammar').

In this study coordination is given special attention, which construction seems to work under similar restrictions in all, or at least in all Indo-European, languages (cf. ch. 7). Several of the criteria for classifying words have been borrowed from or turned out to be used in studies on modern languages. This method seemed not only respectable in itself, but is also advisable on negative grounds: in Latin linguistics, sufficient attention has not been paid to criteria of any kind and the study of syntax has not yet taken the prominent place which it has in modern language studies, especially since the development of transformational generative grammar.

I have used 'knowledge of universals' above in the sense of 'explicit knowledge such as a linguist may obtain about universals'. In a recent study on complementation R. Lakoff (1968) has presented the view that the linguist when working on a foreign language 'does not depend only on the grammar of that language; he also depends on an implicit, inborn knowledge of the nature of language, present in all human beings, a knowledge of what is conceivable in language and what not! ' From this inborn knowledge 'general' or 'universal' grammar derives. The specific grammar of a language, say English or Latin, has to be learned (R. Lakoff 1968: 7-8). A similar argument can be found in Bach (1968: 113). He first remarks that if there were no universals 'it would be a complete mystery how knowledge about one language could throw light on another (as it does)'. This has been argued above. He then proceeds with something similar to R. Lakoff's words: 'the actual rules of the base are the same for every language' and 'In this view it is almost correct to say that language learning by the child consists in finding the transformations which will derive the surface structures of sentences of his language from the universal set of base structures'.

It will be clear that universals of the type I discussed above and those meant (probably) by Bach in the first quotation are different from the kind of universals meant by R. Lakoff and by Bach in his second quotation. In the first interpretation universals are observed facts about natural languages, in the second they are regarded as properties of the human mind (or faculty of speech). In my opinion, Kiparsky (1968: 171) is right in questioning the correspondence between rules formulated by the linguist (among these the universals under my interpretation) and rules which a human being must possess to produce correct utterances. There may be restrictions on concept formation in the human mind which make R. Lakoff's example (1968: 6)

(1) *I devoured for John to do it,

ungrammatical in any language (at least when *devour* is taken literally[5]), but this is an hypothesis which seems to belong to the domain of psychology in the first place; we might, in fact, have to do with a faculty of the human mind to discern sense and nonsense. On 'inborn knowledge of the nature of language' see the criticism by Oller–Sales (1969).

It would seem that a knowledge of universals, as assumed by R. Lakoff, has no heuristic value in studying the structure of a foreign language.

---

[5] Notice the fact that in a figurative sense *devorare* can be constructed with *verba* ('words'). See Thes. s.v. *devorare* 875, 62ff.

2. PROBLEMS OF CLASSIFICATION

In this chapter I will discuss some general problems of classification, viz. the purposes of classification, the types of criteria on which a classification can be based, the relation between these types and, finally, the relative importance of the criteria and the number of criteria required.

2.1. Purposes of classification

Linguistic items can be grouped into classes on account of certain characteristics they have in common. Word classification, such as the classification of adverbs, is a specific instance of this general problem. The purposes of such a classification are to obtain a higher degree of generalization in the description of the specific language the linguist is working on, to make it more adequate since, while classifying, the linguist is forced to state explicitly which items are similar, and in what respects, which items are different, and what is the relation between the various classes to which the items are assigned. The description becomes simpler since identical or similar phenomena can be described together in one statement (Crystal 1967: 25-7; Van Wijk 1967: 235; Schopf 1963: 63). Classification should, of course, be based on a careful analysis of an adequate sample of material (cf. 1.1.).

Once the linguist has reached a satisfactory classification and has thereby left the stage of discovery he may incorporate the classes in the grammar. The way in which this incorporation is effected will be determined by the type of grammar the linguist has in mind. Traditionally the incorporation took the form of a more or less explicit definition[1], like Priscian's adverb

---

[1] Explicit definition does not belong to the stage of discovery. See Robins (1966: 17-9; 1967b: 211-4) contra Bach (1964: 28-9).

definition: 'the adverb is an invariable part of speech that modifies a verb' (cf. ch. 3). One may also indicate the membership of classes in rewriting rules, as was usual in earlier versions of transformational generative grammar (Bach 1964: 27-9). For example,

Adverb → *nunc* ('now'), *heri* ('yesterday'), etc.

The (sub)classes involved may either be closed and then we can enumerate their members, or open, and then we can only characterize them in some way or other[2]. For example, local adverbs (*hic* ('here'), etc.) could be enumerated not only because there are not many of them, but also because in Latin there seems to be no way of adding items to this subclass. On the other hand, the subclass of so-called regular adverbs like *misere* ('miserably'), *feliciter* ('happily') is open, since items may be added any time: the formation of these adverbs is productive.

This study will contain in the first place a discussion of the criteria by which the traditional class of words called adverbs is set up, and of the way this class can be split up into subclasses, and does not aim at a new and complete classification itself.

2.2. Types of criteria

Words have characteristics of four different types and may, consequently, be classified on the basis of four different types of criteria, viz. phonological, morphological, syntactic and semantic criteria.

The familiar word-classes (parts of speech) were set up on the basis of criteria of different types. For example, Priscian's definition of the adverb cited in 2.1. contains a morphological statement ('invariable') and a syntactic one ('modifies a verb'). I will distinguish 'classes of words' and 'word-classes', using 'word-classes' in the traditional sense. I will return to this difference in 2.3. The following sections will be devoted to criteria from the four levels of analysis separately.

---

[2] Gleason (1965: 119) distinguishes between 'list' and 'characterization'. On the distinction 'closed' vs. 'open' see Juilland–Lieb (1968: 53-7). The distinction is not numerical, but qualitative: Pike (1967: 201): 'An open class is one to which new items are known to have been added in recent times, and one to which the linguist may by chance observe a native speaker add new words by borrowing or by direct invention . . .'.

2.2.1. *Phonology*

Phonological criteria, though they may lead the linguist to the assignment of words to phonological classes, are generally considered to be only of moderate use in the establishment of word-classes. Kratochvil (1967: 135-6) mentions stress as a factor in Chinese and Crystal draws attention to an attempt to define some English word-classes by stress as well (1967: 42), but they, too, agree with the unimportance of phonology in this matter. Nor does phonology seem relevant in Latin. Szantyr (: 215) remarks that the preposition is 'tonschwach'[3], in contradistinction to adverbs, with which they are assumed to be related historically, and words of other classes, but this has no overall validity (cf. 3.1.4. on accent in Roman grammatical theory).

2.2.2. *Morphology*

In a morphological classification words might be assigned to various classes depending on whether they are compound or not, etc. It will be clear, that, at least in Indo-European languages, this particular classification would cross-cut almost all traditional word-classes. The main morphological division which suggests itself in Indo-European languages is according to whether words are inflected or not. In fact, this underlies Varro's division of the word-stock of Latin in 'fruitful' and 'barren' words (*L*. 10,14; 8,9-10).

The class of inflected words may then be subdivided according to the syntactic and semantic categories they are inflected for. Varro thus distinguished for Latin four classes: (a) words declined[4] for Case (nominals), e.g. *docilis* ('docile'), (b) words declined for Tense (verbals), e.g. *docet* ('he teaches'), (c) words declined for both (participles), e.g. *docens* ('teaching') and (d) words declined for neither of these categories (adverbs), e.g. *docte* ('wisely').

This classification bears close resemblance to that of Matthews (1967), who divides the Latin lexicon into lexemes, which are characterized for certain so-called morphosyntactic categories, on the one hand, and

---

[3] No enclitics are attached to it.

[4] Varro seems not to have distinguished in his terminology 'inflection' and 'derivation'. Here I take over his term 'declined' as a neutral term. In ch. 5 I will clarify my standpoint with regard to the question of inflection and derivation. I regard Case and Tense as inflectional categories, formation of adverbs as derivational.

particles on the other[5]. I will use both notions in this study. The notion 'lexeme' seems to be particularly useful in the study of inflectional languages.

From antiquity onwards *hortus, horti,* have been described as related forms ('garden'-nominative case and genitive case, respectively). The very use of the term 'case' reflects this idea. A common way of expressing the relationship is saying that *horti* is the genitive *form* of the *word hortus.* The nominative case form has often been considered the basic form of the word: 'casus rectus' (Szantyr: 22), or — in a different framework — as the unmarked case form par excellence, e.g. by De Groot (1948: 462; 1956a: 189)[6].

However, in any sensible definition of 'word' (e.g. Reichling 1969: 33) *hortus, horti,* etc. have to be taken as different words. Still, there must be some way to express the relation between them in spite of their clear morphological and syntactic differences. This is achieved by saying that *hortus* and *horti* are forms of the same abstract lexical entity, which can be called lexeme. In some cases the lexeme can partially be located, so to speak, in some aspect of the forms (e.g. *hort-*), in other cases it cannot be so easily located in this way (e.g. in the case of *iter* and *itineris:* 'route' nom. and gen., respectively). Considering different words as related in this way to the same lexeme is always attractive from the semantic point of view. Moreover, the different forms can be shown to be correlated with the function of the lexeme in the larger construction. For example, if it occurs as SUBJECT in a sentence with a finite verb, the nominative case form (*hortus*) of the lexeme is necessary, if it functions as ATTRIBUTE with respect to another noun the genetive case form (*horti*) is obligatory. The lexeme can be arbitrarily symbolized by the italicized words in capitals (*HORTUS*). Instead of saying that *hortus* and *horti* are forms of the lexeme *HORTUS,* which is inflected for the morphosyntactic categories Number and Case in accordance with its function in the construction, one can also say that *hortus* and *horti* are 'members' of the paradigm of *HORTUS.* Finally, *HORTUS* can be viewed as the abstract symbolisation of the sum of forms *hortus, horti,* etc.

Similarly, *laudo, laudas* ('I praise, you praise'), etc. can be said to be

---

[5] Matthews, too, considers adverbs as inflected forms. I do not agree with him, but pass over this problem here. The term 'particle' is used in a rather vague way in traditional grammar. See ch. 8, no. 2.

[6] Cf. also Greenberg (1966: 95), Hjelmslev (1935: 99-100). Criticism in Fillmore (1968: 6).

forms of the lexeme *LAUDO,* that is inflected for the *morphosemantic* categories Tense, Mood, Person, Voice[7].

Since the differences between the forms of the lexemes are correlated with the syntactic and semantic function the words perform in larger units, a classification of this type is useful, since it is relevant not only to morphology, but also to syntax. Morphosyntactic categories can help to define syntactic classes as well[8], even though there are exceptions. E.g. *nequam* ('bad') must be described as the only member of the paradigm of the lexeme *NEQUAM,* if morphosyntactic categories (Number, Case, Gender) are used in defining the class of adjectives. Of course, the so-called invariable words (particles) can, by their very nature, not be dealt with in this way. These words do not belong to a paradigm, the members of which are chosen in relation to the function in the construction. To assign them to syntactic classes demands purely syntactic techniques. Syntactic analysis was not the strongest aspect of ancient grammatical theory. It is not surprising, therefore, that the traditional definitions of inflectional categories such as noun and verb are much more useful than those of invariables such as adverbs and conjunctions. Cf. Matthews (1967: 165).

It will be clear, however, that a debate may always arise about whether a particular word or a particular paradigm should be considered member of a (larger) paradigm.

I referred to one member paradigms above with respect to *nequam.* Another problem concerns the fact that it is not easy to see how one can decide how many morphosyntactic or morphosemantic categories are necessary. For example why shouldn't we distinguish a morphosyntactic category 'Adverbial' and say that lexemes like *MISER* and *FELIX* ('miserable', 'happy') are inflected for Adverbial on the one hand, for Adnominal on the other, the latter category covering Number, Case and Gender, instead of saying that there is a derivational relation between the particles *misere* and *feliciter* on the one hand and adjectival lexemes *MISER* and *FELIX* on the other? Evidently, a decision can be made only within

---

[7] See Matthews (1965) for a description of Latin verb forms. On 'lexeme' see also Lyons (1968: 197-8) and Matthews (1970: 107-13). I use the term 'morphosemantic' on purpose. As yet, I do not believe in such a thing as 'meaning' of a case (it is a morphological marker of syntactic relations), but I recognize several semantic values in the verb forms (apart from syntactic values).

[8] Hockett (1958: 221) seems to draw a borderline between inflection and syntax, judging from his definition: 'A part of speech is a form-class of stems which show similar behaviour in inflection, in syntax, or both'.

the total framework of the description. I come back to this particular problem later (ch. 5).

2.2.3. *Syntax*

Whereas a morphological classification of words proceeds from a study of the internal structure of words, a syntactic classification is achieved by classifying words in accordance with their syntactic valence, i.e. their ability to enter into certain relations with other words.

Since a word A can be assigned to a certain class on the basis of its relation to one or more other words, e.g. B, which in turn must be assigned to a certain class precisely because of its relation to A (among other words), the establishment of classes is always circular. There is no objection to this circularity and, consequently, there is no reason to follow Kratochvil (1967: 148-9), who thinks that the syntactic classification of words by examining their functional abilities and combinatory qualities 'presupposes that it is known or that it is possible to find out in other ways than through the word-classes themselves what are the functions which words are said to be able to fulfil'. Evidently, there is no such possibility. Function is a relational notion (Chomsky 1965: 68-74; Dik 1968: 154-9)[9], and what functions are needed in the description of language in general or a particular language has to be decided on the basis of the total description (and, of course, the particular type of grammar). Functions have no independent existence nor, for that matter, have categories. Compare also Crystal (1967: 26): 'defining X by Y and Y by X is from the viewpoint of descriptive grammar quite permissible'. For example, *BONUS* ('good') is an adjective since it may have the function ATTRIBUTE with a noun, e.g. *VIR* ('man'), but not with a personal pronoun, e.g. *EGO* ('I'). On the other hand *VIR* is a noun since it may function as HEAD with respect to the adjective *BONUS* and differs from the pronoun *EGO,* which may not fulfil that function. The reason for postulating these functions and distinguishing them from other functions is again that they explain the behaviour of members of these classes as opposed to the behaviour of members of other classes in this particular construction.

The syntactic valence of a word can be determined in three interdependent ways: (a) by observing the constituency of the utterances in which it appears; (b) by omitting it, replacing it and effecting other changes in the

---

[9] Cf. Hjelmslev (1935: 48): 'Les deux ordres de concept se superposent et se traduisent mutuellement'.

expression and checking the results; or (c) by considering whether the word can occur in certain substitution frames (on these see Garvin 1958: 60; Crystal 1967: 43-4; and Wheatley 1970: 48-54).

The former two, especially, are relevant to the assignment of words to classes when the linguist proceeds from a definite corpus. Following Carvelland–Svartvik (1969: 42-3) criteria belonging to these types may be called 'constituent criteria' and 'transformational criteria', respectively. Examples of transformational criteria are: (1) Question. Which question word (if any) should be asked to get this particular utterance as an answer with this particular word? E.g., *Romae habitat* ('he lives in Rome') would be the answer to a question *ubi habitat?* ('where does he live?'). (2) Coordination, viz. which words could be coordinated with this particular word? (3) Permutation. Could word A and word B be interchanged? (4) Omission. If this particular word is left out, would the expression still be 'viable'? (see Garvin 1958: 60, with his reservations about the term 'viable', and 6.1.1. end, below).

These methods presuppose, of course, the presence of one or more informants to answer the questions and therefore the transformational type seems to be inappropriate to the study of dead languages – except insofar as our own judgment on grammaticality in such languages can be relied on (for this problem, see Pinkster 1971: 385). The first type (constituent criteria), however, can be used in a transformational sense, if we compare the constituency of particular utterances. Thus, finding a sentence *Romae habitat,* we cannot ask someone which question word would be appropriate here, but we can look and see whether we find a reliable example of *Romae (habitat)* in answer to a question *ubi habitat?* Or, more generally, whether there is in such answers an example of a word which, tentatively, seems to belong to the same class as *Romae.* This means that syntactic classification of words in a dead language need not be different from classification in modern languages, but will be much more difficult, since attestation is necessary (cf. 1.1.2.). In Latin grammars only the first transformational criterion (question word) is used to distinguish subclasses within the class of adverbs (see below 4.2.).

2.2.4. *Semantics*
A semantic classification can be conceived of in two ways. Most usual is the setting up of categories based on features like 'quality', 'state', etc. Mostly the assignment of a word to such categories on account of its semantic aspect takes place on intuitive grounds, as might be expected in the present

state of semantics. Of course, this is not to say that such a classification is useless. These categories cross-cut the traditional word-classes (see the end of this section).

Another type of semantic classification is the one originated by Reichling. In this theory the vague notion 'meaning' is replaced by the cover term 'semantic aspect'. Several types of semantic aspect are distinguished: (independent) 'meaning', e.g. of words like *cow*; 'semantic value', e.g. of elements like *-s* in *cows;* 'deixis' of words like *this* (Reichling 1969: 42-9; Dik 1968: 251-8). A classification of words according to their type of semantic aspect might cross-cut the traditional word-classes.

As for the first type of semantic classification, most linguists are very sceptical about the possibility of classifying words into word-classes on account of their semantic aspect (e.g. Gleason 1965: 116; V. Wijk 1967: 244; and Kratochvil 1967: 151), i.e. into the same classes that would also be set up on the basis of other (e.g. syntactic) criteria. They doubt whether it is possible to assign a word to a certain class, say adjectives, on account of its semantic aspect, nor do they believe that it is possible to say what categorial semantic aspect members of a certain class (say adjectives) have in common. It will be clear that those, who, in accordance with the second alternative formulation, assume a categorial semantic aspect for each word-class (whether these are similar to the traditional parts of speech or not) ought to be able to assign words to these classes on the basis of their semantic aspect (first alternative formulation). As far as I know nobody has been able to do this.

As an example of the belief in a categorial semantic aspect I cite the following passage from Bally (1965: 113): 'Les catégories lexicales comprennent . . . les sémantèmes virtuels désignant des substances, des qualités, des procès et des modalités de la qualité et de l'action', substantives, adjectives, verbs and adverbs respectively. Similar remarks can be found in Latin grammars, e.g. Kühner–Holzweissig (1912: 253); Ernout–Thomas (1959: 1). If we assume for the sake of the argument that 'quality' is a well-defined notion, we may agree that e.g. *alba* indicates the quality of *domus* in *domus alba* ('white house'). However, the semantic notion quality seems pertinent to *albitudo* ('whiteness') and *albere* ('to be white') as well, which are traditionally called substantive and verb, respectively. That is, the semantic notion 'quality' cannot be taken as characteristic of one (primarily syntactic) class, but is shared by members of several classes. A similar remark can be made about the distinction, clear at first sight, of a class of numerals with a categorial semantic aspect 'number'. In fact, this class comprises words of varying syntactic, morphological and even semantic characteristics (Robins 1966: 17; cf. 2.3.2.). The semantic definitions of adjective and adverb especially, such as those of Bally above, prove, as Hjelmslev (1939: 143) rightly observes, that 'la catégorie est établie par la rection non par la signification; . . . il y a d'autres mots que l'adjectif et l'adverbe qui indiquent la qualité. Si par conséquent on prétend définir une catégorie par la signification, on le fait en assignant une étiquette sémantique à une catégorie établie d'abord par des critériums fonctionnels'.

Those who adhere, like Bally, to the hypothesis of a categorial semantic aspect of word-classes usually assume — implicitly or not — that there is a correspondence between formally distinguished classes and semantic classes. An exponent of this view is De Groot, whose opinion I will discuss in 2.3.2.

2.3.   Classes of words, word-classes and parts of speech

In the beginning of 2.2. I, briefly, drew attention to the difference between 'classes of words' and 'word-classes'. Next, I isolated the levels on which statements about words can be made and accepted the possibility of classification on all levels. On the other hand I have used word-class in the traditional sense ('part of speech') as a class of words which share a number of characteristics belonging to different levels, e.g. the class of adjectives said to be inflected for Case, Number and Gender, to partake in the derivational category 'Degrees of comparison' — two morphological state- ments —, to modify a noun: syntactic statement, and to denote quality (of the noun): semantic statement. I have on several occasions discussed the use of characteristics of a certain level to define words which had been assigned — or at least were believed to belong to — classes established by reason of characteristics which pertain to one or more other levels. In this section I will concentrate on this matter in more detail. The questions to be answered are: (1) is it feasible to define a class by characteristics belonging to different levels and which level should be most important in this respect? ; (2) are there correspondences between classes that are established indepen- dently at different levels and, if so, of what type are they?

2.3.1.   Multi-level-classification and rank of levels
Paul (1920: 352-5) observes that the traditional distinction into parts of speech is insufficient, but that this is inevitable when various criteria from such different levels ('so verschiedenartige Rücksichten') are used. I think that this statement is only correct as long as one feels oneself obliged always

to use criteria from all four levels, in order to assign words to a class. However, one should make only those generalizations which it is useful to make. If then 'the application of all four criteria will result in chaos', as Van Wijk (1967: 247) foresees, this will be a practical problem, which does not follow from the application of criteria from more than one level as such. Another consequence of the application of criteria from more than one level will be that the number of criteria and thereby the number of classes and subclasses grows.

As such, there is no objection to classifying words by all types of criteria. There is only an objection if one limits one's objectives, e.g. to writing a syntax instead of a complete grammar[10]. Another argument for allowing for criteria from more levels is that the levels are not completely independent from each other: a characteristic at one level may always accompany or be connected with a characteristic from another level and thus be predictable. An example of this type might be: 'Latin colour adjectives (semantic subclass) cannot be coordinated with 'normal' adjectives, e.g. *bonus* ('good') (syntactic characteristic). Adverbs are not derived from them (morphological characteristic)[11].

Once criteria from more than one level are accepted the question arises as to which level has the most important criteria for the total description of a language. I agree with those linguists who consider syntactic characteristics most important (e.g. Crystal 1967: 43; Robins 1959: 122-4; Van Wijk 1967: 250). As the latter author observes, words may lack morphological structure, but they do have syntactic valence. Even in an inflectional language like Latin invariable words exist within what are, generally speaking, inflectional classes, e.g. the adjective *nequam* ('bad'), which can be assigned to the class of adjectives only on account of its syntactic valence.

The primacy of morphological criteria for classification has been supported by De Groot and Blatt, for different reasons. De Groot (1948: 445)[12] – on whose definition of word-class cf. 2.3.2. – holds that a classification of words ought to start with morphology since words with the same stem-meaning have different syntactic valences, e.g. *pater* ('father'-nominative), *patris* ('father'-genitive). This objection can be met, of course, by taking account of the notions of lexeme and paradigm. It is true that

---

[10] Fries' objection to using more types of criteria may be due to the limited (syntactic) scope of his study (1957: 67). Cf. Schopf (1963: 64-5).

[11] As far as I can judge this statement may even be correct. At least I find no counterexamples. (I take Plin. *Paneg.* 48,1 *albi et attoniti* ('pale and astonished') as a non-literal use of the colour adjective.) On these adverbs see Löfstedt (1967: 80-1).

[12] De Groot (1964) pays more attention to syntax.

pater has a different distribution from *patris,* if one concentrates on the words as such. If, however, one views these words as forms of the same lexeme (2.2.), one may explain the difference between the actual forms by saying that the forms are determined by the function that the lexeme *PATER* fulfils in the construction in accordance with its syntactic valence. The distribution of *pater* and *patris* is part of the total distribution of the lexeme *PATER.*

The reverse problem seems to be more difficult: if stem and stem-meaning must be the basis of classification of words, *amare* ('to love') and *amator* ('lover') might well be assigned to the same class. But it is not very useful to consider these words to be different forms of the same lexeme, as it is of more explanatory value to say that there is a derivational relation between them, which could be accounted for by saying that the lexeme *AMATOR* is a secondary lexeme derived from the (primary) lexeme *AMARE.* Each of these two lexemes has its own syntactic valence.

Blatt (1952: 27) in his excellent chapter on the parts of speech remarks that it is preferable to base the classification of words on morphology and only then examine the syntactic uses of the classes thus determined. 'Nous éviterons ainsi le cercle vicieux inhérent fatalement au procédé inverse, qui consiste à déterminer d'abord une classe d'après un principe syntaxique et ensuite à en étudier les emplois'. Blatt, regrettably, gives no elucidation of his remark. The type of circularity he is afraid of, if I understand him correctly, is in itself no objection since one should distinguish the stage of discovery from the stage of writing a syntax (cf. also 2.2.3. init.). The criteria which induce a linguist to establish certain syntactic classes are among those that will be given in a syntax as the syntactic properties of the envisaged classes (cf. 2.1.). Of course, what is at stake here is the type of syntax: most ancient and modern grammars concentrate more on the properties of the constituents in a construction in relation to the general properties of the class to which they belong (paradigmatic) than on the properties of the construction and the role of the constituents therein (syntagmatic). Blatt, too, is unable to maintain his principle throughout. The invariables are to be assigned to several word-classes (1952: 33): 'ces classes sont pareillement soumises à des critères purement linguistiques'. These criteria, not unexpectedly, appear to be syntactic, in fact, e.g. in the case of prepositions, the fact of their governing certain case forms.

2.3.2. *Correspondence of levels*

Most modern linguists agree that a one-to-one correspondence between the above mentioned levels of description is exceptional and can as a rule not be expected. For the assumption that such a correspondence must generally be expected Bazell (1952) coined the term 'correspondence fallacy'.

Examples of partial correspondences are well-known. I give two of them. (a) Adjectives of material, e.g. *ligneus* ('wooden') have no corresponding derived adverb (Löfstedt 1967: 80-1). (b) Verbs with a 'punctual' semantic aspect (punctual 'mode of action' or 'Aktionsart') are not constructed with constituents expressing temporal duration (cf. 6.1.2.2. below):

(1)   *I found the book for two hours.

It seems reasonable to postulate that the semantic aspect is responsible for these partial correspondences. Observations of the latter kind are also at the back of the notion 'meaning-class' in R. Lakoff (1968: 165): 'We define a meaning-class in terms of both syntax and semantics, as a set of semantic markers that can function in syntactic rules'. See also on 'congruence in grammatical and semantic classification', Lyons (1968: 166-9).

Several scholars, however, like Jensen (1949: 155) and De Groot (1948; 1964) assume that a complete correspondence between levels is normal. As I said above (2.2.4.), this idea lies also, tacitly, behind the assumption of something like a categorial semantic aspect or 'class-meaning' (Bloomfield 1935: 202-5; 247-51). I will discuss De Groot's opinion in more detail since he applied his view to Latin in his 1948 article.

De Groot's position is reflected in his definition of word-class (1948: 447-8): 'By *word-class* we understand a collection of words of a given language which have a certain categorial element or feature of meaning of their stem in common, in so far as the existence of this common element appears not solely from the investigation of the meaning, but also from the morphological valence of the stem or (and) the syntactic valence of the word'[13], that is, the occurrence of the stem in certain morphological structures and of the word (formed on the stem) in certain syntactic structures. There is an (indirect) relation between syntax and morphology (and even phonology; 1964: 258) in as far as all three are determined by the meaning of the stem.

De Groot bases his view on word-classes on a number of considerations

---

[13] Hockett's remark (1958: 221): 'The part of speech of a word is that of its stem' bears some resemblance to this in its concentration on the stem. This calls forth certain difficulties. See 2.3.1.

(1964: 257-9). The relation between semantics and syntax[14] appears from the valence of e.g. numerals[15]. The relation between semantics and morphology appears inter alia from the fact that verbs can be derived only from certain stems, e.g. *albus* ('white'), *albescere* ('to become white'). The relation between semantics and phonology stands out inter alia with the interjections. Therefore, in De Groot's opinion, it seems a reasonable theory to assume that words of a given language belong to word-classes which are opposed to each other by their categorial semantic aspect. De Groot is well aware that his thesis is, in fact, a postulate and that in practice it will be hard to substantiate the postulate 'that in a given language all words of a certain stem valence class really have a semantic aspect in common', (1964: 259; my translation). Yet, in De Groot's opinion, this should not worry us. It is clear that there exists a categorial difference e.g. between verbs and numerals, though this difference is hard to define. If we want to define it, we may say that the meaning of the category of verbs is 'process', of numerals 'number', while intending these notions in a 'linguistic sense', a concept that remains undefined[16]. 'The terminology only presupposes *that* the verb in the given language really, as such, means something that is especially inherent to the meaning of the verb in this language' (1948: 473). In other words, the postulate is defended by saying that it is a postulate. The postulate itself rests upon observations which are the most obvious that could be cited in this connection. The summary of De Groot's argument shows that his approach is open to the criticism by Hjelmslev quoted in 2.2.4.

The concentration on stem and stem-meaning has the effect of making syntactic differences less important. Thus, *tres* ('three'), *tertius* ('third'), *ter* ('three times') and *terni* ('three each') are assigned to one class alongside *multus* ('much', 'many'), since all undoubtedly have something to do with number (1948: 448-9; 495; 1964: 257). Since De Groot argues from stem and stem-meaning it is not surprising that he holds (1948: 451; 479-80) that 'Adjectives and adverbs, however different their syntactic valence may be,

---

[14] Cf. De Groot (1948: 445): 'equality of syntactic valence as a rule can only be explained from equality – in some respect – of meaning'.

[15] Of course, numerals are not just a collection of ordinary adjectives, adverbs, etc., as might be suggested by the following words from Robins (1966: 17, n. 57): 'the separate chapters on the numerals are merely a pedagogical rearrangement of certain members of the noun, adjective, and adverb classes'. Syntactically there are distinctions from 'normal' adjectives, etc. Compare the example *extremely five houses* in Gleason (1965: 126-7).

[16] Perhaps meant in contrast with what De Groot calls 'ontological' definitions (1948: 429). On these briefly 2.5. below.

are not different word-classes in Latin. They are morphological categories, for which mostly the same stem is used: *longus, longe* ('long' adjective and adverb, respectively). In connection with a particular meaning a stem is sometimes only used for an adjective' — *magnus* ('big'), *parvus* ('small') — 'or only for an adverb' — *tunc* ('then'), *saepe* ('often')[17]. As we see, the general properties of the adjective (that is, in De Groot's terminology, presence of — meaningless — 'syntagmemes' for Gender, Number and Case; derivation of an adverb by a — meaningful — morpheme) are explained on the basis of the categorial semantic aspect of the adjective, which is not given, but only postulated because of these properties. Exceptions, on the other hand, are explained by reference to the specific semantic aspect of the stem, with, however, no further indication of in what respect this semantic aspect is specific so as to exclude for example formation of an adverb. Obviously, in this form this explanation is a postulate just as well, and dependent on the first one at that[18].

De Groot's theory has been applied to Latin adverbs by Bos (1967). The same arbitrariness in postulating a categorial and specific semantic aspect can be found there. Thus, the fact that *bene* ('well') and other so-called adjectival adverbs modify adjectives has to be attributed, according to Bos (1967: 117), to a specific semantic aspect of 'intensity' (cf. 4.2. end, below).

2.4.   Rank and number of criteria. Overlapping classes

If one were to extend the number of criteria ad infinitum, one would ultimately obtain classes with only one member. Logically, there is, of course, no objection to this, but the purposes of classification would not be realized in this way. This implies that somewhere a boundary must be drawn

---

[17] I have taken the examples from p. 480 and added translations of the Latin words. By the way, *parve* occurs rarely: Vitr. 9.4.5. *parve per eos flectitur delphinus* ('the dolphin moves dimly among them').

[18] De Groot did not regard all traditional adverbs as adverbs. For example, *etiam* ('also'), *quoque* ('too'), *fortasse* ('perhaps'), *certe* ('certainly'), *non* ('not') are called 'determining particles, which may determine all kinds of words'. Nonetheless he considers his remarks about the relation between adverbs and adjectives valid for a variety of adverbs, which have different morphological, syntactic and, intuitively, semantic characteristics. Though he has continued in his belief in a categorial semantic aspect, his position with respect to adverbs seems to have changed (1964: 260): 'Thus, under the term 'adverb', various words are grouped together which do not share either valence or meaning' (my translation). In this connection he refers to Roose (1964).

between categorial and individual properties. The latter will be referred to the lexicon. It is not only problematic how far classification should be extended, but also which criterion should be so to say the first. For example, we might extend the analysis by taking modification by 'adverbs of degree' such as *valde* ('very much') as a final criterion for defining adjectives. In that case numerals cannot be said to be adjectives (cf. note 15). On the other hand we might set up in English a separate class of words like *run*, as e.g. Wheatley (1970: 52) thinks feasible (he calls them 'nerbs'). Usually two words *run* are distinguished, one belonging to the class of nouns, the other to the class of verbs. In practice a separate class of 'nerbs' would hardly be useful (Gleason 1965: 124), since we need the two other classes anyway and since the difference noun vs. verb seems of more importance than the fact that some words (or word-forms) belong to both classes.

The question arises, therefore, which criteria are to be considered relevant and which not. We need 'some way of ranking the criteria' (Crystal 1967: 41). One type of ranking would be the assignment of a certain order to criteria from the four levels, as has been discussed in 2.3.1. Leaving levels out of account, choice of criteria can be made on the basis of two considerations: (1) those criteria are most important which apply to most cases (Crystal 1967: 45); (2) those criteria are most important which have most systematic impact, i.e. can be shown to be connected with and predict other phenomena. For example, inflection of the nominals is more important than the fact that diminutives can be derived from them, since inflection is connected with the syntactic characteristics of the nominals (cf. Carvelland–Svartvik 1969: 37-8)[19].

Since the assignment of a word to a certain class is determined by its sharing certain characteristics with other words and since a class may be seen as the 'extension' of a certain number of certain characteristics (Hempel 1965: 139), it is possible that words can be assigned to one class on the basis of some characteristics, to one or more other classes on the basis of other characteristics. There is no objection to this since the *criteria* on the basis of which the words are assigned to more than one class do not overlap. This implies that Bloomfield's remark (1935: 196) that 'However, it is impossible to set up a fully consistent scheme of parts of speech, because the word-classes overlap and cross each other' is incorrect:

---

[19] Van Wijk (1967: 224) observes that 'there seems . . . to be no syntactic principle on which the choice of criteria can be based', but could one expect a *syntactic* principle for ranking syntactic criteria?

consistency of classification and overlapping classes do not exclude each other.

As an example one might think of the class of Latin words like *intra* ('inside') which share characteristics with prepositions on the one hand (governing case forms), with certain adverbs, e.g. *intus* ('inside'), on the other (cf. ch. 9). An example given by Van Wijk (1967: 260) is the infinitive which can be assigned to the class of verbs on some grounds, to the category of nominals on others. Crystal cites as an example adverb and adjective in English.[20]

2.5.   Ontological, psychological and notional definition of word-class

I have not entered into a discussion of a number of studies in which the authors endeavour to establish the categories of things in extralinguistic reality of which the word-classes are supposed to be the linguistic counterparts — 'ontological' in De Groot's terminology (1948: 429). In these studies, e.g. in Otto (1928) notions like 'Dingwort' frequently occur. Nor have I discussed studies in which it is held that word-classes reflect the categorial knowledge the speaker has of the world ('psychological'), e.g. Slotty (1929a, b), with reference to psychological investigation[21]. These studies are quite speculative and have no practical value for writing a grammar or for the classification of linguistic elements. Lyons (1966) shows some points of resemblance to these studies.

2.6.   Conclusion

Words can be assigned to word-classes on the basis of certain criteria. Conversely no class should comprise words which are not in accordance

---

[20] The difference between infinitives and words like *run,* words like *intra* and adverbs and adjectives (in English) is that the infinitive has both the properties of a verb and of a nominal at the same time. For example, in *hoc ipsum nihil agere* (lit.: 'this very doing nothing'; Cic. *de Orat.* 2,24), *agere* governs a noun phrase as its OBJECT (*nihil*) and is modified by a pronoun as its ATTRIBUTE (*hoc*). (More examples in Kühner–Stegmann: I, 666.) With a word like English *run,* Latin *intra,* it is a matter of either–or. We can distinguish two homophones *run* and *intra,* but no homophones *agere.* This fact suggests, of course, that the infinitive should be assigned to an intermediate category of its own.
[21] See also in the bibliography Brinkmann (1950), Hempel (1954), Hermann (1928), Sandmann (1939).

with these criteria. In this respect the traditional parts of speech, especially the class of adverbs, need revision. The criteria by which word-classes are defined may belong to all four linguistic levels. These levels do not show, as a rule, a one-to-one correspondence. There is no objection to assigning a word to more than one class if it has more than one group of characteristics. Most important in the total description of a language is a classification in accordance with syntactic characteristics. A classification of words on the basis of their semantic aspect is difficult. The determination of the semantic aspect of a class which has been defined by other, not semantic, criteria seems a hopeless task. Therefore, it seems not necessary to revise the traditional efforts to find such categorial semantic aspects.

What is most striking in the traditional class of adverbs is the (1) absence of formulation of criteria; (2) absence of syntactic criteria; (3) assignment of words to classes on semantic grounds, though a procedure of semantic classification is absent.

These points will become clear, I hope, in the following chapters.

3. ADVERBS IN ROMAN GRAMMATICAL THEORY

This chapter will be devoted to what Roman grammarians have said about the adverb. It is not my intention to present an exhaustive discussion of the different opinions held by each grammarian, of their sources or mutual relations. Those who are interested may consult Jeep (1893: 268-82). I will give only what seems to be relevant to the modern view on adverbs and confine myself almost entirely to Priscian's *Institutiones grammaticae* and to Charisius' *Ars grammatica*[1].

The definition of the adverb given in most modern handbooks is based to a large extent on what Priscian, Charisius and others have said about it. In their turn, they were heavily indebted to their Greek predecessors. In fact, the very term 'adverbium' is a translation of Greek epirrhema[2]. For the

---

[1] Latin grammarians are cited after the edition supervised by Keil, Charisius also after the edition by Barwick, henceforth abbreviated K. and B., respectively. If no further references are given 'Priscian' means 'Priscian in his *Institutiones*'.

[2] When the Roman grammarians translated the Greek term by *adverbium,* they apparently interpreted 'epirrhema' in a neutral sense: 'what is placed with the verb'. It is possible, however, that epirrhema was interpreted in a more specific sense by some Greeks at least: 'what follows the verb'. Prof. Ruijgh suggested this to me, when we were discussing Apollonius Dyscolus' definition of epirrhema and especially the precise meaning of ἐπιλεγόμενον in this definition, which runs: ἐπίρρημά ἐστι μέρος λόγου ἄκλιτον κατὰ ῥήματος λεγόμενον ἢ ἐπιλεγόμενον ῥήματι (p. 72, ed. Uhlig). Robins' translation (1967a: 33-4; 'part of speech without inflection, in modification of or in addition to a verb') reflects the neutral interpretation of the prefix ἐπι-. Perhaps ἐπιλεγόμενον ῥήματι, a kind of gloss to explain ἐπι- in ἐπίρρημα, should be translated 'following a verb'. That a more specific interpretation along these lines was current among Greek scholars appears from the following remark of the scholiast on Dionysius Thrax (p. 271, ed. Hilgard): εἰ δὲ καὶ προτάττεται καὶ ὑποτάσσεται, πῶς ἀπὸ μιᾶς συντάξεως μόνον ὠνομάσθη; ('If it (the adverb) is both prepositive and postpositive, how could it have been called after one construction only? ').

chapter of Priscian, which I take here as a base, one may readily find almost verbatim parallels in e.g. Apollonius Dyscolus[3]. However, I will neglect these.

Priscian and others endeavour to distinguish between the 'parts of speech' by giving the semantic aspects of each class (Priscian 2,4,17: 'proprietates significationum'), following Apollonius (Robins 1951: 64-5; 1967a: 57), but, in fact, most definitions are mixed (Schopf 1963: 64). They contain information about syntax, semantics and morphology, and we find stray remarks about accent as well. I will now first discuss the definitions and dispersed general observations under these headings, next discuss a few specific subclasses and individual adverbs and, finally, add a remark about the primary importance of word-classes in Roman grammar.

3.1.   General properties of adverbs

3.1.1.   Syntax
The adverb is placed with a verb (Prisc. 2,4,20), 'more suitably' (aptius) before it, just as adjectives are placed before substantives (15,6,39; 16,3,16)[4]. Adverbs may be postponed, Priscian observes, with the exception of all monosyllables such as *non* ('not'), *ne* ('that not'), *dum* ('while'), temporal *cum* ('when'), affirmative *per* ('very'), and *vel*, when meaning *valde* ('very'). There are several subclasses, too, that are usually placed before the verb: adverbia demonstrativa like *en*, *ecce* ('look'), interrogativa like *cur*, *quare*, *quamobrem* ('why'), adverbia hortativa like *heia*, *age* ('come on'), adverbia similitudinis like *quasi*, *ceu*, *veluti* ('like', 'as it were'), adverbia vocandi like *heus* ('hey! '), adverbia optandi like *o*, *utinam* ('would that').

That it was considered normal for adverbs to be placed before the verb may also appear from Charisius (233, 27B. = 181, 17K).), who reports a definition of the adverb as the word-class which precedes a verb ('praeposita verbo'). The same grammarian enters into a discussion about what term would be more suitable: 'praeverbium' or 'adverbium' (252, 21B. = 194,14K.).

---

[3] Cf. Prisc. 17,1,1 on his relation to Apollonius.

[4] Adjectives were regarded in antiquity as a subclass of the *nomen*. They were called *adiectiva nomina* as opposed to *appellativa nomina* and *propria nomina* ('substantives' and 'proper names'; cf. Robins 1951: 41; 1966: 16). I use modern terms in the normal modern sense. If I want to stress in this chapter the different use of terms by Roman grammarians, I will use inverted commas and/or Latin terms.

The relation that exists between adverb and verb is considered the same as the one found between adjective and substantive (15,1,1; 17,5,37). This was a common idea. The Stoics, Priscian reports (2,4,16), called adverbs 'as it were adjectives of verbs' (quasi adiectiva verborum). The meaning of the adverb is added (*adicere*, cf. nomen adiectivum) to that of a verb, or, as we would say with a similar vagueness, the adverb modifies a verb (cf. ch. 6). The parallelism between *prudens homo* and *prudenter agit* ('the wise man' – 'acts wisely') seemed to confirm this idea. This parallelism still plays an important role. Pottier (1962: 52ff.) even uses the terms 'adjectif de verbe' and 'adjectif de substantif'. In the Roman theory it can be found as early as Varro *L*. 8,12, within a different framework originating from Aristotle (see Dahlmann a.1.). He observes that within the category of noun and verb we can distinguish primary and secondary members, *homo* and *doctus, scribit* and *docte* ('man' – 'wise'; 'writes' – 'wisely'), respectively.

As for the relation of adverbs to members of other categories, adverbs differ from prepositions in that they may or may not be constructed with certain case forms (14,1,4), e.g. *intra* ('inside'). A word should be called a preposition if it cannot occur without a case form (15,5,30). Charisius seems to be more practical: if such words govern case forms they are prepositions, otherwise they are adverbs (245, 19B. = 189, 15K.)[5].

3.1.2. Semantics

As has been said, the meaning of the adverb is added to that of the verb. The adverb expresses the quality or quantity or number or time or place of the verb (17,5,38: 'quemadmodum officio adiectivi fungunter adverbia ad significandum verborum qualitatem vel quantitatem vel numerum vel tempus vel locum'). The adverb has no 'complete meaning' (2,4,20: 'perfectam significationem'; 15,1,4: 'plenam sententiam'), except when added to a verb or participle, whereas the verb can have complete meaning without an adverb. In those cases where one uses adverbs without a verb, information from context and/or situation is understood: 'it is necessary that they either refer to verbs said before by another person' (e.g. *bona est superbia?* :: *non* ('is arrogance good? :: no')) 'or that they are said elliptically' ('per ellipsin'), e.g., if someone tells a story one may say *bene*

---

[5] Elsewhere Priscian is prepared to assign a word to more than one class, e.g. *ut, quasi* and *si* to the class of adverbs and of 'conjunctions' (15,6,34-5).

('well'), *diserte* ('clever'), *eloquenter* ('eloquent'). In that case *dicis* ('you speak') is understood ('subauditur')[6].

Adverbs are distinct from interjections. The latter do not only occur without a verb, but also do not need a verb (of emotion) to be understood. The expression of a particular emotion seems to be the very meaning of interjections (Prisc. 15, 7,40; Charis. 246, 27B. = 190, 14K.). In this respect the Roman grammarians differed from Greek scholars, who did not recognize interjections as a class of their own. Of course, these statements (both the one in the preceding paragraph, and this one about interjections) can easily be translated into a syntactic statement. We might say that adverbs have restricted sentence valence (that is, the ability to occur in a one-word-sentence under certain conditions), whereas interjections have sentence valence obligatorily. I will return to this problem in ch. 8.

Though it is maintained by Priscian and others that the adverb has no complete meaning it should be recalled that, according to Priscian (15,5,31; 14,2,12) adverbs differ from prepositions in that they have a definite meaning of their own ('per se habent aliquam certam significationem'), whereas if one would say *de* or *in* one does not know what is meant unless they are constructed with some word, e.g. *de partibus orationis* ('about the parts of speech'), *de loco in locum* ('from place to place').

As we have seen, a distinction is made by Priscian and others between different types of semantic aspect. Verbs (and nouns) may be said to have an independent semantic aspect, adverbs (and adjectives) on the other hand have a dependent semantic aspect. This bears some resemblance (if we ignore temporal and local adverbs which have deixis) to Reichling's treatment of the semantic aspect of noun and adjective (University lectures)

---

[6] Another version of the completeness of meaning is attributed to Palaemon by Charisius (241, 20B. = 186, 30K.). In his version it is claimed that with verbs adverbs are obligatory. The definition and associated explanation run: 'adverbium est pars orationis quae adiecta verbo significationem eius explanat atque implet (cf. Prisc. *Partit.* 474, 26K.). Ita nam cum dico, Palaemon docet, nondum significo satis vim planam verbi, nisi adiecero bene aut male' ('The adverb is a part of speech which is added to the verb and clarifies and completes its meaning. For if I say it like this, Palaemon observes, I do not yet make the meaning of the verb sufficiently clear, unless I add well or badly'). This is probably due to a misunderstanding of Appollonius Dyscolus' definition Ἔστιν οὖν ἐπίρρημα μὲν λέξις ἄκλιτος κατηγοροῦσα τῶν ἐν τοῖς ῥήμασιν ἐγκλίσεων καθόλου ἤ μερικῶς, ὧν ἄνευ οὐ κατακλείσει διάνοιαν. (– περὶ ἐπιρρημάτων 529b, p. 119,6 ed. Schneider). ('The adverb is an invariable part of speech, which modifies the verb forms entirely or partly without which it (the adverb) does not complete its meaning'). The same mistake is made in Greek theory as well. Cf. Uhlig's comment ad Dionysius Thrax 641b, p. 72, Uhlig. For modern views on obligatoriness of adverbs cf. 6.1.2.2. below.

and to the distinction of types of semantic aspect in general (cf. 2.2.4.).

Also semantic in nature is Priscian's observation (15,1,1) that some adverbs, e.g. *sapienter* ('wisely') can be connected with any tense, whereas other ones cannot, e.g. *heri* ('yesterday'). Though, of course, these examples are trivial, the remark might have formed a starting-point for studies on the compatibility of adverbs with (supposed) aspectual verb forms and with various modes of action ('Aktionsarten'). Priscian also observes that there are certain relations between adverb and mood, e.g. *ne* ('that not'), *utinam* ('would that'), *ni* ('if not'), *num* (question word).

3.1.3. Morphology

The adverb is an invariable part of speech (pars orationis indeclinabilis). Thus Priscian (15,1,1). Not all grammarians point to the invariability, nor does Priscian in his *Partitiones* (474, 26K.). Morphologically the adverb shows resemblance to the conjunction and preposition, which are also called 'indeclinabilia' (16,1,1; 14,1,1) as well as to the interjection, as appears from Priscian's general introduction to the invariables (14,1,1). That by 'invariability' Prisican more specifically understands 'lack of congruence' may be inferred negatively from what he says about 'nomina' which are used adverbially ('vim adverbiorum recipientia' − 15,2,7)[7]. These 'nomina' can be identified as having the status of an adverb by their not being declined when they are placed together with[8] various case forms of 'nomina', pronouns, or participles, e.g. *'sublime volans, sublime volantis, sublime volanti'* ('flying high')[9]. Apparently, the 'degrees of comparison' of adverbs were considered to be of a different type and not supposed to make the use of the term 'invariable' incorrect. It is not precisely clear how the relation between comparison in adverbs and in adjectives was seen (Prisc. 15,4,25-6). See 5.3. end.

---

[7] See 3.3. on 'adverbial use'.

[8] 'are placed together with' is intended to translate 'iungantur casibus', which is more neutral than 'are constructed with'.

[9] Of course, one would like to have an example of an adverbially used adjective with a noun or demonstrative. Perhaps Priscian's meaning was, in modern terminology: if a word, which might be considered an adjective, occurs beside a nominal case form, it might theoretically modify the nominal form; if this is not so, this is apparent from the fact that if we put the nominal form in a different construction (e.g. in a passive construction instead of in an active construction) it may occur in another case, whereas the adjective-like word remains unchanged; therefore, it must be an adverb.

3.1.4. Phonology

At several places accent is mentioned as a means of distinguishing adverbs and prepositions (14,1,4; 15,5,39; *Partit.* 475, 3-5 K.; Charis. 245, 10B. = 189, 10K.). Priscian observes that Roman grammarians considered the fact that 'adverbs' (in his theory) followed by a certain case form, e.g. *intra* ('inside') followed by a noun in the accusative case, were accentuated like 'pure' prepositions, as an argument for calling these words prepositions. Priscian's terminology (*gravantur*) suggests that he has 'pitch' in mind. It is at least questionable whether these remarks about the various accents have any more value than remarks on the accents in general. Probably here, too, the remarks are due to the influence of Greek grammarians, for whom the phenomena to which the Latin terms 'gravis', 'acutus' and 'circumflexus' refer, really meant something (Cf. Leumann 1926: 182-3; Allen 1965: 83-4). Another point is that prepositions, being closely related to the noun phrase within the prepositional phrase, probably had weaker stress than adverbs.

3.2. Subclassification and individual problems

Apart from the general characteristics which have been mentioned above, Priscian gives a subclassification of adverbs according to their 'accidentia' (specific characteristics): 'species' ('type'), i.e. whether they are 'primitive' or derived, with a list of adverbs ordered by their endings; 'significatio' ('meaning'); 'figura' ('form'), i.e. whether they are compound or not.

The semantic subclassification is very detailed. Priscian (15,5,28ff.) has 18 subclasses and Jeep (1893: 277-9) gives even more, from various sources. I mention a few interesting items. We find *edepol, ecastor*, etc. as 'adverbia iurativa' ('swear-adverbs'), which would rather seem to be interjections, but occur as 'Beteuerungsadverbien' in Kühner—Stegmann (:I, 796; see 8.2.). *Heia* and *age* are mentioned as 'adverbia hortativa' ('incentives'), the first of which would certainly now be called an interjection. As to *age* ('come on'), Priscian observes (15,6,35), quite unexpectedly in view of his definition, that 'this adverb also has a plural *agite*', e.g. Verg. *A.* 8, 273. Modern grammarians point to the affinity of imperatives and interjections both in semantic aspect (Szantyr: 339) and with respect to syntax (Blatt 1952: 34), in as far as they are said to be no part of the sentence (cf. 8.2.). This resemblance is supposed to explain the so-called 'Interjektionalisierung' (Szantyr: 339) or 'partikelartige Erstarrung' (Hofmann 1963: 37) of certain imperatives. An excellent example is

(1) age igitur intro abite ('come on! go inside! '; Plt. *Mil.*928).

Age must be an interjection and not an imperative singular form of *AGO* ('to carry'), in spite of the formal resemblance to that form, since a singular form would be out of place, as is shown by plural *abite*. What is strange is that 'iurativa' and 'hortativa' are not incorporated within the class of interjections, which Priscian does recognize. We will see later (8.2.) that modern grammarians follow Priscian in this respect.

Remarkable, too, is the subclass of adverbia optativa, such as *utinam, ut, o, si*, wich occur in wishes like

(2) ut illum di perdant ('may the gods destroy him! ').

With the exception of *o* most modern grammarians would call these words (subordinating) conjunctions, a verb of wishing being understood (Kühner–Stegmann: I, 183-4; R. Lakoff 1968: 176-82). Szantyr (p. 330) calls them 'wish-particles', which would be preferable but for the indistinctness of the notion 'particle' (cf. ch. 8, n. 2)[10].

We have seen (3.1.3.) that Priscian pays some attention to the so-called adverbial use of 'nouns'. He also mentions in this connection the use of place names in a certain case form, e.g. *Romae* ('at Rome'), as adverbs of place (15,2,8). Donatus (387, 9K.) goes even further and calls *Romae*, etc., an adverb and not a noun as some 'ignorant scholars' ('imprudentes') do. Compare also among others Charisius 243, 25B. = 188, 9K.; 244, 11B. = 186, 13K.

Priscian does not have a subclass of causal adverbs, which Romanus distinguished according to Charisius (249, 16B. ≈ 192, 10K.). As examples of this subclass Romanus considered *ideo* and *idcirco* ('therefore'). Kühner–Stegmann (: II, 145ff.) and Szantyr (: 515) call these words 'pronominal causal adverbs'[11] alongside *propterea* and other words. Most Roman grammarians (e.g. Prisc. 16,1,5) regarded them as 'conjunctions' along with *quia* ('because'), *itaque, igitur, ergo* ('then', 'therefore', 'so', 'accordingly'), etc., since these words express the logical (or semantic) relationship between propositions (or sentences and clauses) and do not add anything to the meaning of the verb. The class of conjunctions especially makes it clear that semantic considerations settled problems of which class a

---

[10] The treatment of adverbia 'iurativa', 'hortativa' and 'optativa' is due to Greek influence (cf. Dion. Thrax 76ff. ed. Uhlig).

[11] Priscian (16,1,5) calls *ideo* a 'pronomen' used as a causal conjunction.

word had to be assigned to. In the case of the 'conjunctions' the logically (or rather semantically) connecting value was more important than e.g. the syntactic difference in so-called subordinating conjunctions (*quia*) and coordinating conjunctions (*igitur*). And even morphological considerations were more important than syntactic ones, as Priscian's treatment of *ideo* shows. I return to these words in ch. 10.

We find even more remarkable deviations from our standard description in other grammarians. Charisius (242, 19B. = 187, 20K.) reports that Pliny (the Elder) reckoned gerund forms *dicendo, legendo* ('speaking', 'reading' ablative) and *dicendi, legendi* ('speaking', 'reading' genitive) to be adverbs of manner. This treatment seems highly implausible, especially as far as the genitive forms are concerned. Kuryłowicz (1964: 31), however, remarks too that 'The gerund is conceived[12] as an adverb in so far as it represents a subordinate clause denoting the circumstance of the action (time, cause, aim, etc.)'. This observation, along with the ancient ones, in my opinion, suffers from a confusion of function and category (cf. 3.3. below).

That the supines (*doctu* and *doctum* ('(in order) to teach')) were considered adverbs by some people[13] is also reported by Charisius, and Quintilian 1,4,29 points to the resemblance of verbal forms like *factu* ('to do') and *dictu* ('to speak') to adverbs like *noctu* ('at night') and *diu* ('by day', 'long'). As a matter of fact, O'Brien (1965: 100) counts them among adverbs.

We may sum up the above survey by saying that the Roman grammarians combined in the class of adverbs morphologically and semantically divergent words, which were taken to share two characteristics, one morphological (they are invariable), the other (semantic-) syntactic (they modify a verb). It was the latter characteristic that was thought to distinguish adverbs from other invariables, such as conjunctions and prepositions. The rather vague notion 'addition to a verb' (i.e. 'modification') made the assignment of syntactically quite different words to one class of adverbs possible. Therefore the term πανδέκτης which some Stoics used for 'adverb' (Charis. 252, 29B. = 194, 20K.), 'since it takes all within its class', was suitable for the Roman grammars as well.

Most surprising in the definition is the fact that it is not mentioned that some adverbs can modify adjectives and certain other adverbs.

---

[12] Of course, 'is conceived as' is not entirely clear. The gerund, like other nominal verb forms, is produced ('motivated'), in Kuryłowicz's opinion, by transformation (1964: 30).

[13] Among these Pliny, according to Barwick (1922: 28). The ancient theories can be found together in Richter (1856: 7-9).

3.3.   . *Category and function*

Of course, what the grammarians had to say about adverbs had implications for the so-called adverbial use ('constructio adverbialis' — Prisc. 15,2,5) of words belonging to other classes (e.g. *sublime* mentioned in 3.1.3.).

A general remark may be added here about the expression 'adverbial use'. If a word of a certain class did not occur in the way it was supposed to, in view of the definition of that class, it was said to occur 'just like' a member of some other class, instead of being regarded as used in a certain function, which could be fulfilled by members of other classes as well. Function and category were regarded, in a sense, as different sides of the same thing. The categorial (i.e. category- or class-oriented) description of language is perhaps the most characteristic aspect of ancient Roman grammars. This aspect has had, moreover, a profound influence on modern grammars, in which 'substantival use of adjectives', 'adjectival use of substantives', etc. are common notions.

4. THE ADVERB IN LATIN LINGUISTICS

If one compares the definition of the adverb given by Priscian and other Roman grammarians (viz.: the adverb is an invariable word, the meaning of which is added to that of the verb just as the meaning of the adjective is added to that of the noun) with the usual definition in modern Latin grammars — as well as with grammars of modern languages — the main difference turns out to be that nowadays adverbs are said to modify adjectives and other adverbs as well[1].

Most words which are now called adverbs were considered adverbs by Roman grammarians. The overall impression is still one of heterogeneity (Löfstedt 1967: 79; Marouzeau 1949: 11; Booth 1923: IX). The adapted definition is not sufficient to cover the characteristics of these words.

I will examine what modern grammarians have to say about the adverb as far as morphology and phonology, semantics and syntax are concerned. On morphology, I will remark that the classification needs no revision. What is problematic is only the meaning of the term 'invariable'. This term will be discussed in ch. 5. The semantic subclassification, which is in fact the only subclassification given, will appear to be rather unsatisfactory, especially with respect to so-called manner adverbs. The syntactic remarks, finally, if

---

[1] I have tried to find out who was the first to make this addition to the ancient definition. The earliest criticism I encountered was by Julius Caesar Scaliger in his *De causis linguae latinae*, ch. 158: 'Therefore not only is the term 'adverb' a bad construction of the ancient grammarians, but also the definition they gave is unwise, for it is not only a modifier of the verb, but also of the nomen' (that is adjective and, perhaps, substantive). The criticism is also present in Sanctius' *Minerva*, I,17, among whose examples we find instances of adverb + substantive: *semper deus* ('eternal god'), *semper lenitas* ('persistent gentleness'), as well as instances of adverb + adverb and adverb + adjective: *bene mane* ('very early') and *bene doctus* ('very wise'). See also Vossius' admirable chapters III, 2; VI, 16; VII, 61 on adverbs.

understood as a system of generative rules will be shown to produce various types of incorrect utterances and not to produce certain correct ones. In the discussion about syntax the notion of modification will be accepted as such. A further analysis of this will follow in ch. 6.

4.1. Morphology and phonology

The adverb is an invariable word (Szantyr: 170; Kühner—Holzweissig 1912: 255 (using the term 'unflektierbar'); Ernout—Thomas 1959: 1; Blatt 1952: 33, etc.). This characteristic is one it shares with words belonging to other categories, such as prepositions, conjunctions, interjections. For example, Szantyr (: 170) mentions prepositions and particles (see ch. 8, n.2.) as other classes of invariable words[2]. As in ancient Roman grammar it seems feasible to speak of 'comparison of adverbs' (expressions like: *'altissime* is the superlative of *alte*; *diutius* the comparative of *diu'*), which suggests that by 'invariable' is still understood 'uninflected for Case, Gender and Number'. Degree of comparison is apparently not considered an inflectional category. This question will be discussed in some detail in the next chapter. I only mention one exception, viz. Bos (1967: 107), in whose opinion degrees of comparison form 'a system of inflectional categories'.

Apart from pointing to the invariability of adverbs a generalization about the internal structure of all adverbs is impossible. A subclassification according to their morphological structure, on the other hand, is perfectly possible. Such a subclassification has been made from ancient grammarians onwards (ch. 3.2.) and need not be discussed further. The reader is referred to Cupaiuolo (1967). It is self-evident that these morphological subclasses are most useful if they can be shown to be syntactic and/or semantic subclasses at the same time. The best-known example is the number adverbs[3]. Bos (1967) endeavours to show within the framework of De Groot's theory (cf. p. 28-30) that the so-called regular adverbs (ending in *-e* and *-(i)ter*) are such a class. The morphological properties, which are our concern here, are summarized by Bos at p.117: (a) they are formed on the root or stem of adjectives by the suffixes *-e* and *-(i)ter*; (b) as a rule they have degrees of

---

[2] On the value of terms like 'invariable word' see 2.2.2. and ch. 8 (init.).

[3] The strange position of number adverbs amongst the adverbs stands out from the fact that in Kühner—Holzweissig (1912: 253) 'Zahladverbia' are explicitly assigned to the class of 'numeralia', whereas later in the chapter (p. 255) 'numeralia' are mentioned among the 'unflektierbare Wörter'.

comparison, if their semantic aspect allows for it. On their supposed categorial semantic aspect see below 4.2 (end).

Most attention in Latin studies has been paid to diachronic aspects of the adverbs. It has been observed that many, or – less cautiously – most adverbs are former case forms (Löfstedt 1967: 79; Cupaiuolo 1967: 14-5), the shift being due to a process of fixation (Szantyr: 46). An illustration of how this development can be understood is given by Cupaiuolo (1967: 15).

(1) ea malo dicere quae maiores . . . recte atque ordine fecere ('I prefer to tell those things our ancestors did rightly and properly'; Sall. *Cat.* 51,4).

An adverb (*recte*) and an ablative singular case form (*ordine*) are coordinated. If one uses this illustration certain problems arise, which are, briefly: (a) coordination is no proof of diachronic or synchronic *categorial* equivalence; there may be only functional equivalence (cf. 7.3.1.). (b) Under this hypothesis, the ancestor of *recte* would have been marked for case independently, as are e.g. nouns, and not as a result of agreement, as in the case of adjectives (cf. 5.3.).

Kühner–Stegmann (I, 793) remark that adverbs can in a sense be compared with case forms. Proposals to consider adverbs as case forms synchronically, also, (Calboli 1867: 404-6; Hjelmslev 1935; and Fillmore 1968) will be discussed in the next chapter, where the problem will be examined of whether adverbs should be considered as inflectional forms of some lexeme or as particles.

It is self-evident that a diachronic study of adverbs is perfectly respectable but of little use for the synchronic study of these words. In this connection, it should be superfluous to remark that one should avoid confusing diachronic and synchronic morphological classification. However, that both types of analysis are often applied at the same time is apparent from the following discussion of O'Brien (1965: 100-1; 117). One of the subclasses that he distinguishes among the non-regular adverbs[4] are 'adverbials which resemble and occur as locative particles'. Examples are *sīc* ('so'), *istīc* ('there'), *alibī* ('elsewhere'), *alicubi* ('somewhere'), *ibidem* ('in the same place'). Locative particles, with which these adverbs are said to agree in morphological and syntactic respect, are defined, in their turn, as 'uninflected nominal, adjectival and adverbial forms', formed by adding a locative suffix -*i* to the nominal, adjectival and adverbial stem. Examples of

---

[4] I mean those not derived by the suffixes -*e*, -*(i)ter*, -*ies*, -*tim*, -*tus*, following O'Brien (1965: 39).

the adverbial type, which is our concern here, are *ĭbĭ* ('at the point'), *sī* ('on the hypothesis'), *utī* ('how'; translations taken from O'Brien, p. 117).

The question that may be asked with respect to the above description concerns the meaning of the term 'adverbial stem'. For example, what is the stem of *ubĭ* and *sī*? Whereas with the nominal and adjectival locative particles that O'Brien mentions, such as *domī* ('at home') and *tuae* ('at yours/at your home') one can point to a certain derivational relation with the lexeme *DOMUS* ('house') and *TUUS* ('your'), it is not easy to see which stems we should have in mind in the case of *ubi* and *si*. That O'Brien means, in fact, a historical stem appears from his note on p. 106, where he gives a historical derivation of *ubi*[5]. Historically these forms can be considered pronominal adverbs formed by a locative suffix -*ī* < -*ei* (Leumann 1926: 288-9) — that is, with the exception of *tuae,* of course (-*ae* being a merger of genitive singular feminine (disyllabic *ae* < *ā ī*) and locative (monosyllabic *āi*)) and *domī* (nominal adverb). Synchronically, however, there are morphological differences as well as syntactic differences. As the marking of vowel length has shown, we cannot speak about the same suffix -*i* except in a historical sense[6]. Furthermore one might ask what use there is in calling -*i* (if it is accepted as a suffix) a locative suffix. Semantically there is nothing 'local' about *si* and *uti,* and syntactically they behave differently from *ibi, domi,* etc. O'Brien has erroneously equated the historical derivation with synchronic derivation and has drawn conclusions about syntactic and semantic characteristics of the words (correspondence fallacy — cf. 2.3.2.).

As to phonological chacteristics, I have nothing to add to what I reported in 3.1.4.

4.2.   Semantics

That the category of adverbs is a very heterogeneous one from the semantic point of view has been observed in 3.2. with reference to Roman grammarians. In modern grammars the situation is less complicated but far from clear. In Kühner—Stegmann (:I, 792-3) the following subclasses are given: (i) adverbs indicating a relation of place (local adverbs): *hic* ('here'); (ii) time (temporal adverbs): *tunc* ('then'); (iii) frequency: *ter* ('three times'), *identidem* ('repeatedly'), *crebro* ('frequently'); (iv) intensity or

---

[5]   The stem given by O'Brien is **kw-dhei*. Leumann (1926: 124) gives **q^{u}u-dhei*.

[6]   On *ĭbī* > *ĭbĭ* (shortening of the last vowel in iambic words), see Leumann (1926: 101).

degree (intensifiers): *valde* ('very'), *magis* ('more'); (v) quantity or amount (quantifiers); *multum* ('much'), *plus* ('more'); (vi) quality or manner (manner adverbs): *bene* ('well'), *pulchre* ('beautifully'), on the one hand and so-called modal adverbs (sentence adverbs) on the other. The latter comprise (i) affirmative and negative adverbs: *certe* ('certainly'), *sane* ('sure'), *non* ('not'), *neutiquam* ('by no means'), etc.; (ii) adverbs expressing certainty, doubt, etc.: *profecto* ('indeed'), *certe* ('certainly'), *scilicet* ('of course'), *fortasse* ('perhaps'), etc.; (iii) question adverbs: *num, utrum* ('whether'). Kühner—Stegmann (: II, 145-8) mention still another subclass, strangely enough in an entirely different part of their grammar, viz. causal adverbs like *ideo* and *idcirco* ('therefore').

The above subclassification is based on fairly global semantic considerations. Syntactic features of the subclasses are not given[7]. The rough semantic subclassification even overrules distinctions which would become clear by using various question words, as may be seen from Kühner—Holzweissig's subclassification (1912: 253). For example: 'The adverb signifies . . . time in answer to a question 'when', 'since when', 'until when'.' Such question words would, of course, not only specify syntactic characteristics, but semantic characteristics as well. A refinement in the use of questions could be achieved by using larger expressions in which the label of the supposed class is used, e.g. *at what time?* . In English, for example, a question with *how?* in

(2) How did he kill him?

could be answered by (i) *with a gun* and (ii) *gently*. The second answer would be excluded in a more specified question

(3) With what instrument did he kill him?

(Becker 1967b: 15). It goes without saying that the subclassification of adverbs achieved remains far short of such refinement. Of course, this is partly due to the lack of attested questions of this type. See also below 7.1. and Dressler (1970: 31) on the use of questions in Latin.

Since only intuition determines assignment to a subclass, certain decisions are readily open to criticism. For example, the distinction between

---

[7] Only implicitly does it become clear that intensifiers and quantifiers are normally used to modify adjectives, whereas manner adverbs do not properly occur in this way (see below, however). Terms like 'intensifier' are used in this context in the traditional sense, e.g. as they are used in Kühner—Stegmann.

'quantity' and 'intensity', which is present in Kühner–Stegmann, is absent in Kühner–Holzweissig. In Kühner–Stegmann (:I, 792-3) 'intensity' or 'degree' are in contrast with 'quantity' or 'amount'. In Kühner–Holzweissig (1912: 253) a subclass is mentioned, the members of which indicate 'intensity' or 'degree' and 'amount'. In fact, what argument can be found for calling *valde* ('very') an intensifier and *multum* ('much') a quantifier if we neglect the misleading translations and compare these words in (4) and (5)?

(4) (i) valde amare   (ii) multum amare ('to love much').
(5) (i) valde bonus   (ii) multum bonus ('very good').

In fact, this uncertainty is implicitly uttered by Kühner–Stegmann (: I, 793), when they point to the fact that intensifiers and quantifiers are both used for 'gradation of adjectives and adverbs' ('zur Steigerung von Adjektiven und Adverbien'). That is to say (supposing that the semantic distinction could be made), that these words share (at least some) syntactic characteristics, in that both types modify adjectives and adverbs. Notice the fact that this, too, is formulated in a semantic statement only: 'gradation'.

A slightly different phenomenon concerns the so-called adverbs of manner. At first sight this subclass seems to offer no problems. Words belonging to it indicate the way in which the process takes place.[8] However, these words occur as modifiers of adjectives as well. Examples are

(6) (i)   bene mane ('very early'; Cic. *Att.* 4,9,2).
     (ii)   insignite improbus ('remarkably bad'; Cic. *Quinct.* 73)
     (iii) erat ei pecuaria res ampla et rustica sane bene culta et fructuosa ('he had a considerable grazing farm, well cultivated and very productive'; Cic. *Quinct.* 12).

More examples can be found in Kühner–Stegmann (:I, 793-4). *Bene* and *insignite* in the examples seem to express the *degree* of *mane*, *improbus* and

---

[8] In support of this one would like to find examples of these adverbs in coordination with ablative singular forms of *MODUS* ('manner'). I have found one example:
  quae ... novo quodam modo praeclareque dicuntur ('which are said in an original way and brilliantly'; Cic. *de Orat.* 2,127).
Perhaps we can also compare the parallelism in the following example from Plautus:
  decet ... me victitare pulchre, te miseris modis ('it is correct that I live comfortably, you in a miserable way'; Plt. *Mos.* 53-4).

culta et fructuosa, rather than the *manner.* From the semantic point of view they could be called intensifiers.

male ('badly') belongs here, too, in expressions like *male sanus* (Cic. *Att.* 9,15,5), lit. 'badly sane' ('half crazy' in Shackleton Bailey's translation). As Kühner–Stegmann (:I, 794) remark, whether *male* is interpreted as 'to a low degree', as in the example given, or as 'in a high degree' depends on the meaning of the adjective (or adverb) that is modified by *male,* whether it denotes something 'good' or something 'bad'. *male insanus* ('deplorably insane') refers to a high degree of insanity. The case of *male* is also interesting with respect to the importance of the modified item in determining the semantic relation between modifier and head, to which I will return below.

The words that were discussed in the preceding two paragraphs (*bene, insignite, male*) have it in common that they occur as modifiers of adjectives (and adverbs). It might be concluded, then, that it is their occurrence in such constructions that is responsible for their being interpreted as intensifiers. This is the opinion of Kühner–Stegmann (:I, 794) among others: 'in such constructions qualifying adverbs take the value of quantifying adverbs'. It seems, however, that not only the construction is responsible. One factor at any rate, which determines whether a manner adverb will be interpreted as an 'intensifier' concerns the semantic aspect of the word itself. In fact, so-called manner adverbs might just as well be considered intensifiers in constructions with some verbs. For example, *vehementer* ('eagerly', 'strongly' – see Lewis & Short s.v.) might be considered an intensifier not only when constructed with adjectives (7), but also when constructed with certain verbs (8).

(7) suavis autem est et vehementer saepe utilis iocus et facetiae ('jesting and shafts of wit are agreeable and often highly effective'; Cic. *de Orat.* 2,216).

(8) 'inhibere' illud tuum . . . vehementer displicet ('I don't like your word 'inhibere' one bit'; Cic. *Att.* 13,21,3).

In both sentences *valde* could be substituted for *vehementer.* Similarly, *immortaliter* could hardly be said to indicate manner in the following example

(9) quod scribis te a Caesare cottidie plus diligi immortaliter gaudeo ('your writing that Caesar's esteem for you increases daily is an undying joy to me'; Cic. *Q. fr.* 3,1,9).

However, not only the semantic aspect of the word itself is important, but also the meaning of the verb it is constructed with[9]. This explains why *vehementer* in (10) should certainly be interpreted 'in an impetuous manner'. Notice also the coordination with *acriter*.

(10) cum dixerat accusator acriter et vehementer ('when the prosecutor had spoken with shrewdness and energy'; Cic. *Flac.* 21).

The following lines will show that if a manner adverb occurs as modifier of an adjective it need not necessarily be interpreted as an intensifier. In Kühner–Stegmann (:I, 794) and, above all, von Nägelsbach–Müller (1905: 372-6), examples can be found like

(11) sapientis autem civis fuit causam nec perniciosam et ita[10] popularem, ut non posset obsisti, perniciose populari civi non relinquere ('it was the duty of a wise citizen, in dealing with an institution not evil in itself and so dear to the people that it could not be combated, not to leave its defence to a destructively popular leader'; Cic. *Leg.* 3,26).

(12) Lucique Valeri Potiti et M. Horati Barbati, hominum concordiae causa sapienter popularium, consularis lex sanxit, ne qui magistratus sine provocatione crearetur ('and a law proposed by the consuls Lucius Valerius Potitus and M. Horatius Barbatus, men who wisely favoured popular measures to preserve peace, provides that no magistrate not subject to appeal shall be elected'; Cic. *Rep.* 2,54).

According to Kühner–Stegmann the adverb is not used as an intensifier in such cases, but indicates 'in which sense the adjectival concept is conceived' ('bezeichnet ... die Richtung oder Beziehung, in der der adjektivische Begriff zur Geltung kommt'). In (11), *perniciose populari* could be paraphrased – in view of the preceding *popularem* and *perniciosam* –

---

[9] Compare also Greenbaum (1969a: 87) on *honestly* in *Mr. Jones honestly believed our story*, where some informants substituted *really* and *completely* instead of *honestly*.

An interesting textual problem is Cic. *Att.* 1,13,3. The mss. read *Messala vehementer adhuc agit severe* ('Messala at present handles the case very strictly'). Shackleton Bailey follows Purser in reading <*et*> *severe*. There are, in fact, instances of *vehementer et severe* in Cicero. Still, the ms. tradition might just as well be correct, and therefore should be retained. In the emended form *vehementer* is manner adverb ('impetuously'), in the ms. reading it can be taken as an intensifier with *severe*.

[10] Apparently, *ita* is understood as quantifier (or intensifier) as well. Cf. Thes. s.v. 520,51ff.

'popular in such a way (or 'to such an extent') that it is destructive', or in another paraphrase: 'this particular citizen possessed the quality *perniciosa popularitas*'. In the same way we can paraphrase *sapienter popularium* in (12) by saying that the '*popularitas*' of these men was *sapiens*, as opposed to others who showed an *imprudens popularitas*. In the two examples the adverbs indicate what the quality denoted by the adjective was like (one might call it 'qualification in the second degree'), that is, they could be called 'manner adverbs' as they would be in other constructions, e.g. in a non-appositive variant of (12)

(13) qui concordiae causa sapienter populares fuerunt ('who were wisely devoted to the people so as to ensure concord'; cf. Cic. *Dom.* 147)[11].

Most examples might be explained as (11) and (12), e.g.

(14) qui mihi tam crudeliter inimici sunt ('who are so cruelly hostile to me'; Cic. *Att.* 11,10,2).
(15) quisquam ... audet ... tam impie ingratus esse ut ... ('is there anyone, who dares to be so wickedly ungrateful? '; Cic. *Tusc.* 5,6).

The example (15) may, on the other hand, illustrate the fact that semantically the distinction between intensifier and manner adverb cannot be drawn easily in this construction with adjectives either. The lack of *gratia* has to be rather great before it will be called *impia*. We might compare English *damned foolish* and Dutch *heidens moeilijk* (lit.: 'heathenishly difficult') for the use of such words as intensifiers (cf. also *immortaliter* in (9)). Here, too, the semantic aspect both of the adverb and of the adjective are decisive for the interpretation as intensifier or manner adverb. The question remains whether syntactic differences can be found, which accompany these interpretations, and how they can be found. This problem will be discussed later (7.1.).

There are, then, as we have seen, three difficulties in semantic subclassification. Firstly, the semantic subclassification is very global. Secondly, it is not clear what arguments favour the distinction of certain classes (e.g. of intensifiers and quantifiers). Thirdly, several words could semantically be assigned to more than one subclass. (a) Certain words will

---

[11] Another paraphrase might be preferable, e.g. in the case of (12) 'the fact that these men strove after *popularitas* was wise'. The adverb *sapienter* would then be interpreted as expressing judgment (so-called 'Urteilsadverb'). On these adverbs see below 6.3.

be definitely interpreted as 'intensifier' when constructed with adjectives
(and adverbs), as 'manner adverb' when constructed with verbs. (b) Other
words will be considered 'intensifier' when constructed both with adjectives
and with verbs. (c) Other words again will be interpreted as 'manner
adverbs' when constructed with adjectives and also when constructed with
verbs. (d) There are also words that will be interpreted differently with
different adjectives and verbs.

Especially with respect to the so-called manner adverbs of traditional
grammar the facts are much more complicated than grammarians would
suggest. It is certainly too simple to say that the so-called adjectival adverbs
(derivationally related to adjectives and formed with the suffixes -e and
-(i)ter) indicate manner when modifying verbs and may, secondarily, be
used as intensifiers of adjectives (and adverbs). This view is also expounded
by Bos (1967: 117). Her explanation of the circumstance that *acriter*
('strongly'), *flagitiose* ('shamefully'), *graviter* ('vehemently'), *mediocriter*
('moderately'), *stulte* ('stupidly'), *turpiter* ('basely'), etc. occur as modifiers
of adjectives due to a specific semantic aspect of 'intensity' is pertinent
merely to phenomenon (a) above[12].

The difficulty with respect to this class of words is caused by the
assumption that they indicate 'how the process of the verb takes place'. This
assumption can be traced back historically to Priscian's observation that
these words indicate the 'qualitas' of the verb, with which they are
combined (17,38), just as the adjective indicates the 'qualitas' of the noun it
is combined with. In Bos (1967: 122) this idea is expounded along the same
lines as in De Groot's theory. According to Bos the suffixes -e and -(i)ter
convey the semantic value 'in the manner of 'x' where 'x' is the
stem-meaning of the adjective', from which the adverbs are derived (my
translation). Any explanation along these lines makes, in my opinion, the
explanation of manner adverbs as intensifiers, discussed above, quite
complicated[13].

---

[12] Personally, I think that this 'intensity' aspect is only pseudosemantic and is merely
introduced to account for the syntactic phenomenon — modification of adjectives. In
fact, what criterion is there to suggest the semantic aspect 'intensity' in *stulte* (cf. p.
28-30). We should, moreover, distinguish a specific semantic aspect 'locality' as well to
account for *publice* ('publicly'), e.g. in Cic. *Ver.* 5,1. See 7.3.3.

[13] Bos' actual proposal is difficult to understand. Apparently in the adverbs like
acriter, in which Bos assumes a semantic aspect 'intensity', the feature 'intensity'
overrules the semantic value ('manner') of the adverb morpheme -e / -(i)ter.

4.3. Syntax

The main syntactic criterion by which words are assigned to the category of
adverbs is that they modify other words belonging to particular categories.
The adverb modifies (i) a verb; (ii) an adjective; (iii) an adverb. (ii) and (iii)
are usually said to be historically later than (i) (Kühner–Stegmann: I, 792;
Szantyr: 170)[14].

Apart from the ill-defined notion 'modification', which will be discussed
in ch. 6, this definition of adverbs can be criticized in several respects: (a) it
is ambiguous and leads to incorrect interpretations; (b) the use of adverbs is
not restricted to modification of the members of the categories mentioned;
(c) the facts which are covered by the definition are not sufficiently
specified.

4.3.1. Ambiguity of the definition
The definition is ambiguous, given the above formulation and given the
words which are usually assigned to the category of adverbs. The
formulation allows for a wide interpretation (each adverb modifies all
members of all three categories) and a narrow interpretation (each adverb
modifies at least a member of one of these categories). There are, of course,
intermediate interpretations. In fact, if we accept for the moment the
notion of modifying, what we see is that not every adverb modifies all
members of these three categories or can be modified by all of them. Take
the following examples with *heri* ('yesterday'). The definition allows for
them, but obviously some are not correct.

(16) (i)   quando Socrates de iustitia locutus est? :: *valde heri/ heri
            ('when did Socrates speak about justice? ' :: '*very yesterday/
            yesterday').
     (ii)   qualis vir Socrates fuisse videtur? :: *heri bonus/bonus ('what
            sort of man seems Socrates to have been? ' :: '*A yesterday
            good one/a good one').

These trivial examples show that *heri* (itself an adverb) modifies a verb (i),
but not an adjective (ii). *heri* cannot be modified by *valde* (i), nor does it
modify adverbs itself. The wide interpretation is certainly not correct.

---
[14] This definition is, of course, circular in that it defines adverbs by their modifying
adverbs.

Apparently the definition of adverbs would have to be much more specific and a large number of subclasses seems to be necessary. In view of the differences, the class of adverbs would probably be no more than negatively defined, as is actually now the case in the grammars (though without explicit criteria for the other categories and, as we will see, with an insufficient positive criterion — its occurrence as modifier). This means that adverbs would be defined as the class of words, which do not belong to one of the inflectional categories (morphological criterion) and differ from the other non-inflectional categories like subordinating conjunctions, interjections, etc. (syntactic criteria) in certain specified ways.

The refinement in subclassification that could be achieved would be entirely based on the criterion of which words from which subclasses can be modified by the word under consideration. Such classifications can be found in Ahlman (1938) and others. Examination of a few words given below will make clear that these deserve closer inspection. Many adverbs (e.g. local, temporal and causal ones) cannot be modified by intensifiers like *nimis* ('too much'), *valde, tam* ('so (much)'), *quam* ('how (much)'), but manner adverbs can, like *bene* ('well'), *diligenter* ('carefully'), etc., as well as words which have something to do with 'time' and 'place' but seem not to be simply local and temporal adverbs, like *diu, dudum* ('long'), *pridem* ('long before'), *procul* ('far'), *prope* ('near')[15], *saepe* ('often'). It is interesting that several of these last mentioned words occur in a coordination pattern alongside manner adverbs (see 7.3.3.). Intensifiers can themselves be recognized, of course, by their modifying the very words mentioned and, also, by the fact that they can be substituted for *quam* ('how') in a frame consisting of *quam* and those words, or — slightly differently — by their occurring in answer to a question consisting of one of these words and *quam*? ('how?'). (Of course, *quam* itself cannot be discovered in this way.) The intensifiers mentioned do not modify each other, but *valde* can be modified by *tam*, when *valde* itself modifies a verb:

(17) mirabar . . . te tam valde hoc loco delectari ('I was surprised that you are so fond of this place'; Cic. *Leg.* 2,2).

Intensifiers do not modify so-called modal adverbs (**valde fortasse* ('*very perhaps')), but they can be modified themselves by some of the so-called

---

[15] *prope* adverb as well as *prope* preposition:
(1) qui tam prope iam Italiam . . . videret ('who saw Italy only a few miles away'; Cic. *Ver.* 5,160).
(2) tam prope hostem ('so near the enemy'; Liv. 27,33,9).

modal. adverbs. Intensifiers also modify adjectives (except numeral adjectives and adjectives which are probably semantically excluded like *reliquus* ('remaining')) as well as verbs, at least those with 'gradable' meaning.

4.3.2. Adverbs modify members of other categories as well

Whereas in 4.3.1. I discussed the ambiguity of the definition and a few incorrect interpretations of it, I will now turn my attention to the fact that there are adverbs which modify members of other categories, such as preposition phrases, as well. This is especially pertinent to the subclass of so-called modal adverbs. There are many differences among the words that are usually labelled 'modal adverbs'. Many of them occur with many words or phrases which belong to various other categories. I give a few examples with *fortasse* ('perhaps'). I am aware that one might argue about the relationships I assume for the following words. We do not possess intonational criteria with which to determine which word or phrase is actually modified by *fortasse*. In modern languages, however, intonation is often the only criterion which suggests that a modal adverb is constructed with a particular word or phrase, and has no function of its own in the sentence or clause (Ahlman 1938: 35). Besides word order is often illuminating. Both factors are difficult to assess in the study of Latin. Modification is, therefore, difficult to use as a heuristic means. It is always possible that two constituents are merely juxtaposed[16]. In the case of adverbs modification is not overtly expressed as it is in the case of adjectives (agreement with a noun). It is precisely for this reason that coordination, which is as a rule overtly marked — by words like *et* and *atque* ('and') —, is much more useful. However, in spite of these reservations, consider the following examples. The italicized words are regarded as modified by *fortasse*.

(18) (i)   hora fortasse *sexta* diei questus sum in iudicio ('perhaps at the sixth hour of the day I complained in a trial'; Cic. *Dom.* 41).

      (ii)   elegit ex multis Isocrati libris *triginta* fortasse versus Hieronymus ('Hieronymus culled perhaps 30 verses from the numerous works of Isocrates'; Cic. *Orat.* 190)[17].

---

[16] 'juxtaposed' is not understood as 'standing immediately beside each other', but as 'without a mutual relation'.

[17] *fortasse* is not 'almost' but 'perhaps'. It expresses doubt, not a guess about the number. Cf. *illic noster est fortasse circiter triennium* ('he has perhaps been three years or so in our family'; Plt. *Mi.* 350).

(iii) Q. Pompeius ... *biennio* quam nos fortasse maior ('Q. Pompeius, perhaps two years my senior'; Cic. *Brut.* 240).

(iv)   ... Catilinae fuit advocatus, improbo homini, at supplici, fortasse *audaci*, at aliquando amico ('he was Catiline's counsel, a rascal, but a suppliant, perhaps audacious, but once a friend'; Cic. *Sull.* 81).

(v)   mittam ad te exemplum fortasse *Lanuvio* nisi forte Romam ('anyway I shall send you a copy, perhaps from Lanuvium, unless by any chance I go to Rome'; Cic. *Att.* 13,26,2).

(vi)   de meo quodam amore gloriae *nimis acri* fortasse verum tamen honesto vobis confitebor ('I will confess to you my own passion, which is perhaps over-keen, but assuredly honourable'; Cic. *Arch.* 28).

(vii) innocentem fuisse reum quem fortasse *numquam* viderat ('that the man whom he may never have seen was innocent'; Cic. *Cluent.* 131).

(viii) haec fortasse *propter pudorem* in lege reticentur ('perhaps because of shame, these (lands) have not been mentioned in the law'; Cic. *Agr.* 2,37).

Notice that (iii) and (v) – noun, (vi) – noun phrase, and (viii) – preposition phrase, are not covered by the definition.

In fact, the definition of adverb often does not cover what is mentioned concerning adverbs in the grammars and appears implicitly from the examples given. For example, Kühner–Stegmann (:I, 794) mention constructions of adverb and noun as in (19) *plane vir*

(19) at vero C. Marius rusticanus vir sed plane vir cum secaretur ... ('but as a matter of fact C. Marius, a countryman yet undoubtedly a man, when under the surgeon's knife'; Cic. *Tusc.* 2,53)

(examples in Kühner–Stegmann: I, 218-20). Still, they do not assume this fact within their definition. Also, they mention an example of adverb and preposition phrase in their paragraph on manner adverbs that are used as intensifiers.

(20) bene ante lucem ('well before daylight'; Cic. *de Orat.* 2,259).

The only grammar which as far as I know mentions these constructions explicitly is Blatt's (1952: 242-3)[18]

Furthermore, the definition offers no room for the so-called modal adverbs which are said to express the attitude of the speaker towards the content of the expression and to 'have no direct relation to the predicate' (Kühner—Stegmann: I, 793). Perhaps some of the examples of *fortasse* given in (18) belong here. Also, examples like

(21) male reprehendunt ('it is not right for them to blame'; Cic. *Tusc.* 3,34)

(so-called adverbs of judgment in Kühner—Stegmann: I, 795) cannot be handled within the definition. See 6.3. below.

Finally, the definition does not allow for modification of clauses by words that are regarded as adverbs. I give an example with *ne . . . quidem* ('not even')

(21) huic ne ubi consisteret quidem contra te locum reliquisti ('you have not even left him a place where he could make a stand against you'; Cic. *Quinct.* 73).

4.3.3. Inadequateness of the description of adverbs

Even when facts are mentioned the analysis is often not detailed enough. I will demonstrate this with regard to the treatment of constructions of adverbs and nouns. Adverbs are said to be used attributively in such constructions (Kühner—Stegmann: I, 218), or to be used just like adjectives (or even: instead of adjectives; von Nägelsbach—Müller 1905: 306). In many examples this analysis is not complete. For example, *plane* in (19) is not simply an ATTRIBUTE of *vir,* but of *vir* in apposition to a noun, that is in a construction corresponding to

(23) Marius plane vir erat ('Marius was really a man').

In fact, *vir* resembles adjectives as far as its predicative use is concerned[19].

---

[18] It is true that Kühner—Stegmann use 'adverb' less strictly for all constituents (words, phrases, clauses) which occur in what they see as the defining constructions of adverbs (:I, 793), that is as a function label instead of as a category label.

[19] Cf. Fillmore (1968: 84) on *John is quite an idiot.* Generally speaking, if there is a predicative construction in which an adverb is possible, an attributive or appositive construction (the adverb included) is possible as well (cf. Szantyr: 171).

Even in (24) it is doubtful whether *plane virum* means simply 'a real man' and not 'someone who was really a man'.

(24) vidi enim Mytilenis nuper virum atque, ut dixi, vidi plane virum ('I saw the man at Mytilene not long ago and as I said, I saw a man indeed'; Cic. *Brut.* 250).

An incorrect analysis is given, to my mind, of *illic* ('there') in (25)

(25) matrem ... homini illic nobilissimo ac potentissimo conlocasse ('he married his mother to a man who was in high esteem there and had great power'; Caes. *Gal.* 1,18,6).

illic is not attributively constructed with *homini (nobilissimo)*, but is ADJUNCT$_{LOC}$ with *nobilissimo*, just as *illic* would be in a predicative construction

(26) homo illic nobilissimus erat ('the man was in high esteem there')[20].

In this section on syntax I have tried to show that the definition of the adverb does not account for the variety of characteristics that the words have that are thought to be adverbs according to this definition. The last examples show that the investigation of the characteristics of individual

---

[20] Many of the examples given by Kühner—Stegmann and von Nägelsbach—Müller (1905: 306-9) are disputable. I give two examples.

(1) *non tu nunc hominum mores vides?* ('don't you see how men are nowadays? '; Plt. *Persa* 385).

Kühner—Stegmann (:I, 218) translate 'der jetzigen Menschen' (cf. Szantyr: 171). Krebs—Schmalz (1905) s.v. call this use of *nunc* 'griechischartig'. But why not *nunc vides?* ('don't you see now? ').

(2) *discessu tum meo* ('at my departure then'; Cic. *Pis.* 21).

Von Nägelsbach—Müller, Blatt (1952: 243) and Szantyr (: 171) explain *tum* as ATTRIBUTE. Kühner—Stegmann (:I, 20) reject this. Nisbet a.l. agrees with them, because the attributive explanation 'would surely require *meo tum discessu*'. Though most examples given by Kühner—Stegmann present the order 'adjective (or pronoun) — adverb — noun', there is no proof that another order is impossible. Perhaps we may compare Verg. *A.* 1,21: *populum late regem* ('wide ruling people'). At any rate there is nothing which tips the scale either way.

adverbs and of the constructions in which they occur is not detailed enough. An examination of which words occur in which constructions seems necessary. This might be done by looking at which adverbs modify which words, phrases or clauses. On the other hand it is difficult to ascertain whether a word indeed modifies the item it is supposed to modify, since overt expression of the relation is lacking, even if we take the notion of modification for granted. A subclassification based on the relations of modification is, therefore, difficult. Another basis for subclassification (coordination) will be dealt with in 7.3. The main criterion by which adverbs are distinguished from other categories of invariable words will be discussed in ch. 6 (modification).

5. ADVERBS AS DERIVED FORMS

In this chapter I will discuss the question of how we can best account for the fact that the majority of adverbs are related formally and semantically to words belonging to the classes of adjectives, nouns, pronouns and verbs. In principle two solutions are possible:
(1) adverbs are 'forms of' adjectives, nouns, etc. The implication of this solution is that adverbs do not constitute a word-class of their own (are a pseudo-category, as Bergsland (1940: 53) puts it). On 'form of' see 2.2.2.
(2) adverbs are related to adjectives, nouns, etc., but cannot be regarded as forms of them.

In the first solution adverbs are inflected forms, in solution (2) they are uninflected or, in other words, invariable. The formal resemblance is based on a derivational relation. If they are regarded as uninflected, it is not immediately clear how comparative and superlative adverbs are to be described. Should we speak about comparative and superlative forms of adverbs or about adverbs related to comparative and superlative adjectives?

In the traditional view it is held that the adverbs meant here are derivationally related to adjectival, nominal, pronominal and verbal lexemes (or in traditional terminology: are derived from the stems of adjectives, nouns, etc.). It has been suggested, however, from ancient times onwards, that adverbs are not essentially different from inflected forms. Thus the idea that adverbs are words in the 'adverbial case' has been maintained by Chrysippus according to Steinthal (1890: I, 302; criticism in Calboli 1971: 115-22). It has received the approval of Hjelmslev (1935: 4).

The discussion on the advantages of the inflectional view over the derivational view has been focused on the relationship between adjectives and adverbs. As such the problem is relevant for modern languages as well.[1] Bergsland (1940), however, takes adverbs related to the other classes mentioned, into account, too. Three different versions of the inflectional view occur. The first views adverbs and adjectives as forms of the same lexeme, the second regards adverbs as constructed from adjectives by the addition of an empty morpheme, the third regards all four types (adjectival, nominal, etc.) as adverbial case forms.

5.1. Adverbs and adjectives are both forms of one lexeme

In the inflectional view it is held, of course, that adverbs can be accounted for by the constructions which the lexemes they realize enter into. Thus, in *prudens homo* ('the wise man') the actual form *prudens* can be regarded as the realization of the adjectival lexeme *PRUDENS* inflected for the morphosyntactic categories Case, Number, Gender, actually nominative case, singular number and masculine gender in agreement with *homo*. Similarly, in *prudenter fecit* ('acted wisely') *prudenter* could be said to be the realization of a lexeme *PRUDENS* inflected by reason of its standing in a construction with the verbal form *fecit* and exemplifying the morphosyntactic category Adverbial (or whatever one wants to call it). See Matthews (1967: 168). A basic assumption is, of course, that the adverb stands in a relation to the verb (which is open to criticism; see ch. 6) and the argument as it stands neglects the fact that there are adjective–adverb, adverb–adverb and, most important in this context, noun–adverb constructions (cf. 4.3.2.).

Under these assumptions we might combine adverbs and adjectives and set up a class of lexemes which are on the one hand inflected for Adverbial, on the other hand for Adnominal (or whatever else one wants to call it), e.g.

$$PRUDENS \left\{ \begin{array}{l} \text{Adnominal (Case, Number, Gender)} \\ \text{Adverbial} \end{array} \right\}$$

For a somewhat different treatment in the same vein compare Householder (1967: 111; 113) on Greek[2].

---

[1] The relationship between *beautiful* and *beautifully* in English raises similar questions. Robins (1964: 226; 259) and Crystal (1967: 42) maintain the derivational view, Hockett (1958: 210-1) and Greenberg (1966: 88) represent the inflexional view.

[2] *prudens homo prudenter fecit* is the starting point for Bergsland (1940: 53) and resembles Priscian's example (3.1.1.).

Of course, setting up such a class of lexemes would not entirely settle the matter of the invariability of adverbs. There are, after all, 'primary' adverbs like *clam* ('secretly'), *tam* ('so'), *sic* ('so'). It would be extremely artificial to set up a lexeme *CLAM* without realization for the category Adnominal.

5.2. Adverbs as adjectives marked by empty morphemes

Whereas Matthews and Householder do not speak about other types of adverbs, Kuryłowicz (1936: 83-4) makes a clear distinction between adjectival adverbs, like French adverbs ending in *-ment*, and so-called circumstantial adverbs ('de circonstance'). Adjectival adverbs are marked, in Kuryłowicz' opinion, according to their syntactic function with a special 'morphème syntaxique' (*-ment*; = Bühler's Feldzeichen), whereas the lexical meaning of the adjective remains constant.

In his opinion to call these words adverbs would be just as strange as to call a noun which functions as OBJECT of a transitive verb and is accordingly marked with an accusative ending, an adverb[3]. In reality the ending is a 'morphème syntaxique qui ne modifie guère cette valeur' (i.e. the semantic value of the adjective)[4].

Kuryłowicz' position is slightly altered in 1954 (p. 166). He still stresses that the 'cohésion sémantique' between adverb and verb is similar to that between adjective and noun. As for the form of the adverb: 'dans *fortiter agere* ('to act bravely') le morphème *-ter* sert à former l'adverbe, non pas à signaler la subordination de *fortis* par rapport à *agere*. C'est en tant qu'adverbe tout fait que *fortiter* détermine le verbe'. One might say that the adverb ending indicates the lack of agreement which is expressed in the adjective[5].

---

[3] Diachronically Kuryłowicz (1960: 135) accepts an interaction from adverb to case form and vice versa.
[4] Generally speaking, Kuryłowicz pays most attention to the semantic aspects of the stem. Thus *pulchritudo* ('beauty') would be regarded by him as a syntactic variant of *esse pulcher* ('to be beautiful'; 1936: 85; 1964: 29).
[5] Cf. Karcevsky (1936: 107), who calls the adverb a 'déterminant à marque zéro': 'Ainsi par ex. un adjectif passant à la fonction de l'adverbe perd ses valeurs de genre, de cas, de nombre et se dépouille de leurs marques morphologiques'.

5.3.   Adverbs as case forms

The most consistent treatment of adverbs as a pseudocategory is given by
Bergsland (1940), who follows Hjelmslev in several respects[6].
Adverbs 'ne se distinguent pas fonctionellement des formes flection-
nelles' and we should preferably speak of adverbial case forms. Depending
on 'le caractère des sémantèmes[7], qui se combinent avec les morphèmes dits
adverbiaux' we find adverbs among the various parts of speech: adjective,
noun, pronoun and verb. The adverb element[8] serves to connect the
'sémantème' to which the adverb element is attached to a verbal
'sémantème'. The traditionally recognized flexional elements (Case, Number, Gender) function in the same way as relators of 'sémantèmes' (cf.
Hjelmslev 1935: 96).
   Bergsland illustrates the supposed resemblance in 'relator'-character with
an example from Plautus

(1)   recessim dabo me ('I will turn back'; Plt. *Cas.* 443)

(p. 55). It has to be analyzed as *reced-tim dabo me*, *reced-tim* being
derived from the verbal stem *reced-*. A participle (*recedens*) would be
equally possible here, the only difference being that in *recessim -tim*
connects the verbal stem *reced-* with the verbal sémantème *da-*[9], whereas in
recedens a relation would exist between *reced-* and the person element
('morphème personnel') in the complex morpheme *-bo* of *dabo*. We might,
in my opinion, make the objection that the difference in the members
related still has to be accounted for (on the one hand 'sémantème':
'sémantème', on the other 'sémantème':'morphème'). Moreover, the distinction between *crudeliter inimicus* ('cruelly hostile') and *crudelis inimicus*
('cruel enemy'; cf. 4.2. ex.(14)) is quite difficult to account for along these

---

[6] Sandmann (1939: 89-90) follows Hjelmslev in regarding the adjectival adverb as a
case form. Cf. also Calboli (1967: 404-6) for the assumption that
adverbs are synchronically adjectival and nominal case forms. For a dissenting view see
De Groot (1956a: 187).

[7] 'Sémantème' is used in several senses. For the purpose of the present discussion it is
roughly equivalent to 'stem'.

[8] I use the term 'element' instead of 'morphème' in Bergsland's discussion, since he
uses it both in the formal sense (adverb ending) and in a more abstract sense for the
paradigmatic expression of Case, Gender and Number, where a formal connotation can
better be avoided.

[9] Cf. Hjelmslev (1935: 97), on *puer celeriter currit* ('the boy runs quickly').

lines. If adverb endings are regarded as relators, there is not only a difference in members related, but also in type of relation.

Bergsland recognizes, then, several types of adverbs:

(1) prudenter ('wisely') adjectival 'sémantème + adverbial 'morphème'
(2) articulatim ('piecemeal') nominal 's.' + adverbial 'm.'
(3) recessim ('backwards') verbal 's.' + adverbial 'm.'
(4) hic ('here') pronominal 's.' + adverbial 'm.'

There are a number of problems to be solved if one wants to consider adverbs not only as being marked by 'relators', but also as being case forms. Firstly, it would not be easy to explain what case, or rather cases, should be assumed in particular circumstances, and which phenomena could be explained by assuming a particular case. For example, the fourth type (*hic*) is rather isolated. According to Bergsland (1940: 53-4) this is no objection to considering its members as adverbial case forms. This had been suggested before by Hjelmslev (1935: 15), who adds that there are isolated 'normal' case forms as well. Hjelmslev regards *hinc, huc* ('hence', 'hither'), etc. as distinct case forms, which have no parallels in other lexemes where a process of syncretism has made them dissapear (1935: 81)[10]. Regrettably, no further explanation is given. Generally speaking, it is always possible, of course, to describe a word that is traditionally called an adverb as a member of a paradigm of some lexeme (even the only member perhaps). See 2.2.2. and Hjelmslev (1935: 40) followed by Fillmore (1968: 27, n. 35). The question is whether we gain anything by doing so. For example, we might say that *huc* ('hither') is an allative case form of the pronominal lexeme *HIC* ('this'), comparable with *Romam* ('to Rome' − in certain constructions). This allative case could be said to have been merged with the accusative case elsewhere (e.g. *Romam*). However, the profit of this argument is small. The proposal is entirely *ad hoc* (on the allative case see Szantyr: 22 and Kurył̷owicz 1964: 193; 204). On neutralization in general see Kooij (1971: 104-5).

A further problem concerns the fact that there is not much use in calling e.g. *articulatim* a *nominal* adverb based on *articulus* ('member'). In what respects is it nominal? Now, in particular this type shows, in Bergsland's opinion, the connection with case forms quite clearly (p. 63). This solution,

---

[10] Hjelmslev (1935: 97), whose opinion Bergsland follows elsewhere, gives a different treatment of *hinc, hic, huc*. According to him in *Caesar hinc profectus est* ('Caesar proceeded from here') the 'morphème casuel' of *hinc* relates the 'sémantème' *Caesar* to the 'sémantème' *h-*. To me this solution is not attractive either.

however, is quite unsatisfactory in many respects. Bergsland himself remarks that, although *articulatim* shows a resemblance to other case forms [11], it cannot be modified by adjectives (in the usual sense of the term). This means, of course, that the essential syntactic characteristic of nouns does not apply to *articulatim*. Actually, Ahlman (1938: 19-20) and O'Brien (1965: 101; 120) regard the lack of a modifying adjective as a criterion for distinguishing words which could be erroneously regarded as case forms and often were real case forms historically, from real case forms in synchronic analysis. In my opinion they are right.

Even more problematic is the assumption of an adverbial case in adverbs derived from verbs (*recessim*). Bergsland only says that they are infinite forms. This is necessary, of course, to account for the presence of a supposed case element, but seems rather ad hoc. We would like to know what other evidence there is for the existence of these infinite forms, and what is their position as regards the other infinite forms. Here, too, the analysis of the adverb in a verbal 'sémantème' and an adverbial element is not really illuminating. The particular characteristic of infinite forms of verbs is that they share both non-verbal and verbal characteristics (cf. 2.4. and ch. 2, n. 20), such as governing a noun as OBJECT, etc. No such thing is involved here.

Assuming such a thing as an adverbial case is not unproblematic with regard to nominal and adjectival adverbs either. First adjectival adverbs. Bergsland mentions two considerations in favour of explaining adjectival adverbs as adverbial case forms. One of them concerns the fact that comparatives and superlatives have adverbial forms as wel: *prudentissime* ('very wisely') is, in his opinion, the adverbial case of the superlative adjective *prudentissimus* ('very wise') and not, conversely, the superlative of the adverb *prudenter* ('wisely'). I do not see the implications of this observation. The second argument seems stronger. It cannot be accidental, according to Bergsland, that the 'nominative-accusative neuter has the function of an adverb in the comparative *prudentius*' (my translation), that is to say, that the adverb is identical with a 'normal' case form [12].

The objection must be raised here that normal case forms manifest three morphosyntactic categories (Case, Number, Gender). Bergsland (1940: 56) is well aware that we have on the one hand three elements, on the other only one, marking the relation to a verb or another adjective. This

---

[11]   *articulatim* is used as a diachronic argument to illustrate the closeness of adverbial forms and case forms by Meillet–Vendryes (1960: 518ff.).

[12]   Cf. Householder (1967: 113) on Greek.

difference is not surprising, according to Bergsland, as soon as we realize that Case, Number and Gender are not independent categories for the adjective, but depend on the noun (by agreement). There may be cases then, in which the normal flexional elements are lacking. However, this explanation does not get round the fact that the adverbial case operates independently of nouns.

A similar problem turns up in the case of nominal adverbs. The adverbial case could be explained here along the same lines as the normal cases (government by the verb; p. 63). The difference is, again, that in genuine nouns no expression for Case alone exists. Number is always obligatorily present and whereas there is a considerable amount of merging of case forms, singular and plural forms are always distinct. Here, too, Bergsland solves the problem in an unsatisfactory way. He compares the dative and ablative plural forms *mensis* ('tables') and *hortis* ('gardens'), which belong to different declension classes (*a*- and *o*- stems respectively). In the forms cited this difference is blurred. So, Bergsland argues, it needs not surprise us that Number is unexpressed, in nominal adverbs. To my mind it is insufficient to compare a purely morphological phenomenon (*o/a* stem) with a morpho-syntactic phenomenon (Number)[13].

Summarizing the objections raised so far, a major difficulty appeared to lie in the assumption of the existence of adverbial cases of *nouns* and *verbs,* since the supposed nominal and verbal characteristics are absent. It is also difficult to speak about adverbial *cases* of nouns, verbs, adjectives and pronouns, since doing so presupposes (1) isolated case elements, (2) independent marking for Case in the adjective, (3) acceptance of ad hoc types of Case, which are not to be found elsewhere.

As for considering adverbs as marked by an element expressing the relation to the verb (or rather verb, adjective, noun, etc.), this offers some problems as well (*crudeliter inimicus*). If one still prefers this solution and if one ignores the fact that adverbs are not restricted to constructions with verbs and ignores also adverbs like *clam* ('secretly') where the inflexional view has little sense, then there can be no criterion one way or the other for deciding whether a marking element is called derivational or inflexional. If the inflexional view is maintained in spite of all this it becomes senseless to call adverbs forms of adjectives. One should rather speak of adverbial and

---

[13] Moreover, it is clear that the type of argument here differs from the one followed in the discussion of Number in the adjective. The non-marking of Number was explained as being due to the lack of independence of the category of Number in the adjective, whereas, in contrast, Number was said to be independent in the noun.

adjectival forms of one lexeme which is inflected in accordance with adverbial and adnominal constructions (5.1.).

Apart from the difficulties mentioned, there is a semantic observation which supports the derivational view. Adverbs and related adjectives often show a different semantic development. Take e.g. *sane* ('indeed') and *sanus* ('healthy').

On account of the problems that derive from the inflexional view I believe that those scholars are right who assume a derivational relation for the words under discussion (Kühner-Holzweissig 1912: 1003; O'Brien 1965: 39; Robins 1967a: 50-1 — on *docte* ('wisely')). In this explanation we could distinguish in the Latin word-stock a number of particles (2.2.2.) which have a number of syntactic characteristics such that they may be called adverbs. These particles have no synchronic morphological relation to e.g. pronouns and adjectives. Examples are *clam, huc* and *sic.* On the other hand Latin appears to have various morphological devices by which secondary particles can be derived from certain stems. These secondary particles can be called adverbs on account of their syntactic characteristics. These characteristics differ considerably from those of words to which they are derivationably related (in particular from nouns and verbs). In fact, these differences are the reason for not considering adverbs as forms of nouns, verbs, etc.

If the derivational view is taken, the expression 'comparative and superlative of an adverb' is, strictly speaking, not correct. It is better to call *prudentissime* ('very wisely') an adverb that is derivationally related to a superlative adjective which is in turn derivationally related[14] to the adjectival lexeme *PRUDENS*, in spite of instances like *diutius* and *diutissime* (alongside *diu* ('long')), where corresponding comparative and superlative adjectives are lacking. See, however, Priscian (15,4,25-6) for ancient (not attested) *diutior, diutissimus.*

---

[14] In my opinion, it can hardly be maintained that the degrees of comparison can be explained on the basis of the construction in which the lexeme which has then to be assumed occurs. For an inflexional treatment see Matthews (1967: 170; 175) and Hockett (1958: 209-12). An intermediate position can be found in Robins (1964: 260).

6. SYNTACTIC PROBLEMS

In this chapter I will deal with the closeness of relationship ('affinity') between constituents. One aspect of this concept is the optionality of some constituents with respect to others. Optionality vs. obligatoriness of constituents bears on the concept of modification. Since the definition of adverbs is formulated in terms of modification, clarification of this notion is required. It will appear that 'modification' is not clearly defined. In this chapter I will suggest that adverbs occur with at least three different degrees of affinity towards the verb, in other words that adverbs occur at three different levels in the structure of sentences.

6.1. Modification

In the section on syntax of the fourth chapter (4.3.) it was shown, that given the definition of adverbs and given the words that are generally assigned to the category of adverbs, the definition — if conceived of in a generative way — on the one hand allows for constructions which are in fact ungrammatical, on the other hand excludes constructions which are grammatical. The notion 'modification' was accepted without a discussion. However, this notion is not at all as clear as its frequency of use might suggest. Therefore, I will now examine it in detail.

Modification is considered to be related to the notion of optionality of a constituent with respect to another constituent, especially the verb. This notion 'optionality' is problematic as well. It will appear that the notion of modification is closely connected with the sentence model that is tacitly or not assumed in traditional and modern grammar. I will try to reconstruct the model within the framework of which Kühner—Stegmann describe ADJUNCTS and compare it with other models.

6.1.1. Modification interpreted as optionality with respect to the verb
The notion 'modify' (German 'bestimmen'; French 'déterminer') plays an important role in Latin and other studies, but is seldom defined (Swüste 1963: passim; Crystal 1967: 48). Kühner–Stegmann are a notable exception. These authors recognize two main types of modification ('Bestimmung'): (a) modification of the subject, (b) modification of the predicate. By the side of modification of the predicate they recognize 'addition' ('Ergänzung') to the predicate (see below). The subject modifiers are called attributive.

These are the examples of attributive modifiers given by Kühner–Stegmann (I, 19-20; I, 206):

(1) (a) rosa pulchra ('beautiful rose') – noun:adjective.
    (b) pater noster ('our father') – noun:possessive pronoun.
    (c) tres viri ('three men') – noun:numeral adjective.
    (d) hortus regis ('garden of the king') – noun:noun (genitive).
    (e) hortus illius (lit.: 'garden of his' – noun:pronoun (genitive).
    (f) homo de plebe ('man of the people') – noun:preposition phrase.
    (g) tertium consul ('for the third time consul') – noun:numeral adverb.
    (h) Alexander, rex Macedonum ('Alexander king of the Macedonians') – noun:noun phrase in apposition.

In the categorial specification the element before the colon is the head, the element after is the modifier. Except for (c) and (g) this corresponds with the word order in the Latin examples.

What is remarkable in this list is the circumstance that these items are given as examples of subject modifiers, whereas, actually, they are examples of noun modifiers. The reason must be that, since SUBJECT is considered the function which is properly reserved for the category of nouns (cf. Kühner–Stegmann: I, 2), function and category are confused (3.3.). As a matter of fact, the same attributive relation exists when a noun functions as OBJECT, ADJUNCT, etc.

I return now to Kühner–Stegmann's distinction between 'modification of' and 'addition to' the predicate or verb (I, 19-20; I, 251-2). The constituents which are added to the predicate and those which modify the predicate are similar by the very fact that they are related to the predicate (both are called 'objective'), but they are different in as far as 'added' constituents are 'obligatory' ('notwendig gefordert'), whereas 'modifying' constituents are 'optional'. This yields the following scheme

SUBJECT	PREDICATE ('objective')
modification (attributive)	modification
	addition

Examples of obligatory constituents ('addition') are constituents functioning as OBJECT, e.g. the noun *epistulam* in (2a) and the infinitive *proficisci* in (2b).

(2)   (a)   scribo epistulam ('I write a letter').
      (b)   cupio proficisci ('I want to leave').

Another example is *homini* in

(3)   simia homini similis est ('the monkey resembles man'),

(the function of *homini* is difficult to define).

On the other hand, examples of non-obligatory constituents are constituents which denote locality, time, cause, instrument, manner. They may belong to various categories such as preposition phrases, noun phrases, adverbs, e.g.

(4)   puer bene scribit ('the boy writes well').

Constituents like these are often called adverbial modifiers ('adverbiale Bestimmung'), adverbials or adverbs. In this study all these constituents will be said to function as ADJUNCT.

The sentence model that can be deduced from the discussion on Kühner–Stegmann so far, seems to be this: sentences consist of a predicate (usually a verb which is the centre of the sentence (Kühner–Stegmann: I, 2)) to which a subject is subordinated ('untergeordnet')[1]. The predicate can be modified or completed by optional and obligatory constituents. The

---

[1] The relation between subject and predicate has been described in various ways: (a) the subject dominates the predicate; (b) the predicate dominates the subject; (c) subject and predicate are interdependent. See Helbig–Schenkel (1969: 20-5) and below.

subject can be modified by certain constituents as well. Graphically this can
be represented by (5). In the figure I use my own terminology so as to
facilitate a comparison with other models. I will follow this practice with
respect to the Chomskyan model below as well. In particular I will distinguish categorial and functional notions. Brackets indicate optionality.

The fact that in Latin finite verb forms have an implicit (bound)
SUBJECT, which makes an explicit SUBJECT constituent appear optional
(cf. Longacre 1964: 35-6 and ch. 7 n. 8 below) suggests that the SUBJECT
is subordinated to the PREDICATE as Kühner—Stegmann put it. On the
other hand the relation SUBJECT—PREDICATE seems to be closer than the
relation PREDICATE—OBJECT, etc. I have tried to represent the difference
in figure (5).

(5)   sentence

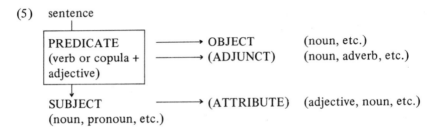

The above figure shares inter alia one important trait with the model of
transformational generative grammar (e.g. Chomsky 1965) in that OBJECT,
INDIRECT OBJECT and ADJUNCT are considered to be dominated by the
PREDICATE (are dominated by the node 'Predicate phrase' in the phrase
marker — Chomsky 1965: 102). They have a different relation towards the
PREDICATE from that of the SUBJECT. The Chomskyan model could be
rewritten in the following way

(6)   sentence

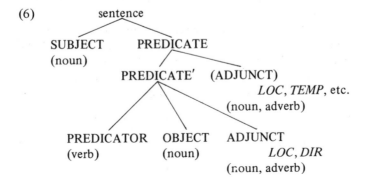

Notice ·the fact that ADJUNCT occurs twice in the tree diagram. Of course, one might suggest two different labels. The reason for speaking of one function 'ADJUNCT' is that there are obvious similarities in semantic and categorial respect on the one ·hand, whereas the difference in relation towards the verb on the other hand is adequately expressed by a difference in level. I return to this problem later.

Optionality of constituents plays a basic role in the distinctions represented in (5) and (6). These distinctions come out less clearly in the tagmemic and functional descriptions (Becker 1967b: 159, n. 20; Dik 1968: 170, passim). In these descriptions the functions dealt with above would be represented in something like (7).

(7)

SUBJECT	PREDICATOR	OBJECT	(ADJUNCT)
(noun)	(verb)	(noun)	(noun, adverb)

In both (6) and (7) ATTRIBUTE would be treated in a manner quite different from its treatment in Kühner—Stegmann, as I indicated above.

The question of which way constituents functioning as ADJUNCTS (e.g. adverbs) have to be placed in the sentence model and, conversely, which model would be necessary in order to describe adequately constituents functioning as ADJUNCT will be given more attention later in this chapter. For the moment I will return to the original question: what is understood by saying that an adverb modifies a verb, adjective or adverb?

The observation in Latin grammars that the adverb modifies the verb in the same way as the adjective modifies the noun (Kühner—Stegmann: I, 792; Szantyr: 170) must be understood to the effect that in adverb—verb constructions the adverb is optional, just as in a noun phrase the adjective is optional. The same holds mutatis mutandis for the relation adverb—adjective and adverb—adverb. Actually, this observation is related to what Priscian said about the adverb (cf. sections 3.1.1. and 3.1.2.), viz. that the adverb has no complete meaning without a verb, whereas the verb has complete meaning without an adverb.

Optionality is the essential criterion in modern use of the term 'modification' as well. Generally speaking, optionality is interpreted in its turn as 'omissibility', i.e. a constituent is said to be optional if it can be omitted from a certain construction without essential consequences for the remaining part (Garvin 1958: 58-9; Greenberg 1963: 14; Ruwet 1968: 399, n. 29; Dressler 1970: 28). Bloomfield (1935: 195) in his discussion of endocentric constructions approaches the problem from the other side: if a constituent can be added to a certain construction without consequences for the resultant phrase it is optional and called 'attribute'. It follows that a test for determining optionality of a constituent (say A) in a given construction (AB) consists in dropping or eliminating the specific constituent (A) and examining whether the resultant construction (B) is still 'viable', 'viable' being specified in the following way[2].

Let XABY be a construction from which A is dropped. B is 'viable' if

(a)   XBY is grammatical and has the same valence as XABY;

(b)   XBY is semantically identical to XABY except for the difference caused by the elimination of A;

(c)   The grammatical status of B and its relations to X and Y in XBY are the same as those in XABY, except for the difference caused by the elimination of A.

If these conditions are fulfilled, A can be said to be optional with respect to B, or, in other words, to be a modifier of B. B, in turn, may be called the head with respect to A.

Most examples that are given of modification concern constructions at the phrase level. In fact, the notion is perfectly workable in explaining the relation between adjective and noun and adverb and adjective (or adverb). Thus if in example (8), *valde* ('very') is eliminated, *bonus* conforms to the conditions given above.

(8)   (a)   puer valde bonus ('the very good boy').

(b)   puer bonus ('the good boy').

If *bonus* is eliminated from the resultant noun phrase (b), *puer* fully conforms to the conditions.

(c)   puer ('the boy').

However, at the clause and sentence level, too, the dropping test seems to deliver clear results. Take the following example in which *a glass of milk* functioning as an OBJECT will be dropped.

(9)   (a)   Each day poor John drinks a glass of milk.

(b)   Each day poor John drinks.

---

[2]   I take 'viable' from Garvin (1958: 58-9).

(9a) is grammatical (part of condition (a)) and conforms to condition (c). However, semantically there is a difference in that in (9b) John is a drunk, or at least drinks alcohol habitually. This is not implied in (9a). Moreover, the second part of condition (a) is not fulfilled. A durative expression can be added to (9b), but not to (9a).

(9)   (a)'   *Each day poor John drinks a glass of milk during the whole afternoon.

       (b)'   Each day poor John drinks during the whole afternoon.

It follows that *a glass of milk* cannot be considered an optional constituent, i.e. a modifier with respect to this particular verb. This would confirm Kühner–Stegmann's remark on the OBJECT constituent. (In the case of other verbs the procedure may prove more difficult to use.)

In the next section we will see that the position of ADJUNCT constituents, which are our concern here, is not as easy to determine.

6.1.2. Problems concerning the optionality or obligatoriness of constituents with respect to the verb

I will now discuss two difficulties concerning modification. The first is of general character and has no particular bearing on ADJUNCT constituents, the second concerns the applicability of the notion 'modification' to ADJUNCT constituents.

6.1.2.1. Optionality is linked with certain conditions.

The term 'optional' suggests that constituents in a construction which are optional with respect to some head cannot occur alone. This is certainly not correct. For example, in question–answer constructions the independent use of adverbs is much more free than in other constructions. We may answer

(10) (a)   eloquenter ('eloquently'),

when a question

(10) (b)   quomodo Socrates de iustitia locutus est? ('how did Socrates speak about justice? ')

has preceded.

There are, moreover, other cases in which no verb is present anywhere in the context. In Cicero's dialogues, for example, there are several examples of the following type

(11) (a)   eloquenter Socrates (lit.: 'eloquently Socrates').
      (b)   bene Socrates (lit.: 'well Socrates').
      (c)   ridicule (lit.: 'ridiculously'; Cic. *de Orat.* 2,245).

In these cases it is understood that some action was ridiculous, good, or eloquent (in the latter case, of course, the action of speaking).

Sometimes the context is clear enough to determine what action is meant, e.g. when, after an expression like (11a), a quotation of Socrates' words follows. Similarly, there are numerous examples like

(11) (d)   tum Cotta ('then Cotta'; Cic. *de Orat.* 1,100),

which are understood as: 'Then Cotta remarked: '. . .'.'

If the adverbs in these examples are characterized as modifiers — as they are — it is clear that one cannot hold that a modifier cannot occur without its head. Apparently, these phenomena do not depend only on syntactic features, but on contextual and situational circumstances as well[3].

6.1.2.2. ADJUNCT constituents defined as optional with respect to the verb. The second problem concerns the fact that is difficult to make generalizations about which constituents in which functions are optional with respect to the verb and which are obligatory. This holds for constituents which are said to function as ADJUNCTS as well. We have seen in 6.1.1. that Kühner—Stegmann mention a number of optional constituents functioning as ADJUNCT. The situation is much more complex, however, than their treatment suggests.

Generally speaking, between two constituents A and B, three relations are possible:

(a) A has to be constructed with B (is obligatory);
(b) A may be constructed with B (is optional);
(c) A may not be constructed with B (is excluded).

The traditional treatment suggests that ADJUNCT constituents belong to type (b). It has been realized, however, that among constituents which are

---

[3] Cf. Priscian quoted in 3.1.2.

traditionally regarded as ADJUNCT constituents, representatives of type (a) and (c) can be found as well. This is the case when ADJUNCT constituents expressing locality, direction, manner and time and duration are involved. I will discuss a few cases to illustrate the general point. Most of them have been discussed within the framework of transformational grammar (Chomsky 1965; Steinitz 1969; Lakoff—Ross 1966). In order to facilitate the discussion I will use transformational terminology in the remainder of this section[4].

As far as Place Adverbials are concerned, there are on the one hand certain verbs with which they are obligatory. Verbs can even be subcategorized on the basis of this criterion (Chomsky 1965: 102; Steinitz 1969: 10-5). Examples are

(12) (a)   John lived at the hotel.
     (b)   *John lived (in the sense of: 'resided').

On the other hand there are examples of exclusion of a Place Adverbial. I take an example from Lakoff—Ross (1966) quoted by Michelson (1969: 147).

(13) (a)   *John was dead in Bayonne (in the sense of: 'was not alive').
     (b)   John was dead.

The fact that certain verbs can be subcategorized with respect to the type of constituent that must or cannot be constructed with them, has been accounted for in transformational grammar from Chomsky (1965: 101-3) onwards. A distinction has been made between *Predicate Phrase* and *Verb Phrase*. The Verb Phrase comprises the verb and obligatory constituents. The Predicate Phrase contains the Verb Phrase along with a number of optional constituents. In Chomsky's opinion, Place Adverbials occur obligatorily with certain verbs within the Verb Phrase and optionally outside the Verb Phrase within the Predicate Phrase. Time Adverbials may optionally be taken as constituents of the Predicate Phrase alongside the Verb Phrase. Graphically this can be represented in the following way.

---

[4] Place Adverbial = ADJUNCT$_{\text{LOCATIVE}}$, etc.

(14)   Sentence

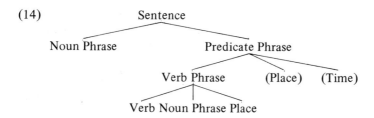

Example (13) has shown already that Place is not always optional. That the same holds for Time appears from (15), also taken from Lakoff–Ross (1966).

(15)   *John lived at the hotel at ten o'clock.

For a Latin example with a Time Adverbial take

(16)   periucundus mihi Cincius fuit a.d. III Kal. Febr. ante lucem ('Cincius is a very welcome arrival before day break, 28 January'; Cic. *Att.* 4,4).

Watt's comment (1964: 397) fits in with this discussion: 'It is odd to find a date and a time combined with *periucundus fuit'*.

Seiler (1968: 348) has presented arguments which suggest that verbs cannot in principle be subcategorized with respect to Time Adverbials. There are, however, restrictions on constructing durative expressions (e.g. *during one hour*) and 'confective' expressions (*within one hour*) with verbs which have a particular mode of action (Aktionsart; Pinkster 1969: 36-9). Furthermore certain tense forms are incompatible with certain Time Adverbials, e.g. *heri laudabit* ('yesterday he will praise'; cf. 3.1.3.). On the other hand I can imagine only a few examples of verbs with which a Time or Duration Adverbial is obligatory. An example of obligatoriness of a Duration Adverbial is Dutch

(17)   (a)   *De oorlog duurde ('the war lasted')[5].
       (b)   De oorlog duurde twee jaar ('the war lasted two years').

Perhaps it is advisable to give priority to the fact that with certain verbs certain constituents are obligatory and to consider types of exclusion mentioned so far, as resulting from individual restrictions on combinability

---

[5]   In case of repetition (*duurde en duurde*) no durative expression is necessary.

of the verb and the ADJUNCT constituent. The low number of examples like (17) would suggest that Duration Adverbials should not be considered as part of the Verb Phrase.

There is at least one consideration about Duration Adverbials that would suggest a totally different treatment. It appears that certain restrictions on combinability with Duration Adverbials may be neutralized or conversely created so to speak by the presence of specific constituents functioning as SUBJECT or OBJECT (Klum 1961: 111-2). For example, French *tomber* cannot as a rule be combined with durative expressions. Such an expression is allowed, however, if *la neige* is SUBJECT.

(18) (a) *Le garçon tombe pendant trois heures.

(b) La neige tombe pendant trois heures.

Examples like these might suggest that it is not the verb alone (its 'Aktionsart') that determines the combinability with a Duration Adverbial. In fact, this phenomenon could be explained by assuming that the Duration Adverbial is part of the combination of Verb Phrase and subject Noun Phrase (cf. figure (14)).

Such a combination is also attractive for explaining the ungrammaticalness of (19b) — cf. (13) above — vs. the grammaticalness of (19a).

(19) (a) The weather was beautiful in Bayonne.

(b) *My sister was beautiful in Bayonne.

It is not 'to be beautiful' as such that excludes a Place Adverbial.

Apart from the Adverbials mentioned so far there are problems with Direction Adverbials and Manner Adverbials as well (Steinitz 1969: 10-5; 35-6; 55; etc.). Thus, a Direction Adverbial is obligatory with German *sich begeben*, a Manner Adverbial with e.g. *sich benehmen*. As for Manner Adverbials consider Marouzeau's observation (1949: 12) on Latin

(20) ruri agere vitam semper, parce ac duriter se habere ('he has always passed his days in the country, lived a sparing and hard life'; Ter. *Ad.* 45-6).

'L'adverbe *semper* est si peu nécessaire que les éditeurs ponctuent en le rattachant à ce qui précède et tantôt à ce qui suit; au contraire, *parce* et *duriter* sont indispensables au sens'[6].

---

[6] Optional in certain constructions, according to Steinitz, are Cause, Manner, Duration, Time, Frequency, Instrumental and Place Adverbials. In my opinion Direction Adverbials belong here, too.

Notice the fact that all adverbials that are obligatory with specific verbs may be optionally constructed with others. These constituents can be considered alike functionally (ADJUNCT) and are at any rate alike semantically (*PLACE*, etc.). Often they are similar categorially. They differ only in the degree of affinity with the verb. Certain verbs demand a particular ADJUNCT just as certain verbs demand an OBJECT (transitive verbs) and most verbs demand a SUBJECT (personal verbs), at least in English and other languages (cf. 6.1.1.).

Just as an OBJECT constituent can be omitted with certain verbs under certain conditions, so ADJUNCT constituents which are normally obligatory, can be sometimes omitted. For example, German *sich verhalten* usually demands a Manner Adverbial (e.g. *ruhig*), but in the imperative (*verhalte dich!*) it can be omitted (cf. Steinitz 1969: 14). Also, certain verbs, e.g. *habitare* ('to live') are normally constructed with a Place Adverbial, which seems to be obligatory. There are, however, examples of *habitare* used absolutely (Thes. s.v. 2475,7) and also of *habitare* + Manner Adverbial.

(21)   habitare laxe et magnifice voluit ('he wanted to live free of restrictions and sumptuously'; Cic. *Dom.* 115).

A Place Adverbial seems to be dispensible if a Manner Adverbial is present.

Conclusion. We have encountered a number of problems concerning optionality and obligatoriness of constituents. It appeared to be incorrect to call all ADJUNCT constituents optional, even though some problems have to be solved with respect to this observation as well. At any rate, it is incorrect to define the category of adverbs (or rather the various subcategories of adverbs) by their *optionally* functioning as ADJUNCT of a verb, or, in traditional terms, by their being modifiers of a verb. Firstly, with certain verbs certain types of ADJUNCT constituents are obligatory. Secondly, with certain verbs certain ADJUNCT constituents are excluded (i.e. cannot be optionally added). What has not been discussed so far is whether it is sensible to speak of the relation towards the *verb* in the way done in traditional and transformational grammar. The few observations on constituents functioning as ADJUNCT$_{DURATION}$ suggest that the distinction of other units (comprising SUBJECT, OBJECT, PREDICATOR and perhaps still others) within the sentence or clause is necessary. This idea of something like a NUCLEUS in the sentence will be developed below.

6.2.   Other types of affinity: NUCLEUS and PERIPHERY

In the preceding section I discussed the distinction between obligatory and optional constituents functioning as ADJUNCT. Obligatory constituents may be said to stand in a closer relation to, or — in other words — to have greater, even maximal affinity with some constituent, in this case the verb, than optional constituents have. Now, within the number of optional constituents certain constituents still seem to have greater affinity towards the verb than others. I will discuss in this section some of the problems which turn up with respect to this type of affinity[7].

By way of an introduction take the proposal by Halliday (1970: 149-50). In his opinion a distinction can be made between 'process, participant, circumstance'. 'Circumstantial elements' (resembling my constituents functioning as ADJUNCTS) seem to be less central to the process than the participant elements. However, 'this .peripheral status is not a feature of all circumstantial elements, which can be subdivided into an 'inner' and 'outer' type'.

(22) He was throwing stones at the bridge.
(23) He was throwing stones on the bridge.

Both in (22), directional, and in (23), locational, the ADJUNCT constituent is optional[8]. Still, the *at* type 'seems to be more central to the process', according to Halliday. This is suggested by the following considerations.

(22)' What was he throwing stones at?
(23)' *What was he throwing stones on?
(22)" *What was he doing at the bridge?
(23)" What was he doing on the bridge?

In practice, however, it will be difficult to decide which constituent is most central. In Halliday's examples the intuitive difference and the different 'transform potential' exemplified in (22)'—(23)" might be explained by the

---

[7] I borrow the term 'affinity' from Becker (1967b: 11).

[8] I presume that the optionality of *at the bridge* differs from the only apparent optionality of a locative adjunct with *habitare*, which can be omitted only under certain conditions (example (21)).

German *werfen* requires an obligatory $ADJUNCT_{DIRECTION}$ according to Steinitz (1969: 13).

fact that the two ADJUNCTS differ semantically. Halliday calls them both 'place'.

The idea that constituents may stand in a closer or less close relation to other constituents in the construction has been put forward in Latin linguistics as well. For example, Booth (1923: IX) observes that 'The adverb of degree, for instance, may be in a closer relation to the modified word than the adverbs of place, time, manner'. Regrettably he gives no further elucidation. Recently Dressler (1970: 35) has suggested that in the example (24) there are various degrees of affinity.

(24)   in Asia venire e montibus in planitiem ('to come from the mountains to the plain in Asia').

in Asia would seem to stand in a less close relation than *e montibus* and *in planitiem* with respect to *venire*. 'Ce fait suggère aussi une certaine gradation des compléments facultatifs'. Compare also Marouzeau (1949: 13-4).

After these introductory remarks I will deal with two problems which can be understood better by assuming different degrees of affinity. The first of these concerns the so-called *ablativus causae* in Latin. The second problem concerns temporal and locative ADJUNCT constituents.

6.2.1. Ablativus causae explained as a marker of a peripheral ADJUNCT$_{MOTIVE}$

A further illustration in Latin of the fact that optional constituents can nevertheless be distinguished in accordance with their affinity towards the PREDICATOR constituent can be found in the characteristics of the so-called ablativus causae and the instrumental ablative in passive sentences[9]. Though in this section no proper adverbs are involved the topic deserves attention since it sheds some light on the function ADJUNCT, especially ADJUNCT$_{MOTIVE}$, in which so-called causal adverbs like *idcirco* ('therefore') occur (cf. chapter 10).

In Latin grammatical studies the ablativus causae is considered a variant of the instrumental ablative. Now, the ablative exemplified in passive sentences like

(25)   voluptate victus est ('he has been overcome by passion'),

---

[9]   Actually, the notion 'affinity' plays a role in Szantyr's discussion (: 132) of these ablatives and the way to distinguish them.

is considered a variant of the instrumental ablative as well. The question arises then, as to how ablativus causae and passive instrumental can be distinguished[10]. The distinction between the two types of ablative is, according to Szantyr (p. 132), that an ablativus causae is 'loosely' constructed with a verb, whereas the relation between verb and passive instrumental is closer. This very difference would even explain the occurrence of both ablatives in

(26) nimis sermone huius irā incendor ('I am very much inflamed with anger by his words'; Plt. *Ps.* 201).

sermone huius is taken as an ablativus causae, *ira* as passive instrumental. Both constituents are optional (for absolute *incendi*, cf. Cic. *Orat.* 132), including the constituent that is the counterpart of the constituent functioning as SUBJECT in the active sentence. We will see that this constituent need not be *ira*.

The difficulty is that syntactic evidence which proves Szantyr's observation correct is hard to find. The collocation as such might be explained, of course, by the fact that, semantically, *sermone* and *ira*, which both function as ADJUNCT, are different, i.e. similarly to the way the collocation of *hoc tempore* ('at this time') and *ira* could be explained in

---

[10] The conception of Case that is behind terms like 'ablativus causae' has a diachronic basis and is in the end determined by the form-meaning-parallelism-hypothesis. Latin grammarians usually try to determine which ablative, genitive, etc. is present in a certain expression instead of taking cases as overt formal characteristics of the functions and semantic roles fulfilled by nominal constituents, without a definite semantic aspect or syntactic value of their own.

This leads to inconsistencies of the following type: in *vinci voluptate* ('to be overcome by passion') the ablative case is explained as a passive instrumental. In *vinci a voluptate* (Cic. *Off.* 1,68; same translation) the ablative is regarded as a separative ablative (*a* is a preposition which means 'by' in passive constructions, but is normally used only with animate nouns). This explanation is claimed to be supported by examples like
ludibrio, pater, habeor :: *unde?* :: *ab illo* . . ('I am made a laughing stock, father! :: by whom? (lit.: 'from which direction') :: by him'; Plt. *Men.* 783-4). In this explanation the fact is neglected that both *voluptate* and *a voluptate* correspond to *voluptas* in the active sentence (which − following the traditional line of arguing − would make an identical explanation of both ablatives more plausible), whereas there is no sense in comparing an ablative case form of a noun as such with a governed ablative form of a noun in a preposition phrase.

(27) hoc tempore nimis ira incendor ('at this moment I am very much
      inflamed with anger').

(See the following chapter on coordination.) In that case the assessment of
sermone as ablativus causae and of *ira* as instrumental ablative need not be
based on affinity. In principle three structures could be assigned to (26).

    (a)   ADJUNCT$_X$ (ADJUNCT$_X$ PREDICATOR)
    (b)   ADJUNCT$_X$ ADJUNCT$_Y$ PREDICATOR
    (c)   ADJUNCT$_X$ (ADJUNCT$_Y$ PREDICATOR)

The brackets indicate greater affinity between constituents. (b) is the
structure underlying (27). Probably (c) corresponds best to the words of
Szantyr (p. 132)[11].

Before examining evidence which might suggest a choice between (a), (b)
and (c), I want, if possible, to make a few things clear with respect to the
syntactic functions SUBJECT, ADJUNCT, PREDICATOR and the semantic
roles *AGENT, CAUSE, INSTRUMENT, PROCESS.* Consider the following
English sentences.

(28) (a)   Someone killed the man with an axe.
    (b)   *Someone killed the man by an axe.
    (c)   The man was killed with an axe (by someone).
    (d)   The man was killed by an axe (*by someone).
    (e)   An axe killed the man.
    (f)   *The man died with an axe (*by someone).
    (g)   *The man died by an axe (*by someone).

My suggestion is that *with* is necessary if an *AGENT* (a human instigator)
or, possibly, a *CAUSE* (an inanimate cause) is either expressed or
presupposed[12]. *axe* is the *INSTRUMENT* used to fulfill the action of
killing, but may be the *CAUSE* (e.g. falling down by chance) of someone's
death. In the latter case an *AGENT* is excluded. The passive is with *by*.
Some nouns may occur as *CAUSE* with verbs like *die*, which might be

---

[11] It is clear that (a) presupposes the possibility of a function + semantic role
occurring more than once in a sentence. This is in conflict with Fillmore (1968: 21) in
whose theory each 'case' only occurs once.

[12] According to Huddleston (1970: 504) 'Instrumental presupposes a (deep structure)
Agentive'. I think that — at any rate in Latin — an inanimate cause is possible, too, on
evidence of (26) and (29a').

considered a lexical passive of 'unintentional killing'. *axe*, however, does not occur in that way. The most difficult case is (28e), which might be explained as an example of SUBJECT$_{INSTRUMENT}$ (cf. Becker 1967 b: 79; Fillmore 1968: 21-5; 7.3.1.3. below), or as an example of SUBJECT$_{CAUSE}$. With the first alternative (28c) agrees, with the second (28d). Personally I think that the second alternative (*CAUSE*) is right.

In the English sentence *axe* clearly belong to the category of instrument words. Consequently the examples (28) are not completely identical with those of (29) with *ira*. Still, something of the above may be valuable for the analysis of the Latin examples (29), be it only the method of analysis.

(29) (a) aliquis me irā incendit ('someone inflames me with anger'; cf. Plt. *Asin.* 420: qui semper me ira incendit ('who always sets me afire with rage')).

(b) irā incendor ('I am inflamed with anger').

(c) iră me incendit ('anger fires me': cf. Cic. *Brut.* 93: (Galbam) naturalis quidam dolor dicentem incendit ('a kind of innate emotion fired Galba')).

(d) irā ardeo ('I burn with anger'; cf. Cic. *Att.* 2,19,5: edicta Bibuli audio ad te missa. iis ardet dolore et irā noster Pompeius ('I hear Bibulus' edicts have been sent to you. Pompey is blazing with wrath and indignation at them')).

(e) aliquid iram incendit ('something kindles the anger'; cf. Cic. *Tusc.* 4,43:... ut auditoris iram oratoris incendat actio ('that the delivery of the orator may kindle the anger of the hearer'))[13].

(a') aliquid me irā incendit ('something inflames me with anger'; cf. *Bell. Alex.* 29: quae res incendit dolore milites ('these tactics filled the soldiers with burning resentment')).

Following the same kind of analysis as in (28) *irā* in (29a) has to be regarded as an *INSTRUMENT* (the case form is genuinely instrumental in the terminology of traditional grammar), *irā* in (29d) a *CAUSE* (case form: 'passive instrumental'), *iră* in (29c) also a *CAUSE*, whereas (29b) is ambiguous as it stands, since in Latin there is no disambiguation like in English (28c) and (d). In fact, the 'active' parallel may be (29a) as well as (29c). The case form, consequently, is either genuine instrumental or passive instrumental. In (29a') *irā* has to be taken as an *INSTRUMENT*, *aliquid* as a

---

[13] Thes. s.v. *incendo* reads *oratio* instead of *actio*, wrongly.

CAUSE. In (29a) *aliquis* is *AGENT*, of course. (29e) has been added solely in order to make clear that a complete description of the semantic roles which *IRA* may fulfil with respect to *INCENDO* requires even more distinctions.

The examples show that two constituents may be related to *INCENDO* functioning as SUBJECT and ADJUNCT, fulfilling the semantic roles *AGENT* or *CAUSE* and *INSTRUMENT* respectively, for active sentences. In passive sentences constituents are closely related to the PREDICATOR constituent in the function ADJUNCT, fulfilling the semantic roles *AGENT* or *CAUSE* and *INSTRUMENT.* The latter combination might represent he structure exemplified by our initial example (26)

(26)   nimis sermone huius irā incendor:

ADJUNCT$_{CAUSE}$ ADJUNCT$_{INSTRUMENT}$ PREDICATOR$_{PROCESS}$

This is actually alternative (b) mentioned on p. 86. Both constituents are related to the verb (and both are optional).

However, there are constructions which bear resemblance to the *PROCESS CAUSE* type (29b-d), but are, in fact, different. Examples are (30) and (31):

(30)   ei vel aetate vel curae similitudine patres appellabantur ('these men were called 'Fathers' by reason either of their age or of the similarities of their duties (to those of fathers)'; Sall. *C.* 6,6).

(31)   quod ego non superbiā neque inhumanitate faciebam ('this I did neither from arrogance nor churlishness'; Cic. *de Orat.* 1,99).

aetate and *similitudine* could not be *CAUSE* of the *PROCESS appellabantur*, but they explain the fact that these men were called '*patres*'. The sentence is not the passive counterpart of

(30)' eos vel aetas vel curae similitudo patres appellabat ('their age or the resemblance of their task called them 'patres').

In (31) *superbiā* and *inhumanitate* could not be *CAUSE* of *faciebam* in view of the presence of an *AGENT* (*ego*). On the other hand they are not *INSTRUMENT* either, but are the motive because of which *id faciebam.* In traditional terms the ablative case form is not a genuine instrumental nor a passive instrumental, but, actually, 'ablativus causae'.

The difference between (29) and (30)-(31) lies precisely in the circumstance that in (29) *IRA* is closely related to the *PROCESS,* whereas the ADJUNCT constituents in (30)-(31) are not related to the *PROCESS* alone, but to the *PROCESS* + other more closely related constituents. The question is whether there is only a difference in affinity (comparable with alternative (a) on p. 86) or a difference in semantic role as well (comparable with alternative (c) on p. 86). The first solution is suggested by the fact that the nouns which occur in the ways described are all abstract nouns and often identical. Still, I think that the second solution is correct. In (30)-(31) the constituents discussed could be answers to questions with *cur?* ('why'). Such a question would probably be excluded in (29). The difference in semantic role might be labelled MOTIVE[14]. Both ADJUNCT $_{MOTIVE}$ and ADJUNCT $_{CAUSE}$ are marked by the ablative case if they are fulfilled by noun phrases (ablativus causae and passive instrumental, respectively)[15].

The distinction between ADJUNCT $_{MOTIVE}$ and ADJUNCT $_{CAUSE}$ is, consequently, not a matter of affinity only. The difference between these constituent types is often blurred by grammarians. Consider the following remark from Kühner—Stegmann (:I, 395) about the ablativus causae ('Ablativ des Beweggrundes'). According to them this ablative is often accompanied by a passive participle, e.g.

(32) (iustitia) eas res spernit et neglegit ad quas plerique inflammati aviditate rapiuntur ('justice scorns and cares nothing for those things, which most people are inflamed with desire for'; Cic. *Off.* 2,38).

The point is that *aviditate* is *CAUSE* with respect to the *PROCESS inflammati* and not *MOTIVE* with respect to *rapiuntur* + closer constituents. The sentence might be paraphrased

(32)' aviditas plerosque inflammat ut ad eas res rapiantur ('passion inflames most people with desire for those things')

---

[14] In order to make clear that a noun functioning as ADJUNCT $_{MOTIVE}$ (ablative case form) may answer a question with *cur?* I mention one example:
si me arbitrabare isto pacto ut praedicas, cur conducebas? :: *inopia, alius non erat* ('if you thought me the kind of person you say, why did you hire me? :: A shortage. No one else to be had'; Plt. *Ps.* 799).
[15] *MOTIVE* and *CAUSE* can hardly be distinguished in Latin, as we have seen. In Dutch *MOTIVE* seems to have a much greater mobility in the sentence than *CAUSE.*

(a late parallel for *inflammare ut* can be found in Thes. s.v. 1455, 50). In many cases the addition of a passive participle (for the sake of brevity I put it this way) would change the status of the ablative case form from *MOTIVE* to *CAUSE* with respect to the *PROCESS* as expressed by the participle[16].

Now, it is the ADJUNCT$_{MOTIVE}$, which complicates the analysis of (26). The analysis might run

(26) nimis sermone huius irā incendor:

$$\text{ADJUNCT}_{MOTIVE} \ (\text{ADJUNCT}_{CAUSE} \quad \text{PREDICATOR}_{PROCESS})$$

that is agreeing with alternative (c) on p. 86. The sentence might, therefore, have two active counterparts

(26) (b)   sermo huius me irā incendit (cf. p. 87).
      (c)   sermone huius irǎ me incendit.

Alternative (a) of p. 86 (two ADJUNCT$_{CAUSE}$ constituents at different levels) seems unlikely, since apparently *CAUSE* does not occur twice with respect to one PROCESS. In favour of (b) one might adduce (29a') and the fact that one would not readily expect *sermone huius* in answer to a question with *cur?* ('why'). In favour of (c) one might point to the quotation given with (29d) and the consideration that there, with *ardet, irā* will have to be understood as *CAUSE* (lexical passive of (29c)) and *iis* as *MOTIVE.* Personally, I prefer the analysis given for (26b)[17].

We have seen that there is reason to assume a difference in degree of affinity towards the verb even with optional constituents. Constituents functioning as ADJUNCT$_{MOTIVE}$ are not closely related to the verb, whereas the equally optional constituents functioning as ADJUNCT$_{CAUSE}$

---

[16] Contingently in (32), if *inflammati* was not present, the noun phrase *aviditate* could be *CAUSE* with respect to *rapiuntur.*

[17] In the light of the preceding discussion there is a priori nothing against accepting an ablativus causae and a passive instrumental within one sentence, as Meusel refused to accept (ad Caes. *Gal.* 4,34,1). He consequently suggested deleting *novitate pugnae* in *quibus rebus perturbatis nostris novitate pugnae . . . Caesar auxilium tulit* ('Caesar brought help to our men embarrassed by the situation by the unusualness of the fight'). In the manuscript version *quibus rebus* would be instrumental, *novitate pugnae* ablativus causae (cf. Barwick, K. 1943. *Gn.* 19, 93-4). The point is, of course, that it is difficult to see why these ablatives have to be regarded as different: *quibus rebus* refers to the preceding context which is a description of the *novitas pugnae.* See Seel (1960).

are closely related to it. As far as this particular
explanation is, probably, that within each sentence
made between a *nuclear* and a *peripheral* part. Long
observed that the main criterion for judging which
and which peripheral, is obligatoriness. 'All obligator
(although not all nuclear tagmemes are obligato.,,.
constituent functioning as ADJUNCT$_{CAUSE}$ we have to do with a nuclear
constituent which is optional, and does not differ in this respect from
ADJUNCT$_{MOTIVE}$ which is peripheral. Notice the fact that this is only
relevant in passive sentences: SUBJECT$_{CAUSE}$ is not optional.

6.2.1.1. *NUCLEUS and PERIPHERY.*

Observations like the above suggest
that in each sentence a distinction should be made between two parts which
stand in a relation to each other that could be called a relation of
NUCLEUS vs. PERIPHERY. It is the verb, or rather the constituent
functioning as PREDICATOR (also copula + adjective) that determines
what belongs to the NUCLEUS. Each verb has a number of open slots,
which can be filled by constituents in specific functions.

Within the NUCLEUS the relation between the verb and the other
constituents can be conceived of in two ways. Either (i) the verb is seen as
the centre to which a varying number of constituents are assigned, together
forming the NUCLEUS, or (ii) the NUCLEUS is regarded as consisting of a
number of constituents at one level among which is the verb. Conception (i)
is comparable with Tesnière's conception (e.g. 1959: 14 and passim) and
would account for the importance of the verb in governing the number and
nature of nuclear constituents. Conception (ii) bears some resemblance to
the functional model described above (p. 75). Its advantage over (i) is that
it does not suggest that the presence of a SUBJECT constituent, etc.
depends on the presence of the verb (Dik 1968: 164-7). On the entire
matter see now Helbig—Schenkel (1969: 20-5). The main difference from
the transformational model (cf. (14) above) lies in the different status of the
SUBJECT constituent, which has lost its 'privileged' position with respect to
the verb.

It is perhaps useful to represent the two conceptions graphically. Many
details have to be left out, since they are not very clear to me at this
moment.

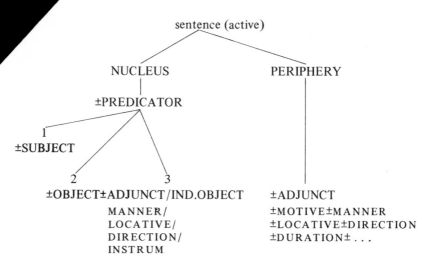

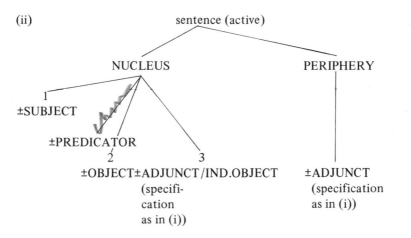

I have only given a semantic specification of ADJUNCT and have left out all categorial specification. The figures (1,2,3) are related to the typographic indications '/' and '±'. They do not represent any sort of order. What I mean is that only a maximum of three nuclear constituents can be found with a verb, but never both an ADJUNCT and an IND. OBJECT constituent at the same time, as far as I can judge. '/' is meant to indicate this exclusion. '±' means that collocation is allowed. For ADJUNCT this means that within the NUCLEUS only one ADJUNCT constituent is allowed (coordination excluded, of course), whereas in the PERIPHERY a variety of ADJUNCT constituents is allowed.

The conception underlying the two models is primarily syntactic and semantic roles are regarded as specifications on syntactic functions: ADJUNCT$_{MANNER}$, etc. I do not imply that a semantic approach is impossible or worse (*MANNER*$_{ADJUNCT}$, etc.). As a matter of fact one semantic role may occur in various functions and, similarly, one syntactic function may cover various semantic roles. My reason for adopting the first strategy is that it is much easier to start from the formal side of language (lexical syntactic category and syntactic function) than from the semantic side (semantic lexical category and semantic role). A slightly complicated version of the representations (i) and (ii) will be discussed in the next section[18].

6.2.2. *ADJUNCT constituents specifying place or time*

In addition to the preceding problem which concerned two constituents that are both optional, but still differ in affinity, since one is nuclear, the other peripheral, I will now discuss the fact that between two or more non-nuclear constituents there is a difference with respect to what seems their respective affinity to the verb. The constituents meant specify temporal and local relations (ADJUNCT$_{TEMP}$, ADJUNCT$_{LOCATIVE}$, etc.).

In a study, which seems to have escaped the notice of most grammarians, Müller (1895) has drawn attention to what he calls a 'predilection for local and temporal parataxis instead of hypotaxis' in Latin. Further evidence for this phenomenon has been presented by Hache (1907: 13-29) and Onnerfors (1956: 117). The following examples illustrate the phenomenon. They exemplify ADJUNCT$_{LOCATIVE}$, ADJUNCT$_{DIRECTION}$, ADJUNCT$_{SEPARATIVE}$, and ADJUNCT$_{TEMP}$.

---

[18] I am not very sure about ADJUNCT$_{INSTRUMENT}$ and IND. OBJECT. I am thinking of pairs like:
Dono tibi librum ('I give a book to you') *IND. OBJECT OBJECT.*
Dono te libro ('I present you with a book') OBJECT ADJUNCT$_{INSTRUMENT}$.
As for sentences like:
doceo te linguam latinam ('I teach you the Latin language'), perhaps we should postulate a peripheral OBJECT to account for the fact that we have passive (a) but not (b).
(a) *linguam latinam doceris* ('you are taught the Latin language').
(b) **lingua latina te docetur.*

(33) ... Postumiam ... domum ad se venisse (lit.: 'that P. had come to
      him in his house'; Cic. *Att.* 12,11).
(34) domi esse apud sese archipiratas dixit duos ('he declared that he had
      two pirate captains in his house'; Cic. *Ver.* 5,73).
(35) in Lysandri ... statua in capite corona subito exstitit ('on the statue
      of Lysander, a crown suddenly appeared on the head'; Cic. *Div.* 1,75).
(36) nos ... hinc Romā qui veneramus ('we who had just arrived from this
      place in Rome'; Cic. *Agr.* 2,94).
(37) his ego tamen diebus ludis scaenicis ... dirupi me paene ('these days
      during the performances on stage I almost overstrained myself'; Cic.
      Fam. 7,1,4).
(38) postero die luce prima movet castra ('the following day at daybreak
      he removed the camp'; Caes. *Gal.* 5,49,5).

There is even an example with three ADJUNCT$_{DIRECTION}$ constituents.

(39) dictator ... Teanum in hiberna ad exercitum redit ('the dictator
      returned to the army in the winter quarters at (lit.: to) Teanum'; Liv.
      23,24,5).

It is impossible to explain the occurrence of more than one local and
directional ADJUNCT constituent by considering one nuclear, the other
peripheral. The phenomenon is not restricted to those verbs with which
such a constituent is obligatory. In particular, example (39) shows that
nuclear versus peripheral is not relevant here. The constituents specify in
narrowing circles locative, directional, separative and temporal relations.
This phenomenon seems restricted to constituents in these functions.
    The question is whether we should make a difference in kind within
these ADJUNCT types or allow for iteration of the same ADJUNCT. The
first alternative has been suggested by Becker (1967a: 113; 1967b: 59).
According to him for the sentence

(40) I live at 2165 Newport in Ann Arbor,

'the proper analysis probably requires two different location tagmemes,
perhaps Loc$_{area}$ and Loc$_{point}$'. To me this proposal seems unattractive
since the phenomenon is not restricted to two constituents as is shown by
(39). Secondly, the distinction 'area' vs. 'point' is relevant only when there
are two constituents as in (40). Only then there is some sense in calling
2165 Newport 'point', *in Ann Arbor* 'area'. The distinction is useless in the
case of one constituent.

(41) I live at 2165 Newport.
(42) I live in Ann Arbor.

Thirdly, the question of which constituent specifies which, can only be decided by one's knowledge of the world. Steinitz (1969: 54) discusses this phenomenon in German and illustrates it excellently with the following examples.

(43) (a)   In der Stadt, auf dem Berg steht noch der Sockel des ₁
             Müller-Denkmals.
      (b)   Auf dem Berg, in der Stadt steht noch der Sockel des
             Müller-Denkmals.

If, in extralinguistic reality, there is a mountain in the town (43a) is correct. Reversely, if on the mountain there is a town (43b) is correct[19].

It seems better, in view of the above considerations, not to consider the apparent uncorrect application of coordination rules (see next chapter) as decisive evidence in favour of setting up several 'subfunctions' like 'area' and 'point'. What is necessary, of course, is a description of the specification relations that are possible between such constituents.

Conclusion. We have seen in this section (6.2.) that constituents that are optional with respect to the verb do not stand in the same closeness with respect to the verb. The examples were of different types. One type could be shown to be nuclear in spite of its optionality (ADJUNCT$_{CAUSE}$). The other types resemble each other in being peripheral. They differ nonetheless in their affinity towards the verb, or perhaps better, in their affinity towards the NUCLEUS. This phenomenon is not restricted to constituents which fulfil different semantic roles and different functions, but is also present in locative and other expressions where semantic role and function are identical. It is not easy to see how such differences in affinity can be expressed in the description of sentences, not to speak of the graphic representation of sentence structures. At any rate it is clear that by calling a constituent a modifier of the verb many subtle distinctions are obscured.

---

[19] With different intonation (43a) might mean: 'the town that is on the mountain'; (43 b): 'the mountain which is in the town'. In that case the second constituent would be ATTRIBUTE.

6.3.   The problem of modal adverbs and disjuncts

In 6.2.1.1. it has been observed that a distinction between nuclear
ADJUNCTS and peripheral ADJUNCTS is attractive. Nuclear ADJUNCTS
are closely related to the PREDICATOR, whereas peripheral ADJUNCTS
are not. The main distinguishing factor are relations of presupposition
between the verb and specific constituents. There is, actually, little reason
to concentrate on the relation between peripheral ADJUNCTS and the
PREDICATOR alone. They could, in fact, better be described as AD-
JUNCTS with respect to the entire NUCLEUS.

In traditional grammar certain adverbs have always been considered as
modifiers of the sentence rather than as modifiers of the predicate (or verb),
viz. the modal adverbs (sentence modifiers, sentence adverbs). According to
Kühner–Stegmann (:I, 793) these adverbs modify the proposition, the
content, as such, while indicating the opinion of the speaker about it. Cf.
4.2. and 4.3.2. above[20]. A number of such adverbs has been given in 4.2.

A similar subclass of adverbs is mentioned in studies of other languages.
The best and most complete study on these adverbs and related expressions
is, in my opinion, Greenbaum (1969a). He uses the term *disjunct*, 'a term
suggesting their lack of integration within the clause to which they are
subordinate' (p. 25). Disjuncts 'express an evaluation of what is being said
with respect either to the form of communication' – *style* disjuncts – 'or its
content' – *attitudinal* disjuncts. I cite one example of each type, (44) style
disjunct, (45) attitudinal disjunct.

(44)   Briefly, India faces famine because there too are many people and too
        little food (Greenbaum 1969a: 82).
(45)   Certainly, he ate a lot (Greenbaum 1969a: 98).

These examples may illustrate the fact that more adverbs than are usually
considered to be modal adverbs behave similarly to them with respect to
syntax and semantics. Many adverbs are used in this way. In Latin grammars
little attention is paid to this phenomenon. Szantyr (: 827) devotes a few
lines to this problem in his part 'Stilistik' in a chapter on brachylogy and
pregnant expressions[21]. The idea is that such usage constitutes a peculiar

---

[20] Kühner–Stegmann's words run: '... sondern auf die Aussage selbst, den
Gedanken, bezogen werden und diesen näher bestimmen, indem sie das Verhältnis des
Gedankens zu der Überzeugung des Redenden angeben'.
[21] References to Thes. s.v. *male* 241,58ff. and s.v. *bene* 2118,70ff. ('well'; 'badly').
(Szantyr has wrongly *bene* 2,118,72.)

brevity of expression. It is, however, doubtful whether it should be regarded as an example of brevity. Though, as we will see, it is difficult to determine how many examples of this use are present in our texts, the phenomenon may have been as normal as in English. The contention in many studies (e.g. Kühner–Stegmann: I, 795) that Latin equivalents of *notably, probably*, etc. are lacking and that Latin uses copula + adjective constructions instead, may be due to lack of clear criteria. I will briefly discuss these constructions (e.g. *notum est* + subject complement; *verisimile est* + subject complement – 'it is well-known that'; 'it is probable that') below.

All Latin grammarians, as far as I know, only speak about what I will henceforth call 'attitudinal disjuncts' (Kühner–Stegmann: I, 795; Szantyr: 827). Hence the label 'Adverb des Urteils' in Szantyr (l.c.). Still, there are examples which may be compared with style disjuncts as well. Thus, Thes. s.v. *brevis* 2187,18 remarks that *breviter* ('briefly') is a short expression equivalent to *ut breviter dicam* ('in order to put it briefly') in

(46) Narbonensis provincia . . . amplitudine opum nulli provinciarum postferenda, breviterque Italia verius quam provincia ('the province of Narbonne is by the vastness of its wealth the equal of any other province: it is, in a word, not so much a province as a part of Italy'; Plin. *Nat.* 3,31)[22].

The best treatment, albeit a short one, is given by Kühner–Stegman(:I, 795). They observe that disjunct use is not restricted to adverbs alone, but can be shown for other adverbial expressions as well, e.g. *ut vere dicam* ('speaking the truth'). See Thes. s.v. *dicere* 973, 29ff. Adverbs and related expressions used in this way 'actually contain the predicate', according to Kühner–Stegmann (:I, 795)[23]. Comparable is a remark by Koestermann (1963: 124) on

(47) leviore flagitio legatum interficietis ('a lesser crime would be to kill a commander'; Tac. *Ann.* 1,18,3).

This is an example of extreme brevity, according to Koestermann: 'Stärkste

---

[22] On *verius* see below p. 100.

[23] An impressionistic description of the disjunct use of what would seem to be a manner adverb can be found in Nisbet–Hubbard (1970: 28) on *(ferrum) quo graves Persae melius perirent* ('the sword whereby the Parthian foe had better perished'; Hor. *Carm.* 1,2,22). They remark: 'As so often the adverb carries the weight of the sentence'.

Komprimierung des Gedankens. . . . Der Abl. modi steht an Stelle eines zu erwartenden Hauptsatzes *levius flagitium erit si . . .*' ('the crime will be smaller if').

Though disjunct use of adverbs has been noticed, no criteria are given for identifying such uses. Hence decisions are often quite arbitrary. For example, one case which was one of the first to be called to attention (by Madvig) could in my opinion be explained in two ways.

(48) num stulte anteposuit exilii libertatem domesticae servituti? ('was it foolish of him to prefer the freedom of exile to the slavery at home? '; Cic. *Tusc.* 5,109).

It is undoubtedly correct to say that *stulte* expresses the conviction of someone judging the process of *anteponere libertatem servituti* ('to prefer freedom above slavery') by the very qualification 'stupid'. The question is, however, whether this conviction is expressed by a constituent which is ADJUNCT$_{\text{MANNER}}$ in the sentence or is DISJUNCT set apart from the rest of the sentence. Madvig's paraphrase, which can be found in his commentary on *De Finibus* 4,63,

(48)' stulte fecit quod anteposuit ('it was stupid that he preferred'),

is no proof of the second alternative. Two factors may have influenced Madvig's paraphrase. Firstly, the assumption that *stulte* must mean 'in a stupid manner'. Secondly, *stulte* is obviously the communicative centre of the sentence.

Similarly, the example mentioned by Kühner–Stegmann (:I, 795)

(49) non meā culpā saepe ad vos oratum mitto, patres conscripti, sed vis Iugurthae subigit, . . . ('it is no fault of mine, Fathers of the senate, that I often address an appeal to you, but I am forced to by the violence of Jugurtha'; Sall. *Jug.* 24,2),

may be paraphrased 'it is not my fault that' etc., but grammatically *mea culpa* could just as well be explained as ADJUNCT$_{\text{MOTIVE}}$[24]. The same question can be raised with respect to Koestermann's comment on example

---

[24] A number of highly debatable cases can be found in Seyffert–Müller (1876: 107). I wonder whether it is accidental that a remarkable number concern passive verb forms like *dicitur obscene* ('it is filthy to say').

(47). Of course, with *leviore flagitio* a judgment is passed on the intended act of killing. Yet, syntactically there is no reason to interpret *leviore flagitio* differently from other cases of ablativus modi.

Even with the word *certe* ('certainly'), which is one of the modal adverbs given by Kühner–Stegmann, there is room for doubt. In the Thes. article a distinction is proposed between (a) *certe* pertaining to the entire sentence or clause, (b) *certe* pertaining to single words. However, the examples of *certe scire*, which is interpreted along the lines of (b) (s.v. 932,57), are open to discussion. Some examples might be better interpreted, in my opinion, along the lines of (a). Thus *id certe scio* is ambiguous: (a) 'I certainly know this' (disjunct) vs. (b) 'I know this for certain' (manner, or perhaps intensifying, adverb) – opposite of *incerte scire* ('not know for certain'; Plt. *Epid.* 505).

It is impossible to draw conclusions about he syntactic characteristics of disjuncts on the basis of the examples which are given in Latin studies. If, hypothetically, we accept as undebatably disjuncts all examples in the Thes. article on *certe* which are interpreted as pertaining to the entire sentence or clause, we find great variation in word order and clause and sentence type. The only criterion which may work is that *certe* may occur as an answer to a neutral (yes–no) question (cf. Ahlman 1938: 36-7). Manner adverbs and other adverbs, as well as related expressions, could not be expected in such an answer (see ch. 8).

(50) miser ergo Archelaus? :: certe, si iniustus ('Archelaus is therefore wretched? :: Certainly if he is unrighteous'; Cic. *Tusc.* 5,35).

The usefulness of this criterion is impeded by the lack of examples. For example, how do we know that one could answer the question

(48)" servituti libertatem anteposuit? ('did he prefer freedom to slavery? '),

with *stulte* ('stupidly yes')?

Other criteria which might be of some use in the study of Latin adverbs would seem to be: (a) non-occurrence in interrogative sentences and clauses; (b) non-occurrence in imperative sentences; (c) exlusion from being intensified, restricted or focused by words like *valde* ('very'), *quam* ('how'), *quidem* ('at least'), etc. These and other criteria work sufficiently in English (Greenbaum 1969a: 84-5; 111-27). *stulte* would be rejected as an example of a disjunct in (48) on account of criterion (a) and so would *certe* in

(51) certen <non> longe a tuis aedibus . . . Romulus Proculo . . . dixerit se
deum esse? ('is it a fact that Romulus told Proculus that he was a
god, not far from your house'; Cic. *Leg.* 1,3).

However, one cannot be certain.

The lack of criteria is equally vexing in cases where these adverbs are not
disjuncts with respect to the main part of the sentence or clause, but are
constructed with smaller constituents, as they often are (4.3.2., cf.
Greenbaum 1969a: 197-201). I give one more example.

(52) rem haud dubie utilem ('an undoubtedly useful matter'; Tac. *Hist.*
1,46,4).

In many cases one might argue about which constituent the adverb has to be
constructed with, as I remarked in 4.3.2. Generally speaking only semantic
considerations are decisive (Ries 1928: 67-8). Moreover, how could adverbs
in such constructions (modifier of an adjective) be distinguished from other
adverbs which are also modifier of an adjective (i.e., are at the same level)?
I return to this problem in 7.1.

Though syntactic characteristics of disjuncts are not clear at present, a
decision may be reached in individual cases by examining the possibility of
using other constructions instead of the one under consideration. Several of
these parallel constructions have been mentioned.

(a)   *breviter = ut breviter dicam.* Cf. ex. (46) + preceding comment
(b)   *certe = certum est* + subject complement. One might point to
the parallelism in

(53) moriendum enim certe est et incertum an hoc ipso die ('for it is
certain that we must die and, for aught we know, this very day'; Cic.
Sen. 74).

If this parallel were decisive, *certe* in (51) would certainly be regarded as a
disjunct. Notice the fact mentioned above (p. 97) that adjective + copula +
subject complement is the normal or complete construction according to
many grammarians. Many modal adverbs in Kühner—Stegmann have no such
parallel construction, some of them quite naturally, because their being
incorporated into the subclass of modal adverbs only reflects the residual
character of this class (e.g. the question word *num*, 'emphatisizer' *quidem*,
negator *non* ('not')), others, because there is no corresponding adjective
(*fortasse* ('perhaps')). But even *verius* in (46), which might be considered a

disjunct, could not be replaced in that sentence by *verius est* + subject complement ('it is more true that . . .').

    (c)   *leviore flagitio* = *levius flagitium erit si.* (Cf. ex. (47) and p. 98)

    (d)   *stulte* = *stulte fecit quod.* (Cf. (48)).

The use of parallel constructions raises questions both with respect to the choice of particular parallel constructions and about the status of parallel constructions in general. If a particular paraphrase is available, what does this tell us about the structure of the original expression? To me it seems necessary not only to search for paraphrase, but to point to syntactic characteristics as well. Paraphrases alone might be used, of course, as a heuristic method the outcome of which has to be confirmed by syntactic observations. Greenbaum (1969a: 82-4; 94-5), for example, gives not only a number of 'correspondences' as he calls parallel constructions, but also a number of syntactic considerations. Parallel constructions alone are only an indication of semantic relationship[25].

Conclusion. We have seen that adverbs and other expressions occur at still another level in the sentence or clause (apart from the nuclear and peripheral levels discussed in 6.2.). Such so-called disjunct use can not only be accepted for some of the modal adverbs, but also assumed for adverbs which as a rule occur as ADJUNCT$_{MANNER}$, e.g. *stulte*. The difficulty is that apart from semantic considerations — sometimes confirmed by the presence of parallel constructions — there are no formal characteristics in Latin to prove that an adverb has to be regarded as a disjunct in a given construction.

Nevertheless it seems sensible to revise the analysis of sentences presented in 6.2.1.1. to the effect that a sentence (or clause) is said to consist of two parts, which could be called CENTRE and DISJUNCT, the CENTRE comprising NUCLEUS and PERIPHERY:

(54)

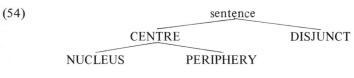

(cf. 6.2.1.1.).

When I was revising this chapter I saw an article by Schreiber (1971) which deals with problems like these as well. In a transformational framework he considers sentence adverbs to be derivationally related to adjective + copula + complement constructions (cf. ex. (53) above) and notes a few other restrictions on their formation.

7. SUBCLASSIFICATION OF ADVERBS

In the preceding chapter I endeavoured to show that generally speaking the relationship of adverbs towards other constituents (both in the phrase and, also, particularly, in the clause or sentence) is much more complicated than the notion 'modify' in the traditional definition would suggest. In this chapter I will discuss three criteria by which adverbs can be classified in a dead language even in those cases where there are no differences with respect to the constituents the adverbs are combined with. For example, in 4.2. a semantic distinction was observed between e.g. *vehementer dicere* ('to speak impetuously') and *vehementer displicere* ('to displease strongly'), manner adverb and intensifier respectively from the semantic point of view. The question was mentioned of whether there are syntactic differences corresponding with the semantic ones. This chapter will be devoted to questions like this. The three criteria discussed are (1) the use of question words; (2) word order; (3) coordination. Coordination will be shown to be most useful.

7.1. The use of question words

In the following examples we find several adverbs constructed with adjectives. These adverb—adjective combinations are constructed with a noun. This can be expressed as follows: Noun ((Adverb) Adjective)(cf. 4.2. – the adverbs are italicized)

(1)   (a)   laudo hominem *valde* nobilem

('I praise the very famous man').

(b)   laudo hominem *vehementer* nobilem

          ('. . . the very famous . . .').

(c)   laudo hominem *sapienter* nobilem

          (lit.'. . . the wisely famous . . .'; cf. (11)-(13) in 4.2.).

(d)   laudo hominem *fortasse* nobilem

          ('I praise the perhaps famous man'; cf. (18) in 4.3.2.).

(e)   laudo hominem *illic* nobilem

          ('. . . famous there . . .'; cf. (26) in 4.3.3.).

(f)   laudo hominem *haud dubie* nobilem

          ('. . . undoubtedly famous . . .'; cf. (52) in 6.3.).

Intuitively, these adverbs seem to belong to different subclasses though they share the characteristic of being optional with respect to an adjective as their HEAD.

These differences could be brought to light by examining which questions (or question types) these sentences might occur as answer to. Such questions might be

(1)   (a')   quam nobilis est homo quem laudas? " :: valde nobilis est ('how famous is the man you praise? :: very famous'): intensifier.

       (b')   quam nobilis . . .? :: vehementer nobilis est ('how famous . . .? :: very famous'): intensifier.

       (c')   ? quomodo nobilis . . .? :: sapienter nobilis est ('in what way is the man famous? :: wisely') : manner.

       (c")   ? nobilisne est . . .? :: sapienter nobilis est ('is the man famous? :: wisely yes'): attitudinal disjunct[1].

       (d')   nobilisne est homo quem laudas? :: fortasse nobilis est ('is the man famous? :: perhaps'): attitudinal disjunct[1].

       (e')   ubi nobilis est homo quem laudas? :: illic nobilis est ('where is the man famous? :: there'): local.

       (f')   nobilisne est homo quem laudas? :: haud dubie nobilis est ('is the man famous? :: undoubtedly yes'): attitudinal disjunct[1].

The status of each adverb in (1a-f) is assessed by transforming the

---

[1] A more attitudinal disjunct-like paraphrase would seem to be *putasne nobilem esse hominem quem laudas?* ('do you think that the man whom you praise is famous? ')

adverb—adjective construction into a predicative construction[2]. The difficulties which present themselves are obvious. What evidence do we have that e.g. *vehementer* in (1b) may be used in answer to a question with *quam*? Similarly, how do we know that questions (1c') and (1c") are allowed, and, if both are correct, how can the difference be proved in a given text? The employment of questions is a useful method, but gives clear results in the study of modern languages only, where informants are at hand and where the linguist can use his own knowledge (see ch. 1). In a study which has to base its conclusions on the data contained in a corpus which presumably has no examples of most of the question—answer pairs given above, other methods seem to be necessary.

7.2. Word order

One criterion which indeed seems suitable in a study of a dead language is word order. Whereas it has been remarked in the preceding chapter that word order is not very useful when a decision has to be made in a given text about the correct analysis of a particular expression, it might be useful for formulating generalizations about different subclasses of adverbs. Bos (1967: 117), for example, observes that the so-called regular adverbs (ending in *-ē* and *-(i)ter*, such as *pulchre* ('beautifully') and *fortiter* ('bravely')) tend to be placed as closely as possible to the verb, whereas the so-called pronominal adverbs like *hic* ('here'), *ibi* ('there'), as well as members of a residual class containing e.g. *clam* ('secretly'), *paene* ('almost'), *huc* ('hither'), *ita* ('so'), *quondam* ('once') show the opposite tendency[3]. I pass over the circumstance that many of the words given by Bos cannot be simply regarded as modifiers of verbs so that it is only of partial interest to examine their relative position with regard to the verb: several of the words modify adjectives and adverbs and e.g. *hic* ('here') could be called a modifier of the NUCLEUS in at least some cases. This has been discussed in ch. 6.

Taking Bos' observations as they are, I examined a sample of the adverbs

---

[2] Of course, it remains problematic whether there are differences between e.g. (a') and (c'). Intuitively, *quam* is a constituent within the adjective phrase *quam nobilis*, whereas *quomodo* is an ADJUNCT at the clause level.

[3] Bos' subclasses are in the first place morphological (cf. 46; 54). The morphological distinctions are supplemented by a few syntactic characteristics. Both morphological and syntactic characteristics are finally explained by reference to the semantic aspect of the stem.

she mentions. I used Merguet's indexes on Cicero's oratorical and philosophical works. I have accepted as valid the distinctions which Merguet makes such as 'adverbs modifying verbs', 'adverbs modifying adjectives', etc. My assumption was that all adverbs may occupy odd positions with respect to the verb, especially when they have a certain emphasis (Kühner–Stegmann; II, 613-4; Szantyr: 410; Löfstedt 1933: 397-402; Marouzeau 1949: 11-33), but that here is a priori nothing which suggests that one adverb should be emphasized more often than another (see however on *hic* below). Given a sufficient number of instances we can simply use statistics to determine the average relative position with respect to the verb.

In the following list I give for each adverb (a) the number of examined instances; (b) the percentage of items occurring before the verb; (c) the percentage of items which occupy the place immediately before or after the verb; (d) the percentage of items placed before the verb in such a way that three or more words are placed between the verb and the adverb; (e) the average 'distance' of adverbs from the verb, if they are placed before the verb, distance being computed in terms of the number of intervening words. I first give examples which belong to Bos' group of regular (adjectival) adverbs. Since these adverbs are for the greater part relatively rare, I give an overall survey of this group and deal only with three of them separately in order to demonstrate that as far as relative distance is concerned generalizations are dangerous. There are probably stylistic differences between the oratorical and philosophical works, but my results are not reliable enough at this juncture to show this.

(i) regular adverbs[4]

(a)	(b)	(c)	(d)	(e)	
358	81%	63%	12%	1.	total
114	87%	70%	10%	0.7	*graviter* ('seriously')
70	76%	57%	12%	1.	*aperte* ('openly')
31	93%	36%	20%	1.5	*celeriter* ('quickly')

(ii) pronominal adverbs

132	95%	12%	55%[5]	2.1	*hic* ('here')
80	95%	25%	33%	1.7	*ibi* ('there')

[4] *acriter* (39), *alte* (17), *aperte* (70), *aspere* (8), *audacter* (21), *celeriter* (31), *fortiter* (36), *graviter* (114), *pulchre* (11), *stulte* (8).
[5] This high percentage may be due to the fact that *hic* is a kind of transition marker in a continuous text ('at this moment').

(iii) residual group (Bos 1967: 116)[6]

(a)	(b)	(c)	(d)	(e)	
37	100%	58%	17%	1.	*clam* ('secretly')
101	88%	38%	40%	2.	*repente* ('suddenly')
116	96%	43%	31%	1.	*vix* ('hardly')
57	83%	84%	0	0.3	*paene* ('almost')
200	99%	54%	18%	1.2	*ita* ('thus', 'so')
188	94%	43%	21%	1.5	*sic* ('so')
207	83%	52%	26%	1.5	*iam* ('already')
60	80%	28%	29%	1.4	*quondam* ('at one time')
66	66%	42%	23%	1.6	*interdum* ('sometimes')
138	83%	50%	34%	2.2	*semper* ('always')

Table (iii) calls for some comment. It is remarkable that 40% of the examples of *repente* are placed two or more places from the verb. The only explanation I can think of is the very meaning of *repente*. It is often placed at the beginning of the sentence. *paene* is found immediately before the verb in 84% of the examples. The explanation might be (hypothetically) that *paene* can be constructed with members of many categories, and could therefore be constructed with many constituents in a sentence with the result that unless a rather fixed position with respect to the verb is observed ambiguity would arise. Distance would be in inverse proportion to the valence of the word. It is not easy to explain, however, why the same would not hold for *vix*, which could be expected, moreover, to cluster with the verb on account of its enclitic nature. In addition, it is not easy to see what explains the low percentage of occurrences of *quondam* immediately before or after the verb.

What is remarkable about the results given in the columns of the tables is that there exists no clear relationship between the figures. One cannot simply say, for example, that if the adverb does not cluster close to the verb and if it occurs frequently in fourth (or more distant) position in front of the verb, then its distance will be great. Take, for example, *quondam*. This suggests that other factors are concealed behind the figures. One might think of phonological (euphony) and syntactic ones, e.g. constraints on word order, if adverbs (and other constituents) in different functions are present in the sentence. What is clear if one compares (i)-(iii), is that there is no evidence for Bos' remark that members of the subclass of regular adverbs

---

[6] I have not examined all examples of *ita, sic* and *iam*, but have stopped near 200.

behave in a way systematically different from the adverbs given in (ii) and
(iii). It is true that in column (d) the figures of the regular adverbs are lower
than those of the other adverbs (exceptions *clam, ita, sic* — not
surprisingly), but the figures in column (c), which are actually relevant to
Bos' assertion, do not allow generalizations.

All this supports Marouzeau's conclusions about relative position of the
adverbs (1949: 33), which is relatively free if the word does not belong to a
group (e.g. an adjective phrase). With respect to the relative position of
adverbs and verbs which do not as a rule constitute a group (see ch. 6.) this
could be expected to be less fixed. The tables prove that there is no
remarkable difference between the adverbs in this respect.

7.3.   Coordination

In my opinion the best criterion for the syntactic and semantic subclassification of adverbs (and other linguistic phenomena) is coordination, especially
if — but not only if — conclusions have to be drawn about a dead language.
Coordination has been used by Ahlman (1938: 29) with Finnish adverbs. He
observed that, within the category of adverbs, subclasses could be
distinguished inter alia by their being mutually incompatible as far as
coordination is concerned. In modern linguistics the use of coordination as a
heuristic means 'for the initial determination of phrase structure' has been
stressed by Chomsky (1957: 36) and has been demonstrated on the topic of
adverbs by Steinitz (1969: 46-55).

I will briefly set forth the rules which, in my opinion, underlie
coordination. These rules will appear to be of two main types: syntactic and
semantic. It goes without saying that the need of both types of rules has
consequences for the grammatical model and the kinds of information to be
handled in a grammar. In the Introduction and in ch. 6 attention has been
given to this problem.

In discussing the rules which have to be set up I will deal with violations
of these rules. Many of such violations have received attention in Latin
studies. Next I will formulate some sorts of procedure for using coordination as a heuristic test. In the end of this section I will give a demonstration
of the application of this procedure to Latin adverbs.

7.3.1.   Restrictions on coordination
Chomsky (1957: 36) and traditional grammar (e.g. Kühner—Stegmann: II,

2; 555-6) consider coordination as a device by which two or more linguistic expressions which have some part in common can be reduced to one shorter, and complex, expression. Accordingly, Kühner–Stegmann (:II, 555ff.) explain coordination in a wider context of 'brachylogy', i.e. brevity of expression which can be supplemented by information from the immediate context.

They give the following examples of coordination:

(2)   (i)   Cicero eloquentissimus fuit ('Cicero was very eloquent').

     (ii)   Hortensius eloquentissimus fuit ('Hortensius was very eloquent').

     (iii)   Cicero et Hortensius eloquentissimi fuerunt ('Cicero and Hortensius were eloquent')[7].

In Kühner–Stegmann's opinion, the reduction which is assumed in (2 iii) is comparable with the reduction in comparative expressions. Take the following example of so-called *comparatio compendiaria* ('shortened comparison'), quoted by Kühner–Stegmann (: II, 556).

(3)   ingenia . . . nostrorum hominum multum ceteris hominibus omnium gentium praestiterunt ('as for ability, our fellow-countrymen have far excelled the men of other race'; Cic. *de Orat.* 1,15).

Another type of reduction is exemplified by the example (4).

(4)   conferre vitam Trebonii cum Dolabellae ('compare Trebonius' life with Dolabella's'; Cic. *Phil.* 11,9; Szantyr: 217).

Now, whereas the idea that coordination has to be regarded as some sort of reduction (hence the term 'conjunction reduction') is attractive in (2), it breaks down in other cases (Dik 1968: 72-92). One of the irreducible cases cited by Dik (p. 90) is

(5)   The King and Queen are an amiable pair.

It cannot be reduced to (6)

---

[7] The process of coordination is seen not only as a synchronic phenomenon by Kühner–Stegmann, but is supposed to reflect the historical development of human language as well. See ch. 11.

(6)   *The King is an amiable pair and the Queen is an amiable pair.

It seems better, then, to consider coordination one of the means of recursion in natural language. Coordination is, in fact, *linear recursion* (Becker 1967a: 110; 1967b: 56; Dik 1968: 92-4; 114-5) as opposed to nesting recursion exemplified by

(7)   The man who saw the boy who killed the dog that chased the cat has been shot.

Certain structural elements in an expression may be 'repeated' in the same position. For example, if it is correct to say

(2)   (i)   Cicero eloquentissim(us) fu(it),

then it is also correct to say

(2)   (iv)   Cicero et Hortensius (et . . .) eloquentissim(i) et sapientissim(i) (et . . .) fu(erunt) et appellat(i sunt) (et . . .) ('Cicero and Hortensius (and . . .) were very eloquent and wise (and . . .) and were called (and . . .) like that')[8].

It is immediately clear that repetition of an element is restricted by certain conditions. The following sentence would undoubtedly be ungrammatical.

(8)   *Cicero et tunc eloquentissimi fuerunt ('*Cicero and then were very eloquent').

On the other hand (9) would be correct.

---

[8]   A description of this example of coordination requires a decision about the way in which the relationship between Number of the SUBJECT constituent and Number of the PREDICATOR has to be described. Two possibilities are open:

(i)   congruence of Number between S and P is seen as governed by S;
(ii) the S constituent is in apposition to a bound SUBJECT in the verb form, with which it agrees in Number (Longacre 1964: 35; Dik 1970).

The second alternative is better, in my opinion. My description is nonetheless in accordance with alternative (i), because this alternative is usually followed. In this way my remarks on coordination can be better compared with Kühner–Stegmann's treatment.

(9)   Cicero tunc eloquentissimus fuit ('Cicero was then very eloquent').

Apparently there must be some kind of equivalence between two constituents in order to allow coordination between them. If such an equivalence is lacking coordination is forbidden. In that case the constituents, if they can be combined at all, are merely juxtaposed (on this term ch. 4, n. 16)[9]. Conversely, coordination and juxtaposition tell something about the constituents involved. In the case of adverbs these phenomena may tell us which adverbs are equivalent and which are not.

For constituents to be equivalent a number of conditions must be fulfilled. These conditions have been discussed most profitably by Becker (1967a; b) and Dik (1968). Much of what follows can be found in their publications. These conditions concern category, syntactic function, semantic role, semantic aspect of the coordinated members and selectional restrictions between the coordinated members and the constituent they are constructed with.

7.3.1.1.   Categorial equivalence.   It has often been suggested that coordination is allowed between constituents if these are categorially equivalent. This opinion seems to be held by Chomsky (1957: 36) and others[10] and was also implicitly present in traditional grammar. This is apparent from the fact that coordination patterns of adverb & noun, adverb & preposition phrase, etc. are often mentioned as if they were exceptional. Take e.g. Kühner—Stegmann (:II, 24) and Thes. s.v. *et* 873,27ff. Related to this opinion is probably the observation by Eklund (1970: 17): 'When a present participle is coordinated with a substantive, this coordination indicates that the present participle has the general value specific to the substantive'. The participle is then said to be used as a substantive[11].

Evidently, this approach is not correct, as has been shown inter alios by Marouzeau (1949: 11) with respect to adverbs.

---

[9] It is interesting to see that grammarians were confused about mere juxtaposition. Thus, Hache (1907: 23) explains expressions like *ibi tum* ('there then') as instances of asyndeton. The point is, of course, that no coordination is allowed in this case. Similarly, I have not found examples of the (modern?) phraseological expression *hic et nunc* ('here and now') in classical Latin. On asyndetic coordination 7.3.2. (end) below.

[10] Chomsky speaks about 'constituents of the same type', Steinitz (1969: 54) also assumes a relation between the possibility of coordination and equivalence of (sub)category. See, however, her discussion of the status of the subcategories of adverbs which she distinguishes (especially pp. 63-9).

[11] Confusion of category and function also plays a role (cf. 3.3.).

(10) *recte* atque *ordine* fecere ('they did rightly and properly'; Sall. *Cat.*
      51,4): adverb & noun.
(11) utinam ... *ex animo* ac *vere* diceres ('would that you were sincere and
      genuine in saying'; Ter. *Eun.* 175): preposition phrase & adverb.

Compare also from the sample made by Hahn (1930: 98; 126; 139; passim)

(12) concordes animae *nunc* et *dum nocte premuntur* ('souls harmonious
      both now and while wrapped in night'; Verg. *A.* 6, 827): adverb &
      (temporal) subordinate clause.

Examples like these occur quite frequently and there is no reason to assume
that there is something unusual about them. Notice the fact that the
coordinated constituents behave similarly with respect to questions introduced by question words like *quomodo* ('how') and *quando* ('when').
Apparently categorial equivalence is not essential, although, as we will see, it
certainly plays a role in coordination.

7.3.1.2. Functional equivalence. The examples (10)-(12) could be explained if it is assumed that constituents may be coordinated if they are
equivalent as to syntactic function. This idea has been worked out most
consistently by Dik (1968: 25-32; passim). He argues that two or more
constituents may be coordinated if they are functionally equivalent and
stand at the same level of structural hierarchy. The latter condition is
necessary in order to explain the fact that in an expression like

(13) fides populi Romani ('the faithfulness of the Roman people'),

there are two HEAD–ATTRIBUTE relations, but no coordination: *Romani*
is ATTRIBUTE within the phrase *populi Romani,* in which *populi* is HEAD.
The phrase *populi Romani* is, in turn, ATTRIBUTE within the entire phrase
(13), in which *fides* is HEAD. *Romani* is said to be ATTRIBUTE on a lower
level than *populi Romani.* The notion 'level' also takes care of

(14) multi cives boni ('many good citizens').
(15) multi et boni cives ('many good citizens').

The translations obscure the fact that in (14) *multi* is ATTRIBUTE of the
phrase *cives boni,* whereas in (15) *multi* and *boni* are both ATTRIBUTE of
the noun *cives* (examples in Merten 1893: 10f). Thus, though (14) and (15)

are semantically closely related, they must be assigned different syntactic structures.

Similarly, there is a difference of level that forbids coordination of *bene* and *latine* in expressions of the type *bene latine loqui* ('to speak correct Latin').

(16) quia (Curio) latine non pessime loquebatur ('because Curio used a Latin which was not so bad'; Cic. *Brut.* 210, cf. Von Nägelsbach– Müller 1905: 375-6)[12].

The notion of level underlies, in fact, the distinction of NUCLEUS vs. PERIPHERY as well. Whether two different functions have to be assumed, or two different levels, can be solved only within the entire system: one might contend that in (16) *latine* and *pessime* fulfil different functions, which would explain the absence of coordination (see also the discussion in 6.2.1. above). However, the very existence of examples of coordination might suggest a distinction of level. I would certainly follow this alternative in (16) on evidence of (17), from which it can be inferred that *latine* is an adverb of manner.

(17) plane et latine loquuntur (lit. 'they speak clearly and Latin'; Cic. *Phil.* 7,17).

The idea that functional equivalence is involved seems to have occurred to Kühner–Stegmann (:II, 555). They remark that reduction takes place 'when two or more coordinated sentences have some constituents in common which stand in a similar grammatical relation' (my translation). The notion of level can be found in Latin studies as well (Kühner–Stegmann: II, 32; Nisbet 1961: 160).

7.3.1.3. Equivalence of semantic role. Whereas the incorporation in the theory of coordination, of functional notions and of the notion 'level' is a help for (10)-(12) and (16), it has been shown that equivalence of this kind

---

[12] Even if one is convinced that *latine loqui* is an idiomatic phrase on account of expressions like *latine scire* ('to know Latin'), the structure has to be described in terms of a distinction of level. Comparable, then, is *non quo libenter male audiam* ('not because I like being abused'; Cic. *de Orat.* 2,305). *libenter* and *male* cannot be considered members of the same subcategory (I mean *male* in the expression *male audire*). There is also a difference of level: *libenter* modifies *male audire* as a whole.

is not a sufficient condition for coordination. Becker (1967a: 115-6; 1967b: 61-2) and Fillmore (1968: 21-2; 1969: 115-6) have reintroduced traditional semantic notions like *AGENT, GOAL,* etc. alongside syntactic functional notions like SUBJECT, OBJECT, etc. (see ch. 6 and Introduction).

The usefulness of these semantic notions, for which I use the term 'semantic role' following Halliday (1970), is apparent in instances of coordination as well. Consider the following example taken from Becker (1967b: 62):

(18)   John hit Bill with a stone.
(19)   A stone hit Bill.
(20)   *John and a stone hit Bill.

In (18) and (19) *John* and *a stone* are syntactically SUBJECT. If functional equivalence alone were sufficient (20) should be grammatical. That this is not true has something to do with the circumstance that, semantically, *John* is *AGENT*, whereas *a stone* is *INSTRUMENT* both in (18) and (19). (See now also Huddleston 1970: 504 on *INSTRUMENT* and 6.2.1 above.)

Before proceeding to the next section it may be useful to point out that here is no one-to-one correspondence between semantic aspect and semantic role. For example, not only do instruments function as *INSTRUMENT,* but nouns of other semantic subclasses are also possible.

(21)   John hit Bill with his wife.

The scene referred to is rather picturesque, to be sure, but the sentence is correct. In Dutch we have an expression which runs lit.

(22)   He swabbed the floor with his wife.

Of course, such expressions are often odd. It is the job of the linguist to explain this oddness. See now also Kooij (1971: 113-5).

7.3.1.4. Relations between semantic aspects of constituents.   Even if the condition of equivalence of function and semantic role is met there are facts which point to further semantic conditions on coordination (Becker 1967a: 117; 1967b: 65). Take the examples (23)-(27) from Vergil's *Aeneid.* They all have a peculiar effect and have, consequently, attracted attention, e.g. in Hahn (1922; 1930).

(23) pariterque oculos telumque tetendit ('he levelled eyes and shaft alike'; Verg. *A.* 5,508).

(24) oculos dextramque precantem protendens ('uplifting eyes and pleading hands'; Verg. *A.* 12,930-1).

(25) ut tandem ante oculos evasit et ora parentum ('when at last he came before the eyes and faces of his parents'; Verg. *A.* 2,531).

(26) qui carmine laudes/ Herculeas et facta ferunt ('who in a song acted out the praise of Hercules and his deeds'; Verg. *A.* 8,287-8).

(27) (ferre iubet) pallam signis auroque rigentem ('he bids him bring a mantle thick with figures and gold'; Verg. *A.* 1,648).

(23)-(27) were probably not incorrect, judging from the number of occurrences, and were perhaps even deliberately employed for their particular effect in poetic and rhetorical style. What makes these examples odd is not a break of equivalence of function or of semantic role. I cannot figure in what way the members of the coordination would differ in these respects. What seems to be left is the semantic aspect of the coordinated members.

For example, in (27) the gold is the material which is used for the embroidery (cf. Hahn 1922: 193). Vergil might have used *aurum* alone to refer to the *signa*, or at least to inform the reader that the robe was embellished with gold, whereas *signis* alone could never have informed one that they were manufactured of gold. In (26) *laudes* and *facta* are not independent of each other: the praise given to Hercules concerns Hercules' deeds[13]. In (25) *oculos* stands in a 'part of' relation towards *ora*. One could perhaps even better say that *oculos* and *ora* are synonymous in this case. The same thing may have been expressed twice for metrical reasons[14]. At any rate, in (25)-(27) the reference of the coordinated members is partially the same[15].

(23) and (24) are more complicated. The oddity of the coordination of *oculos* and *telum* in (23) could be explained by saying that the first member is 'human', the second 'not—human' (Lausberg 1960: 353), or, preferably,

---

[13] A quite different explanation is given by Servius (a.l.): 'The old men only sang the praise of Hercules, the young men acted out his deeds by gestures as well'. In this – in my opinion wrong – explanation zeugma would be involved.

[14] That metre favoured the use of (25)-(27) may be inferred from Servius' comment on Verg. *A.* 1,61: *molemque et montes* ('mountain masses'; lit.: 'masses and mountains').

[15] Numerous 'examples involving terms not mutually exlusive' from Vergil are to be found in Hahn (1930: 224-44).

'inalienable' vs. 'alienable' (cf. Lyons 1968: 301). Yet, *oculos* and *dextram* in (24) are both inalienable and still give rise to a similar effect.

In some of the examples one might argue that, following the reduction hypothesis, one of the reduced expressions underlying the complex one is incorrect. For example, in (23) *telum tendere* seems to be correct (at least in poetry), whereas *oculos tendere* seems less correct[16]. Similarly, *manum dextram protendere* is normal, but *oculos protendere* is not. However, in this way we cannot explain why coordination is excluded or odd in cases which could be reduced to correct expressions. Thus, (28i) and (ii) are correct, but we would hardly expect (iii).

(28) (i)   oculos conicere in aliquem ('to turn one's eyes to someone'; cf. Cic. *Cluent.* 54).
      (ii)   tela conicere in aliquem ('to throw spears to someone'; cf. Caes. *Gal.* 1, 26).
      (iii) *oculos et tela conicere in aliquem.

It appears that not only are the semantic aspects of the coordinated members involved, but also their respective selectional restrictions with respect to the constituent they are constructed with, in this case the verb. Apparently, there should be identity, at least compatibility, of these relations towards the verb.

7.3.1.5. Violations of restrictions on coordination. We have seen, that on the one hand there are syntactic restrictions on coordination, on the other hand semantic restrictions. The latter concern the semantic role of the coordinated members, the semantic aspect of each of the members, and the relationship towards the constituent with which the members are constructed. Violations of these restrictions are possible. I have discussed a number of them in the preceding sections. I will give some more attention to them now.

Many of these violations have received attention in Latin philology. The most extensive study, to my knowledge, is Hahn (1930). She deals with questions of coordination in Vergil. The study falls into two parts: (i)

---

[16] *oculos tendere* is read by Nonius (411,2 M.) in Lucr. 1,66 instead of *tollere* ('to raise') and accepted by West (1969: 161-2) on account of the military context.
    Nonius cites as an instance of *tendere* being equivalent to *dirigere* ('to direct') Verg. *A.* 2,405: *ad caelum tendens ardentia lumina* ('uplifting to heaven her blazing eyes').

'members parallel logically' (i.e. semantically) 'but not grammatically'; (ii) 'members parallel grammatically but not logically'. A number of the examples in this chapter are taken from Hahn's book.

Not a few oddities which follow from violation of the rules of coordination have been discussed by Latin scholars in the chapter on so-called *hendiadys*, and *zeugma* and *syllepsis*[17]. Thus, the examples (27) and (26) would probably be taken as instances of hendiadys. Perhaps (25) as well. Proposals on a precise definition of hendiadys have failed until now (Hatz 1886: 3-11; Szantyr: 782-3). The reason for this is precisely that, grammatically, there is nothing unusual about such expressions (conditions regarding categorial and functional equivalence are observed), whereas semantically it is open to dispute whether the semantic relationship between the coordinated members is such that a definition of hendiadys, e.g. the one given in Kühner–Stegmann (:I, 26) applies. This definition runs: 'The peculiarity of this type of expression lies in the fact that two words (especially substantives), one of which is semantically subordinate to the other[18] — so that what is expressed by the semantically subordinate substantive ought to have been expressed by an attributive genitive case form of this substantive or by an attributive adjective — are coordinated in the same case by *et, que* and *atque (ac)*. Both words refer to the same thing[19], but illustrate it from a different angle, to the effect that they supplement each other and together constitute one concept ('Begriff')'. Given this definition the coordinated constituents in (26) might be paraphrased 'the praiseworthy deeds of Hercules' and *laudes* and *facta* might be said each to refer to one aspect of the same thing. Similarly, instead of *signis auroque* in (27) *signis aureis* ('golden figures') might have been expected. Many other cases, e.g. those from Cicero given in Hatz (1886), are disputable, however. What makes Kühner–Stegmann's definition problematic is their remark that 'one concept' is constituted and their calling one member subordinate to the other.

The examples (23) and (24) are usually treated as instances of zeugma[20]. In fact, in particular zeugma and syllepsis cover many of the violations of coordination, syntactic as well as semantic though these notions and the

[17] These notions are not well-defined. See below. It may also be rewarding to examine examples of so-called apo koinou constructions.
[18] 'der Begriff des einen dem des anderen untergeordnet'.
[19] 'bezeichnen dieselbe Sache'.
[20] Cf. Williams (1960) ad Verg. *A*. 5,508; Szantyr (: 833); Lausberg (1960: 353); Lussky (1953: 290).

difference between them have never been clearly defined (Szantyr: 832)[21].

One attempt to define zeugma can be found in Lussky (1953: 285). The definition runs: 'Zeugma is a figure of speech in which two nouns are joined to a verb strictly suitable to only one of them, but easily suggesting another verb suitable to the other noun'. This definition would exclude many of the cases described as 'instances of zeugma'.

Firstly, those cases would be excluded under the definition in which the verb is suitable to both nouns. Accordingly, Lussky (p. 287) finds no difficulty with

(29) si et in urbe et in eadem mente permanent ('if they remain in the city and in the same spirit'; Cic. *Cat.* 2,11).

He takes '*permanent* literally with *in urbe*, figuratively with *in eadem mente*'[22]. Of course, we may not assume zeugma in (29), but this does not make this just ordinary Latin. Secondly, those cases would be excluded in which the verb is only suitable to one of the nouns and does not easily suggest another verb. Now, the trouble starts again with the words 'easily suggesting'. Lussky and Austin (a.l.) hold that in

(30) longa tibi exsilia et vastum maris aequor arandum ('a long exile and a vast distance of sea you must plough'; Verg. *A.* 2,780),

it is not easy to supply a verb from *arandum* to go with *exsilia*. They explain the sentence as ellipsis: *longa tibi exsilia erunt* ('your exile will be long'). Of course, those who assume zeugma consider it not particularly difficult to supply a verb from *arandum.* In addition, it is questionable whether it will always be so easy to find a verb to explain the ellipsis. Lussky's treatment of the second type is the more unattractive since it proceeds from the reduction hypothesis and, also, from a static view on language. It seems that these coordination patterns widen the use of a verb and 'create' figurative use. It is unlikely that one could say *exsilia arare*, but one could perhaps say *longa exsilia et vastum aequor arare.*

---

[21] I do not agree with Szantyr (: 832) that the distinction between syntactic and semantic zeugma (and syllepsis) is useless, though often a decision between them may be difficult and sometimes they may overlap.

A history of the notion 'zeugma' and the relation towards syllepsis and apo koinou can be found in Sievers (1907: 7-19).

[22] In particular *et . . . et* ('both . . . and'), which is stronger than *et* alone, is found (Szantyr: 833).

Lussky's definition certainly clarifies the treatment of many instances which are considered zeugmatic. However, it does not account for the phenomena within a wider domain of coordination. The use of the term 'zeugma' by Lussky covers only one of the types of deviant coordination suggesting that the other deviations are normal. It seems preferable to me not to search for new definitions of traditional notions, but to try to single out the various conditioning factors.

(i) The examples (23), (24) and (30) can be explained as violations of the rules of compatibility of semantic aspect and relation towards the constituent (i.c. the verb) they are constructed with (aspect 7.1.3.4.). Violations of this particular type are often found as instances of zeugma. The coordinated members are categorially equivalent (i.c. substantives).

(ii) Violations of semantic role are common as well. Apart from example (29) consider

(31) inceptoque et sedibus haeret in isdem ('and he sticks to his purposes and his place'; Verg. *A*. 2,654).

Whereas *in urbe* in (29) and *sedibus* in (31) could be considered as ADJUNCT$_{LOC}$, *in eadem mente* and *incepto* could not. Examples like these are often considered as zeugma as well.

(29) and (31) might perhaps be described as instances of violation of type (i) as well. The difference between these two examples and the cases cited under (i) is that in (i) we seem to have no difference as to subtype of OBJECT, whereas these examples exemplify different ADJUNCTS. But this may have something to do with the nature of the function OBJECT. Generally speaking one might argue about violations of semantic role thus that what is involved is a difference in relationship with the verb. Thus, in (18) a different act of hitting is implied from that in (19), viz. intentional vs. unintentional. *hit* in (18) could be described as *cause to hit*, as *hit* in (19). If a situation is imagined in which, for example, *John* is falling down a hill together with *a stone*, (20) is not really odd at all. However, this description is merely a rephrasing of the observation that *John* in (18) is *AGENT*, whereas *a stone* in (19) is *INSTRUMENT* or something like that. Moreover, assuming so to speak of two different *hit* verbs would obscure the fact that *hit* is one of those verbs which allows for the variation of structure

exemplified in (18)-(20): being one of the verbs that can be associated with three nominal constituents[23].

(iii) There are also examples of syntactic violations, e.g. (32) and (33). (32) is mentioned as an example of syllepsis in pseudo-Iulius Rufinianus *De schematis lexeos 2*.

(32) *his* quidam *signis* atque haec exempla *secuti* ('by such tokens and led by such instances'; Verg. *G.* 4,219).

(33) praemissus . . . *orator* et subdole *speculatum* Bocchi consilia ('sent as a spokesman and to spy out secretly the plans of Bocchus'; Sall. *Jug.* 108,1).

In (32) the noun phrase (ablative case form) *his signis* functions as an ADJUNCT$_{MOTIVE}$. It is coordinated with a participle which functions as a PREDICATIVE COMPLEMENT of the SUBJECT (cf. Hahn 1930: 122). In (33) a noun (*orator*) which functions as a PREDICATIVE COMPLEMENT of the SUBJECT is coordinated with a supine I functioning as ADJUNCT$_{PURPOSE}$.

These examples are also interesting in that they show that the interpretation of the participles, neutral in themselves, is forced so to speak in the direction of the semantic role of the constituents they are coordinated with. Neither (32) or (33) are semantically surprising, but both are syntactically divergent.

7.3.2. Procedure

Given the restrictions formulated in 7.3.1. it must be possible to obtain an insight into the syntactic and semantic characteristics of constituents in a linguistic expression (e.g. of adverbs) by examining which constituents in which functions they can be coordinated with and, conversely, with which they cannot. Next it must be possible to classify words, phrases, etc. by these characteristics.

A question which has to be raised is whether the examples of coordination that are found in our texts and, like the ones discussed so far, are in conflict with the theory of coordination briefly sketched above

---

[23] Of course, the notion of semantic role would be useful in the description of those ADJUNCTS which are not in a type of relation towards the verb like that of *a stone* towards *hit* in (18)-(20), for example *yesterday* and *in the mountains*, unless one preferred a large number of syntactic functions instead of one function ADJUNCT.

should be marked as deviant or should be accepted as normal cases. The latter strategy would imply that the theory is not applicable to Latin and would demand another theory which would also explain the examples mentioned, whatever the theory would be like. In my opinion there are several considerations which are in favour of the theory that I have expounded. The first consideration is, of course, the circumstance that a very high percentage of coordination structures can be explained by the theory. Secondly the fact that ancient grammarians paid attention to the stylistic effect of the divergent examples suggests that they did not fully conform to the norm. Thirdly, considering them deviant is the more attractive since this can be explained in terms of violations of the rules of coordination given above[24].

Given this positive conclusion concerning the value of the theory it seems sensible to use it heuristically in defining the syntactic and semantic properties of adverbs. The procedure that will eventually yield a subclassification of the traditional category of adverbs will be as follows:

(a)   if two or more constituents are coordinated, they are (i) at the same level; (ii) equivalent as to grammatical function, semantic role and semantic relation with respect to the verb, adjective, adverb, etc. with which they are constructed;

(b)   if two or more constituents are juxtaposed, they are (i) not equivalent in the sense given under (a) and/or (ii) not at the same level; a decision can be reached only within the overall system;

(c)   proviso: the corpus may contain violations of the rules given under (a) and under (b); they can be discovered to be such in the light of the overall system;

---

[24]   Textual problems are involved as well. Take the following example from Caes. *Gal.* 6,37,1. All good mss. read *hoc ipso tempore et casu Germani equites interveniunt* ('at this very moment and by accident German horsemen intervened'). *et* is omitted in the later mss. and by most editors, including Seel in his recent Teubner edition. Constans, however, (Budé edition) retains *et*. In the opinion of Meusel, Seel, and others this is impossible, since this would imply *hoc ipso casu* ('by this very accident'), which is obviously nonsensical. Yet, this is not the point. *hoc ipso* may and must belong to *tempore* alone.

Syntactically, the members of the coordination (*hoc ipso tempore* and *casu*) are equivalent as to grammatical function (ADJUNCT) and on the same level. They are not equivalent, however, as far as their semantic role is concerned (De Man 1965: 14). Hence the expression is odd and has to described as being in conflict with the rules of coordination. Only prejudice about Caesar's style could apparently settle the question of whether a unanimous ms. tradition had to be put aside. In my opinion it ought not to.

(d)   necessary condition: a sufficient number of examples.

It is self-evident that the proviso (c) is necessary in order to avoid unpleasant conclusions as I will now illustrate.

(34)   omnia cursim et properantes transmittunt ('they pass over everything hastily and in a hurry'; Sen. *Ep.* 2,2).

(35)   recte et vera loquere ('speak truly and honestly! '; Plt. *Capt.* 960).

In (34) the wrong conslusion might be: (a) *cursim* functions as a PREDICATIVE COMPLEMENT of the SUBJECT (cf. *properantes*); (b) *properantes* functions as an ADJUNCT$_{MANNER}$ (cf. *cursim*). Similarly in (35): (a) *recte* functions as an OBJECT (cf. *vera*); (b) *vera* functions as ADJUNCT$_{MANNER}$ (cf. *recte*).

Apparently, the correct explanation is that *cursim* and *recte* function as ADJUNCT$_{MANNER}$. Coordination is present against the rules on semantic grounds. *properantes transmittunt* and *properanter transmittunt* and *vera loquere* and *vere loquere*, respectively, are semantically equivalent, though syntactically different.

In favour of the analysis of (35) we might adduce

(36)   de quo recte et verissume loquitur Atreus ('of which Atreus speaks correctly and with perfect truth'; Cic. *N.D.* 3,68).

In favour of (34)

(37)   cursim et breviter attingere ('to touch hastily and briefly'; Plin. *Ep.* 1,20,2).

It is possible, of course, that certain adverbs will appear to occur frequently both coordinated with certain constituents and also juxtaposed with them. An example is *diu* ('long' — see next section). This must have implications for their classification.

Improper coordination constitutes a difficulty. Take the English example (38)

(38)   John went home and in a hurry.

Becker observes (1967a: 134) that it cannot be considered an example of genuine coordination as appears from the fact that it is impossible to effectuate a permutation of the two coordinated members as one group

(38)' *Home and in a hurry John went,

whereas it is possible to separate the members and place *in a hurry* in front

(38)" In a hurry John went home.

Such examples are, moreover, often recognizable by a particular intonation. In Latin improper coordination is less easy to handle. An example is

(39) vah! vapulabo hercle ego nunc, atque adeo male ('oh Lord! I'm in for a beating now, and a bad one, too! '; Plt. *Truc.* 357).

adeo male is added so to speak as an afterthought, *vapulabo* being understood. In particular *et . . . quidem* is used in this way (Krebs–Schmalz 1905: I, 523-4). Whether a coordination pattern has to be considered as genuine or not can only be decided on the basis of the rules formulated and cannot be established on formal grounds.

One point has been left out of the discussion until now, viz. when can we speak of coordination in Latin, or rather, in what way is coordination expressed in Latin. Coordination is overtly expressed in Latin by the following *coordinators* (on these, Dik 1968: 34-55; cf. also ch. 10 on so-called coordinating conjunctions). The copulative coordinators are *et, atque, ac, -que, cum . . . tum, et . . . et, ut . . . ita;* the alternative coordinators are *aut, vel, sive . . . sive, -ve;* the adversatives are *sed, at.* Semantically and syntactically there are differences between the three subclasses given, but they all share the characteristics of linking constituents which conform to the conditions discussed in 7.3.1. Semantically related words like *tamen* ('still') do not occur like this. On the semantic differences between the subclasses see Dik (1968: 271-81). On the syntactic differences between the subclasses (of English *and* and *but,* not differing much from Latin *et* and *sed*) see Greenbaum (1969a: 28-32; 1969b).

There is also non-overt coordination, viz. so-called asyndeton. This type of coordination is not different in its general characteristics (Dik 1968: 31-4), but is of no assistance as a heuristic test, of course. A few examples can be found in Kühner–Stegmann (:II, 151). An example of copulative asyndetic coordination is

(40) omnes sapientes semper feliciter absolute fortunate vivere ('that all wise men at all time enjoy a happy, perfect and fortunate life'; Cic. *Fin.* 3,26).

Apart from the fact that from the heuristic point of view asyndetic coordination is less usefull, the precise interpretation of possible examples is not always clear. Take the example given by Kühner—Stegmann as asyndetic.

(41) aperte tecte quicquid est datum libenter accepi ('I gladly received what was given openly or secretly'; Cic. *Att.* 1,14,4).

This could be interpreted 'what was given openly or secretly', i.e. as an example of alternative asyndetic coordination. Shackleton Bailey (a.l.), however, compares examples like English 'bitter-sweet', 'in the sense that Pompey's praise was neither open and direct nor so veiled as to be imperceptible'. In this way the expression would not be regarded as asyndetic. Though, in my opinion, Shackleton Bailey's interpretation is not correct — at least there are not enough parallels which might prove such a usage in Latin — there always remains room for debate.

I have not used asyndetic coordination in the following section.

7.3.3. Application to some Latin adverbs

Given the procedure sketched in 7.3.2., I collected examples of adverbs occurring in coordination or in juxtaposition. I mainly used Merguet's lexica of Cicero's oratorical and philosophical works. To this collection, which is quite extensive, I added stray instances I found when reading Latin texts or that can be found in other studies. The collection contains not only instances of adverbs and adverbs, but also adverbs and noun phrases, adverbs and prepositional phrases, etc. Obviously, I was not particularly interested in cases like (34) and (35) given above and (42).

(42) (virtus) quae et semper et sola libera est ('(virtue) which is free for ever and alone'; Cic. *de Orat.* 1,226)[25].

These are not very useful in classifying adverbs.

As so often the results of the investigation are not really startling. Still they are useful, since in contrast with intuitive assignment to certain subclasses they are based on objective observations. Of course, certain results are in conflict with intuition. For the purpose of this study (see

---

[25] See Thes. s.v. *et* 882,46 and Kühner—Stegmann (:II, 24) for more examples. Add Cic. *Att.* 2,19,5; *Imp. Pomp.* 47.

Introduction) it seems sufficient to discuss a few instructive cases. I will confine myself to adverbs that would seem to belong to the subclass of manner adverbs.

This subclass contains most of the so-called adjectival adverbs. Their syntactic homogeneity appears from their frequently occurring in coordination patterns with each other.

(43) (i) audacter et aperte dicere ('to speak boldly and frankly'; Cic. *Q. Rosc.* 16).

    (ii) breviter aperteque scribere ('to write briefly and plainly'; Cic. *Fin.* 2,100).

    (iii) libenter audacter libereque dicere ('to speak as one pleases, boldly, and freely'; Cic. *S.Rosc.* 31).

Judging from their meaning it is not surprising that *clam* ('secretly') and *palam* ('openly') belong to the same class.

(43) (iv) aperte palamque dicere ('to speak plainly and openly'; Cic. *Ver.* 18).

Instances of coordination suggest that other words such as *derecto* ('straightly'), *fortuito* ('accidentally'), *merito* ('justly'), *secus* ('otherwise'), *singillatim* ('one by one') and *temere* ('rashly') belong to the same subclass.

(44) (i) cur non derecto et palam regionem petiverunt ('why didn't they go to the region directly and openly'; Cic. *Agr.* 2,44).

    (ii) movebatur . . . immoderate et fortuito ('it moved without a rule and by chance'; Cic. *Ti.* 48).

    (iii) recte facis et merito et pie ('you act rightly, justly and dutifully'; Cic. *Leg.* 1,63).

    (iv) partem maximam . . . beate aut secus vivendi ('the main factor in our happiness or the reverse'; Cic. *Fin.* 4,59).

    (v) quid singillatim potius quam generatim atque universe loquar? ('why should I take them one by one instead of speaking in general or comprehensive terms? '; Cic. *Ver.* 5,143).

    (vi) libidines temere et ecfrenate . . . incitarentur ('passions are driven recklessly and uncontrollably'; Cic. *C.* 39).

Members of the class of manner adverbs are often found in coordination with ablative case forms of nouns and noun phrases (cf. Szantyr: 117).

Sometimes a distinction between adverbs and noun (phrase)s is difficult to make (cf. 5.3.). Examples are *casu* ('accidentally'), *ritu* ('according to custom'), *more* ('according to usage'), *ordine* ('properly'), *iure* ('rightly'). I quote two instances.

(45) (i) quae (officia) iudicio, considerate constanterque delata sunt ('which are performed with judgment, considerately and firmly'; Cic. *Off.* 1,49).

(ii) confiteretur . . . et magno animo et libenter ('he would confess proudly and gladly'; Cic. *Mil.* 80)[26].

Such coordination patterns prove that the term 'ablativus modi' has some justification.

We also find instances of coordination with prepositional phrases, in particular with the prepositions *sine* ('without'), *cum* ('with'), and *ex* ('according to'). Again a few examples.

(46) (i) quae sunt . . . varie et ad tempus descriptae ('which have been formulated in varying forms and for the needs of the moment'; Cic. *Leg.* 2,11).

(ii) temere prosiluisse . . . atque ante tempus ('that they sprung forward thoughtlessly and before the right time'; Cic. *Cael.* 64).

(iii) dies bene et ex praeceptis tuis actus ('a day well spent and in accordance with your lessons'; Cic. *Tusc.* 5,5).

Finally, there is an instance of a manner adverb coordinated with an ablative absolute phrase.

(47) nec sapienter et me invito facit ('he does this unwisely and against my wish'; Cic. *Cael.* 16).

It has been observed in 4.2. that words which seem to be regarded as manner adverbs can be called quantifiers or intensifiers under certain circumstances. These observations were only based on semantic considerations. An investigation into coordination patterns in which these words may occur gives syntactic support, though the evidence is small. For example, *acerbe* ('severely') will probably be regarded as a manner adverb in

---

[26] An excellent example from Sallust is *Jug.* 97,4: *non acie neque ullo more proelii sed acervatim . . . incurrunt* ('they attacked not in order or with any plan of battle but in swarms').

(48) libidinose . . . et acerbe et avare populo praefuerunt ('they indulged in licence and in cruelty and greed towards the people'; Cic. *Rep.* 2,63).

In (49), however, its very occurrence alongside *penitus* ('deeply', 'thoroughly')[27] confirms the idea that *acerbe* indicates not so much (or not only) the quality of 'hatred', but also its intensity.

(49) acerbe et penitus oderat ('he hated him bitterly and intensely'; Cic. *Cluent.* 171).

Similarly *leviter* ('lightly', 'slightly') might be considered a manner adverb (being an adjectival adverb), but will be taken rather as an intensifier in (50).

(50) non qui leviter nocet sed qui nihil nocet ('not the man who is guilty of a slight offence, but the man who is guilty of none'; Cic. *Tusc.* 5,41).

A similar problem arises with respect to *publice* ('publicly') and *privatim* ('privately'). On the basis of morphological considerations they might be taken as manner adverbs. The two words are often coordinated.

(51) privatim et publice laudent ('they praise him both unofficially and officially'; Cic. *Font.* 32).

However, coordination of *privatim* with *in fanis* ('in temples') in (52) and the fact that the two words do not occur in coordination with 'normal' manner adverbs — at least not in my corpus — suggest that they have to be set apart.

(52) in urbibus et privatim et in fanis invidiosa res est ('whether in private possession or in temples, the thing creates hatred in the cities'; Cic. *Leg.* 2,45).

(Cf. juxtaposition with *apertissime* in Cic. *Ver.* 5,1.)

On closer inspection the assignment of *palam* to the subclass of manner adverbs is not as clear as I suggested above. A few examples suggest that it

---

[27] I must confess that I find difficulty with the construction in Cic. *Div.* 1,13: *'cum (mare) subito penitusque tumescit'* ('when the sea begins to swell suddenly and totally').

can be compared with *publice* and *privatim* in some sense. In Cic. *Pis.* 23 the manuscripts read

(53)   arma . . . luce et palam comportarentur ('weapons were brought in in daylight and so that everybody could see it').

(cf. 1.1.2.). Nisbet (1961: 86) prefers the old conjecture *luce palam*, being 'the normal expression' in Cicero (e.g. *Sest.* 83). The actual problem is, of course, whether *luce* and *palam* can be coordinated. The expression *luce palam* itself can be interpreted in two different ways: (i) *luce* and *palam* are equivalent in some respect and are coordinated asyndetically; (ii) *luce* and *palam* are not equivalent and are juxtaposed. In the first interpretation the manuscript reading of (53) is correct, in the second it is not, unless, of course, *palam* has the characteristics of two subclasses, both the subclass of manner adverbs (this would explain juxtaposition in the expression *luce palam* and coordination with *aperte* in (43iv)) and to the subclass of temporal adverbs (which would explain coordination in (53)). Although, again, the evidence is scanty, I believe that this argument is correct. Equivalence with *luce* would explain the occurrence of *palam* juxtaposed with manner adverbs, as in (54).

(54)   apertissime repugnarunt, cum et recusarent et palam fortissime atque honestissime dicerent ('they openly fought the measures, protesting against them and saying courageously and honourably before all . . .'; Cic. *Cluent.* 153).

Another implication would be that examples of *palam* coordinated with temporal adverbs such as *luce*[28] are to be found. Nisbet (l.c.) quotes two examples adduced by A. Klotz in favour of the manuscript reading:

(55)   Pompeius clam et noctu, Caesar palam atque interdiu (exercitum educit) ('Pompeius secretly and by night, Caesar openly and by day'; Caes. *Civ.* 3,30,3).
(56)   dumque haec luce agerentur et palam ('when this was going on in the light of day and before the eyes of all'; Amm. Marc. 24,4,21).

Nisbet does not consider these satisfactory parallels. Perhaps not for what is

---

[28]   *luce* is a temporal adverb. Compare Cic. *Tul.* 47: *permittit (lex) ut furem noctu liceat occidere et luce* ('the law allows one to kill a thief both at night and by day').

'normal' in Cicero, but they are from the point of view of coordination. There is, moreover, a slightly different but semantically quite close parallel in (57).

(57) Thessalonicam omnibus inscientibus noctuque venisti ('you came to Thessalonica without telling anyone and by night'; Cic. *Pis.* 89).

It seems best to assign *palam* to two classes[29].

I will now discuss a few adverbs that would intuitively seem not to belong to the subclass of manner adverbs, but are often found coordinated with them, viz. *multum* ('(very) much'), *saepe* ('often'), and *diu* ('long').

For example, *saepe* would seem to be an adverb of frequency on account of (58).

(58) ut (Pompeius) in senatu non semel sed saepe multisque verbis . . . salutem imperi . . . adiudicarit ('that P. assigned to me in the senate, not once but often and at length the credit of having saved the empire'; Cic. *Att.* 1,19,7).

In particular the comparative form *saepius* is found coordinated with *semel* ('once') and *iterum* ('once more').

(59) semel atque iterum ac saepius . . . coacti sunt ('once and twice and more often they are compelled'; Cic. *Font.* 26).

It is not surprising, then, that *saepe* can be found juxtaposed with temporal and manner adverbs, (60)-(61) and (62)-(63) respectively.

(60) cum saepe antea . . . tum me consule ('often earlier and also in my consulship'; Cic. *Flacc.* 67).

In (60) the coordination is between *antea* and *me consule*.

(61) quamquam id quidem cum saepe alias tum Pyrrhi bello . . . iudicatum est ('yet this very question has been decided on many occasions before, but particularly in the war with Pyrrhus'; Cic. *Off.* 3,86).

---

[29] Another solution would be to assign *aperte* in (43iv) and *obscure* and *occulte* elsewhere to two subclasses.

One could, of course, hold that (53) has to be explained as irregular coordination, as is (42). This seems less feasible to me in view of the parallels cited.

In (61) the coordination is between *alias* and *Pyrrhi bello*.

(62) persaepe esse severe ac vehementer vindicatum ('punished again and
      again with sternness and vigour'; Cic. *Ver.* 5,133).
(63) scripsit . . . et multis saepe verbis et breviter aperteque in eo libro . . .
      mortem nihil ad nos pertinere ('he argued repeatedly and at length
      and also stated briefly and plainly in that book that death does not
      affect us at all'; Cic. *Fin.* 2,100).

In (63) *multis verbis* is juxtaposed with *saepe*[30].

It appears, however, that not only is *saepe* found juxtaposed with these
adverbs, but also coordinated with them. Consider the contrast between the
temporal adverb *nuper* ('lately') and *saepe* in (64) and coordination of *saepe*
and the ablative noun phrase *bello Punico secundo* ('in the second Punic
war') in (65).

(64) sicut et tu ipse nuper et multi viri boni saepe fecerunt ('as you did
      lately and many good men have often done'; Cic. *Flacc.* 86).
(65) plena exemplorum est nostra res publica cum saepe, tum maxime
      bello Punico secundo ('our own country has many instances to offer
      throughout her history and especially in the second Punic war'; Cic.
      Off. 3,47).

Similarly, there are instances of *saepe* coordinated with manner adverbs:
(66)-(69)

(66) saepe et palam . . . dixerat ('he had frequently and publicly said . . .';
      Cic. *Ver.* 2,102)[31].
(67) haec . . . liberius ab eo dicuntur et saepius ('these things are discussed
      by him more freely and more often'; Cic. *Fin.* 2,28).
(68) et saepe et iure vexatus ('often and rightly assailed'; Cic. *Phil.* 3,23).
(69) vehementer erat et saepe vexatus ('he was assailed furiously and
      often'; Cic. *Cluent.* 113)[32].

We have seen so far that *saepe* can be assigned to at least three subclasses
judging from the coordination patterns in which it occurs: frequency,

---

[30] Cf. (58) above, where *multis verbis* is coordinated with *semel* and *saepe*.
[31] *et* is omitted in cod. O – 'fortasse recte' in A. Klotz' opinion.
[32] Unless *vehementer* is an intensifier (quantifier) here.

temporal and manner adverbs. In addition, *saepe* is coordinated with quantifier *multum* and duration adverb *diu*.

(70) quas (lacrimas) pro me saepe et multum profudistis ('which (tears) you have often and copiously poured out for me'; Cic. *Planc.* 104).
(71) saepe et diu ad pedes iacuit ('he often and for a long time prostrated himself at their feet'; Cic. *Quinct.* 96).

Now, it is interesting that *multum* and *diu* show a similar variety of use as *saepe* (they are not coordinated with temporal adverbs, however). Thus, *diu* is found coordinated with manner adverbs (72), but also juxtaposed (73).

(72) quae singillatim ac diu conlecta sunt ('what I have acquired singly and through a long period of years'; Cic. *Div. Caec.* 72).
(73) Pansa sine causa paulo ante tam accurate locutus est tam diu? ('did Pansa without a reason make such a precise and lengthy speech just now? '; Cic. *Phil.* 12,6).

Also it is found coordinated with *multum*.

(74) haec diu multumque et multo labore quaesita ('all this, acquired for a long time and often and by earnest labour'; Cic. *Sul.* 73).

The examples of *saepe, multum* and *diu* suggest that these words have to be assigned to several subclasses as far as their syntactic characteristics are concerned. Proceeding from the semantic point of view they would probably each be assigned to one subclass.

Whereas in the above examples no distinction of level was assumed to explain the juxtaposition of adverbs, this now seems necessary in order to account for the juxtaposition of manner adverbs and other constituents functioning as ADJUNCT$_{MANNER}$ in the examples (75)-(80). Several types can be distinguished.

In (75) it seems reasonable to call *lepide* ('pleasantly') a nuclear ADJUNCT$_{MANNER}$ as opposed to *miro modo atque incredibili* ('in an extraordinary and incredible way'), which is peripheral.

(75) miroque modo atque incredibili hic piscatus mihi lepide evenit ('wonderfully and unbelievably this fishing expedition turned out very pleasantly'; Plt. *Rud.* 912).

In (76) and (77) one might feel inclined to assume a kind of specification like that described in 6.2.2. for time and place ADJUNCTS.

(76) ita facillime quae res totum iudicium contineat . . . intellegetis ('by this means you will most readily understand on what the whole issue depends'; Cic. *S. Rosc. A.* 34).

(77) at stulte . . . qui dissuaserit. quomodo stulte? ('it was foolish to plead against it. How was it foolish? '; Cic. *Off.* 3,101).

In (78) it seems reasonable to say that whereas *alio modo* ('in another way') is constructed with *perfici, facile* ('easily') goes with *possit*. Compare also (79).

(78) quam facile vel aliunde vel alio modo perfici possit ('how easily can it be attained with assistance from some other source or in some other way'; Cic. *Tusc.* 4,74).
(79) nec facere aliter ullo modo possumus ('we cannot possibly do otherwise'; Cic. *Off.* 3,101).

(See, however, on *nec . . . ullo modo* also n. 33.)
   Example (80) is less easy to explain.

(80) etsi ea . . . quamvis ad aetatem recte isto modo dicerentur ('though those things were rightly said thus, for any age whatever'; Cic. *Tusc.* 5,27).

I would suggest that *recte* is a DISJUNCT.
   The difference between the examples (75)-(80) and the examples of *palam, saepe,* etc. is, that there is no reason to assign these words to let's say the subclass of frequency adverbs or what have you. They do not occur in

coordination patterns with words other than manner adverbs or other constituents functioning as ADJUNCT$_{MANNER}$[33].

Conclusion. In this chapter I have discussed three means of achieving a better subclassification of adverbs, namely the use of question words, examination of relative position with respect to the verb, and coordination. I hope that this sketchy discussion of manner adverbs has sufficed to show that given a theory of coordination as expounded above, the use of coordination as a heuristic method is most promising and gives the most objective results even if a number of less clear-cut cases remain.

---

[33] *quomodo* ('how') occurs coordinated with e.g. *unde* ('whence'), *quando* ('when? '), *a quibus* ('by whom') in questions, which seem to offer greater freedom. See, however, also (78). Two examples: *quaero unde (constantia) nata sit aut quo modo* ('whence or how would consistency be engendered? '; Cic. *Acad.* 2,23). *quo modo . . . haec aut quando aut a quibus inventa dicemus* ('how, when and by whom shall we say that these things were invented? '; Cic. *Div.* 2,80).

nullo modo ('by no means') and less clearly *ullo modo* ('somehow') and *quodam modo* ('in some way') can be regarded as negators and quantifiers. Consider *nullo modo*, coordinated with *vix* ('hardly') in Cic. *N.D.* 2,20: *ut profluens amnis aut vix aut nullo modo . . . corrumpitur* ('just as a running river almost or entirely escapes pollution'). Therefore, juxtaposition with *facilius* ('easier') in Cic. *fr.* I,12 is not surprising. One may compare Dutch *geenszins, enigszins.*

8. ADVERBS AND OTHER INVARIABLES

Morphologically, adverbs resemble words that are usually assigned to other categories such as interjections, prepositions, subordinating and coordinating conjunctions. Their common characteristic is that they are all indeclinable, invariable, or whatever one wants to call it, that is, they do not belong to the inflectional nominal and verbal categories[1]. A common denominator for words belonging to the classes mentioned, that is often found, is 'particle'. In fact, 'particle' is as good as any other term as long as it is used consistently in a morphological sense, as it is by Matthews (1965; cf. 2.2.2.). Since in Latin linguistics (but also elsewhere; see e.g. Ruijgh 1971: 99 on Greek), the notion 'particle' is often used in syntactic sense as well, or rather in several syntactic senses, I will avoid it and use rather the term 'invariable'[2].

---

[1] On *nequam* see p. 21.

[2] 'Particle' is used for all so-called coordinating conjunctions (Szantyr: 473-514; Ernout–Thomas 1959: 437ff.; Blatt 1952: 329-37). Cf. ch. 10.

Secondly, for both coordinating and subordinating conjunctions. Thus Szantyr (: 170) opposes adverbs to prepositions and particles.

Thirdly, for all invariables. In the same vein we find such usages as 'partikelartige Erstarrung' (Szantyr: 133, explaining for the development of *quare* ('why') from an ablative case form to an adverb).

Then, with a greater vagueness, 'particle' is used for the relative *qui* ('who') by Marouzeau (1953: 83).

A fifth variety is offered in the new Oxford Latin Dictionary. Each entry is provided with information about the (sub)class to which the word belongs. Thus, *aut* ('or') is called 'conjunction'. The term 'particle' is applied to *autem* ('however'), that is to a word which is usually assigned to the category of coordinating conjunctions, just like *aut*. (Continued on p. 136.)

Actually, there are a number of syntactic (as well as semantic) differences between adverbs and other invariables, to which I will now turn. The first and most important distinguishing criterion that I will discuss is the criterion of 'sentence-valence' — I borrow the term from Van Wijk (1967: 240-1). Adverbs are said to be capable of occurring independently, in one-word-sentences, whereas e.g. prepositions are said not to occur in this way[3]. On the other hand, it has been observed that interjections do not occur other than independently. I will try to show that this criterion is difficult to apply in Latin in the first place and, secondly, intersects with the traditional class of adverbs.

8.1.   Adverbs as optionally free forms

The only Latin grammar, in which the sentence-valence criterion is used is O'Brien (1965). He observes (p. 39-40) that adverbs optionally occur as free forms, in contradistinction to interjections, which obligatorily occur in that way, and other invariables, which never occur as free forms[4]. Kuryłowicz (1964: 21), too, considers the occurrence of traditional adverbs as free forms the primary criterion by which they can be differentiated from prepositions[5].

Finally, Blatt (1952: 33) distinguishes 'les particules et adverbes numéraux multiplicatifs'. Prof. Blatt kindly explained to me in a letter that he wants to distinguish between *semel* ('once'), *bis* ('twice'), etc. on the one hand — multiplicative numeral particles — and *primum* ('for the first time'), *iterum* ('for the second time'), etc. on the other — numeral adverbs.

Only the third use agrees with the use made of the term by Matthews. Of course, there would be no objection to the other senses in which the term is used, provided they were used consistently. This is not the case.

[3] Quotation of isolated words should be left out of account, of course.

[4] I do not follow O'Brien's terminology throughout, in order not to complicate the discussion. His grammar is written from the tagmemic point of view.

The term 'free form' as opposed to 'bound form' has become familiar in linguistics since Bloomfield (1935: 177ff.): 'Forms which occur as sentences are free forms' (p. 178). The following discussion might be used to demonstrate that Bloomfield's definition of the word as a 'minimum free form' (p. 178) would exclude a large number of candidate-words and is therefore unattractive.

[5] The relationship between adverbs and prepositions is considered in ch. 9. On words like *intra* ('inside'), which share characteristics with 'pure' prepositions and adverbs see 9.1.

Most words which may occur independently are not likely actually to occur in one-word-sentences unless in an appropriate setting of context and/or situation, e.g. only if an appropriate question precedes or, conversely, if an appropriate answer follows. These words may be said to have 'restricted sentence-valence' (Van Wijk 1967: 241).

The sentence-valence criterion is applicable in the study of modern languages (cf. Roose 1964: 22-3; Greenbaum 1969a: 25). In Latin syntax, however, it is much more problematic, due, of course, to the fact that the Romans were not writing to facilitate our linguistic studies[6]. Some words which, on the basis of analogy with modern languages, one would expect to occur as sentences, do not in fact so occur, but in such cases it is difficult to determine whether, in fact, they could not occur in this way. For example, I expected *enim* and *nam* ('for')[7] which are usually considered coordinating conjunctions, not to occur in one-word-sentences and this assumption has proved correct. On the other hand, I would have expected *ideo* ('therefore'), a causal adverb (cf. ch. 10 end) to have sentence-valence, but I have not been able to find examples. This criterion can therefore not be decisive in Latin. (For general problems of attestation see 1.1.2.)

Now, the lack of examples of independent use of a word need not force us to reject a word as an adverb if it shares characteristics with other candidate-adverbs which do occur independently. For example, in answer to a question introduced by *ut* ('how')

(1)   quaeris ego me ut gesserim ('you ask how I comported myself'; Cic. *Att.* 4,18,1),

we find *constanter et libere* ('firmly and frankly'). Immediately following we find

(2)   ille . . . ut ferebat ('well, how did he take it? ')

and the answer *humaniter* ('pleasantly'). We might extrapolate this finding and assign sentence-valence to *moleste* ('with difficulty'), *bene* ('well'), *suaviter* ('pleasantly'), etc. without looking for examples, since they share other characteristics with *constanter, libere* and *humaniter*.

Extrapolation is less easy, however, in the traditional subclass of modal

---

[6] On the difficulty of using questions in Latin, cf. Dressler (1970: 31).
[7] On *nam* and *enim* see my note 14 of ch. 11, where I discuss the translation with 'for'.

adverbs. In view of the heterogeneity of this subclass we should like to find the occurrence of each word in one-word-sentences actually attested. The results of such an inquiry into attestation are quite disappointing. I will now deal with a few of the problems that turn up, especially since O'Brien pays no attention to actual use of the criterion.

In my section 6.3. I have referred to the traditional view of modal adverbs as being words that modify a sentence and I have shown how this view is unclear and incorrect. I proposed to divide the sentence into two parts which stand in a relation CENTRE:DISJUNCT to each other. Since modal adverbs can be regarded in a sense as a comment on the content of the entire sentence, they might be expected to occur in questions in which the content of the sentence as a whole is questioned, i.e. in so-called neutral or yes—no questions[8]. In modern languages like English and Dutch possible answers to such questions are *yes, no, perhaps, certainly*, etc. Latin questions of the type meant are introduced as a rule (Szantyr: 460) by particular question-words (*num, nonne, -ne*)[9]. Independent occurrences of modal and other adverbs can also be expected in expressions in which someone comments on (agrees or disagrees with) the words of a previous speaker. As an example take

(3)   frugi tamen sum, nec potest peculium enumerari :: fortasse ('I am an honest man and my money is uncountable :: perhaps'; Plt. *As.* 498-9).

A number of modal and other adverbs that occur in one-word-sentences can be found in the grammars in chapters about answering a question with 'yes' or 'no' (Kühner—Stegmann: II, 531-2; a monograph on the subject is Thesleff 1960). It is well-known that words equivalent with English *yes* and *no* do not exist in Latin. Accordingly attention has been paid to how a Roman did express agreement or disagreement with the words of another. One thing should be kept in mind: *yes* and *no*, Dutch *ja* and *nee*, differ from

---

[8] For such questions cf. Szantyr (: 456ff.) who calls them 'Bestätigungsfragen' as opposed to 'Ergänzungsfragen' which are introduced by words like *quomodo* ('how').

[9] Strangely, these question words are traditionally taken as adverbs themselves (Kühner—Stegmann: I, 793), though they share no characteristics with most other words belonging to the traditional class. They do, of course, only occur in interrogative sentences and consequently cannot be expected to occur independently as the answer to a question.

Similarly, question words introducing disjunctive questions (Szantyr: 465), viz. *utrum* and *an*, though differing from the above mentioned question words never occur alone.

traditional adverbs in English and Dutch in at least one respect: they never occur in construction with other constituents in a larger expression. The question

(4)   Did John come home?

may be answered by *yes* or *no*, but the answer cannot be added to

(5)   *John yes (no) came home.

On the other hand *certainly*, in answer to (4), could be expanded

(6)   John certainly came home,

(cf. Hempel 1965: 232 on German). This indicates that the sentence-valence criterion cannot be reversed automatically. Roose (1964: 69) seems to attach little importance to this: he takes *ja* and *nee* in Dutch as modal adverbs ('modaliteits-adverbia') along with *werkelijk* ('really').

Whereas equivalents of *yes* and *no* are lacking in Latin, equivalents of *certainly*, etc. do exist (cf. 6.3.). Of course, in individual cases it will be difficult to supplement these words, for example

(7)   'at sic malo' inquies 'quam cum exercitu'. certe; sed ... ("Better thus', you will say, 'than with an army at his back'. Assuredly, but ...'; Cic. *Att.* 7,9,3).

If one would like to supplement *certe* in (7), one might do it in the following way: 'assuredly it is better that he hands over his army than that he retains his army, but ...'.

Generally, among the instances of words that can be used so to speak instead of 'yes' and 'no' in Latin (Kühner–Stegmann: II, 531-2) we should distinguish between those that fit in with the construction of the remarks that elicit the comments or answers we are dealing with and, on the other hand, those which do not. Examples of the latter kind are *(non)ita, ita vero, ita est* ('it (really) is (not) so'), cf. Thes. s.v. *ita* 519,59-520,19. Thus, in

(8)   (indicat) gladiatores emptos esse Fausti simulatione ad caedem ac tumultum? 'ita prorsus; interpositi sunt gladiatores' ('these gladiators were purchased for murder and riot on a pretence that they were

furnished for Faustus? 'Exactly so; gladiators were intruded"; Cic. *Sull.* 54)

ita in this sense could not be a constituent in the preceding sentence if this were not a question but a declarative sentence (e.g. an answer). The manner in which the buying took place is not in discussion. In fact, *ita* could be supplemented only by *est* or something like it[10]. The degree to which a word fits in with the construction of the expression it refers to and, similarly, the degree in which a word has a clear meaning without appealing to expressions in the context of which it might be a constituent, and thirdly, the degree of individual semantic aspect of a word determines the equivalence of the word to English *yes* and *no*. As far as I can judge the strongest candidates are *ita* and *etiam.* See (8) and (9)

(9)   aliud quid? etiam: quando te proficisci instinc putes fac ut sciam ('what else? oh yes, let me know when you think of leaving Rome'; Cic. *Att.* 2,6.2).

Cf. Kühner—Stegmann (: II, 52); Shackleton Bailey's note on Cic. *Att.* 4,5,1; Priscianus 17,14,86.

The other words which Kühner—Stegmann (:II, 531) mention as occurring in answers to express agreement or disagreement can be said — with the proviso given above — to fit in with the pattern laid by the preceding expression. These words are *sane* ('indeed'), *vero* ('certainly'), *admodum* ('quite so'), *omnino* ('by all means'), *certe* ('certainly'), *scilicet* ('of course'), *minime* ('by no means'), *non* ('not')[11]. With the exception of *minime* they are all referred to as modal adverbs (expressing 'Bejahung', 'Versicherung' and 'Verneinung') as well. When these words are used in answers they seem not to refer to constituents of preceding sentences, as they could do theoretically, but to sentences as a whole. For example, in

(10) tu . . . orationes nobis veteres explicabis? :: vero, inquam, Brute ('won't you go over with us those early speakers? :: certainly, Brutus, I said'; Cic. *Brut.* 300),

---

[10] *prorsus* in example (8) could be inserted in the preceding sentence. The problem would be different, of course, if a manner adverb (e.g. *quomodo*) preceded.

[11] It is claimed by O'Brien (1965: 95) that negative words ('negators') do not occur independently. However, *non* does, although rarely (Krebs—Schmalz 1905: II, 159). I do not suggest, of course, that *non* is syntactically similar to *minime, sane,* etc. in other respects as well.

vero might theoretically stress *tu*, but, in fact, refers to the question as a whole.

From the list of modal adverbs in Kühner–Stegmann (:I, 793) the following words seem unlikely to me to have sentence-valence: *nē* ('truly'), *profecto* ('certainly'), *saltem* ('at least'), *quidem* ('indeed'), *equidem* ('truly'), *haud* ('not'), *nē* ('not'). It may be true, then, that adverbs are distinguished from prepositions and conjunctions in that the latter can not occur independently, but within the subclass of modal adverbs especially, the criterion is problematic. Intuitively, within this class a differentiation with regard to the applicability of the criterion seems possible. In practice the criterion delivers meagre results.

8.2.   Adverbs as non-obligatorily free forms as opposed to interjections

Whereas there is some sense in saying that adverbs may optionally occur in one-word-sentences, they differ from interjections in that they are not restricted to use in one-word-sentences according to O'Brien (1965: 95). This view on interjections resembles that of Blatt (1952: 34): 'les interjections, c'est-à-dire des indéclinables qui, sans faire partie de la proposition, présentent à eux seuls un sens complet (cf. le vocatif, l'impératif)'[12].

Now, what is less clear in Latin is the fact whether interjections occur as constituents of larger expressions or not. Apparently, we find almost all case forms of noun phrases[13], notably accusative (Szantyr: 48; Kühner–Stegmann: I, 273) and dative (Szantyr: 93; Kühner–Stegmann: I, 341) in construction with interjections (*ah, o, (e)heu, vae*) and other words that — being curses — are called 'Beteuerungsadverbien' by Kühner–Stegmann (:I, 796), such as *hercle, edepol, ecastor, mecastor*. Examples are *heu me miserum* ('alas poor me') and *vae mihi* ('woe is me'), respectively. Expressions like these should be regarded, in my opinion, as independent groups, which are not constituents of the larger expressions after, before, or — parenthetically — inside which they are found. One might maintain, of course that within the group a syntactic relation exists between interjection and noun phrase (and, similarly, between 'Beteuerungsadverb' and noun phrase). This relation could account for the particular case form. Interjections could no longer then be regarded as 'obligatorily free forms'. Perhaps one should

---

[12]   See also 3.2. init. on *age*.

[13]   The ablative case is the only exception.

explain the phenomenon as due to the specific sentence type (exclamation)[14]. The reason is that noun phrases do occur in these same forms in exclamatory sentences, even when no interjection (or 'Beteuerungsadverb') is present[15].

The syntactic properties of *hercle* and other 'Beteuerungs-adverbien' mentioned above and their relationships towards other adverbs and towards interjections is not very clear. From the fact that they occur juxtaposed with some affirmative modal adverbs (cf. 4.2. init.) like *profecto, equidem, nē* we might infer that they are different from these (coordination procedure (b) in 7.3.2.)[16]. On the other hand they differ from interjections by occurring much more frequently in non-exclamatory sentence types without being understood parenthetically, as seems to be necessary when exclamations occur inside sentences, e.g.

(11) quem fugis - a - demens? ('oh fool, whom do you flee? '; Verg. *Ecl.* 2,60)[17].

hercle, etc. do occur beside interjections, e.g.

(12) heu hercle! ne istic fana mutantur cito ('oh my Lord! How fast these here temples change hands'; Plt. *Rud.* 821).

They do not often occur independently.

We may conclude from the above remarks that it is useful to regard *hercle*, etc. as a separate (sub)class, the syntax of which has still to be studied. They do occur as constituents in larger expressions. In this respect they may be different from interjections though even the use of these within constructions cannot be denied without further comment.

---

[14] Historically, the case form in some examples can be accounted for as a product of government by the interjection. Cf. Szantyr (: 48) on the accusative with *em*, a former imperative (= *eme*, 'take').

[15] An exception to this, it is true, appears with the dative. Noun phrases in the dative case ('dativus commodi' according to Kühner–Stegmann, l.c.) are only found in exclamatory sentences if an interjection (usually *hei* or *vae*) is present.

[16] Burckhardt (Thes. s.v. *equidem* 722,53) uses the notion 'particulae affirmativae' to cover *certo* (*certe*), *ecastor, hercle*, etc. as well as *credo* ('I think'). The notion then becomes less useful.

Most examples of juxtaposition can be found in Plautus. My conclusions are mainly based on what I find in Gonzales Lodge's lexicon.

[17] We might read '-*a demens*-' as one parenthetic group. On the relation between *a* and *demens* in this case, see above.

Conclusion. The criterion of sentence-valence seems useful, but is difficult to use both positively (what words have sentence-valence or only have sentence-valence?) and negatively (what words cannot occur independently?). This is not to say that a detailed investigation into what words and phrases may occur independently in what contexts is not useful.

9. THE RELATIONSHIP BETWEEN ADVERBS AND PREPOSITIONS

This chapter will mainly deal with diachronic observations, since the relationship between adverbs and prepositions is seen in most grammars in a historical perspective. Since, however, conclusions are often drawn from this as to their synchronic relationship a discussion seems in place here. First, however, I will make a few remarks about the synchronic relationship itself in so-called classical Latin.

9.1. The synchronic point of view

Synchronically the main difference between prepositions and adverbs is that the former do not occur independently without case forms (Kuryłowicz 1949: 131; O'Brien 1965: 101). We could leave the topic with this observation, if no intermediate type of words existed which share the characteristics of 'pure' adverbs and 'pure' prepositions. The fact of the existence of such words was mentioned in 3.1.1. with reference to Priscian 15,3,30. Thus, in answer to a question

(1)   ubi locum sepulturae dederunt? ('where have they given a place for burial? '),

we may say *intra urbem* and *in urbe* ('inside town', 'in town') alike. We might also answer *intra* ('inside') alone. *in* alone would be ungrammatical. In cases like these *intra* will be understood with respect to some place known to the speaker (and/or hearer), inside which the burial can take place. Grammatically, however, *intra* is independent. The semantic dependency is less outspoken in examples like

(2)   (animalium) tota illorum ut extra ita intra forma humanae dissimilis est ('just as their outward form is wholly different from that of man, so is their inner nature'; Sen. *Dial.* 3,3,7),

(*extra* and *intra* function as ATTRIBUTE with *forma*, judging from word order and content). The ungrammaticalness of *in is confirmed by Priscian's words (15,3,30) that *e, ex, a, abs, de, pro, sub, in*, and others 'never do occur without caseforms'[1].

Other words of the intermediate type to which *intra* belongs probably never occurred independently, but can be recognized without difficulty. An example is *ad* when meaning 'about' in expressions like

(3)   occisis ad hominum milibus quattuor ('after about 4000 men had been killed'; Caes. *Gal.* 2,33,5).

If *ad* were a preposition there would be an accusative case form governed by it. In the examples, *milibus* (ablative case) is part of a normal ablative absolute construction. A similar argument holds for occurrences of *praeter* ('except'), *prope* ('about') and *iuxta* ('alike'). See Kühner–Stegmann (:I, 575-9).

These words have different characteristics and can be compared with different subcategories of adverbs. Only words like *intra* ('inside') and *ante* ('before') seem to have sentence-valence. I have not been able to discover any different syntactic behaviour between these words and semantically related pure adverbs: *intra* vs. *intus*[2], *prope* vs. *fere, ante* vs. *antea*[3]. Apart from the presence of an appropriate case form, words like *intra* may have been understood without difficulty by their accent (cf. 3.1.4.). They probably had weaker stress when used as a preposition than when used as an adverb. This may be compared with the difference of stress in comparable English words according to whether they are prepositions or adverbs (Dietrich 1960: 19-21).

Kühner–Stegmann (:I, 578-9) mention the different behaviour of pure prepositions and members of the intermediate type in coordinate constructions. If two or more prepositions are to govern one noun, each preposition governing a different case, the conflict which arises from the difference is

---

[1] Cases like *in Ciceronis* (scil. *libro*), 'in Cicero's (book)', constitute a different phenomenon.

[2] *intus* is rarely used as a preposition (Thes. s.v. 107, 55-68), the first example being Apul. *Met.* 8,29,6.

[3] See Thes. s.v. and Krebs–Schmalz (1905) on *prope*.

solved by constructing the first preposition with the noun, the second with an anaphoric pronoun.

(4)   in urbem et ex ea ('to and from the town', lit.: 'to the town and from it').

This solution is unnecessary if one or more[4] of these prepositions 'can be used as an adverb'. In that case no pronoun needs to be inserted, so to speak.

(5)   in urbe et extra ('in and outside town', lit.: 'in town and outside')[5].

Words of this intermediate type may be assigned to a subclass of their own (something like 'adverb-prepositions)[6] or we may distinguish pairs of homophones: *intra* preposition vs. *intra* adverb. The latter solution is in my opinion preferable when semantically there are considerable differences as well, as in the case of *ad* ('towards' preposition) and *ad* ('almost' adverb).

9.2.   The historical point of view

The relation between adverbs and prepositions is for the greater part seen in a historical perspective. As is often the case, however, in Latin grammatical studies, conclusions are drawn about the synchronic structure from diachronic argumentation. Therefore, it seems appropriate to discuss the relationship between adverbs and prepositions from the diachronic viewpoint in some detail. It will be inevitable to touch on certain aspects of case theory.

---

[4] Kühner–Stegmann (:I, 579) speak only about the last preposition. There are cases, however, in which the former 'preposition' can be used as an adverb: *quae ante et post et in ipsa re facta . . . erunt* ('what has preceded, followed, and accompanied the event itself';*Rhet. Her.* 4,68).
[5] It is understood that we should keep calling *extra* a preposition and not an adverb, though, actually, there is no governed case form. One might maintain that we should, in fact, prefer the term 'adverb'. Syntactically there is not much to say against this. Semantically it is unattractive.
[6] Calboli (1963: 361) calls *plus* ('more') in expressions like *cum equis plus quingentis* ('with more than 500 horses'; Liv. 40,32,6), and related words, 'avverbi preposizioni'. In my opinion there is no reason not to call *plus* an adverb comparable with *fere* ('almost'; Van der Heyde 1930: 127), since it lacks the distinguishing characteristic of prepositions, viz. governing a case form. Notice the fact that *plus* in the example occurs within a preposition phrase introduced by *cum.*

Prepositions are said to have developed from original adverbs (among others Kühner–Stegmann: I, 491; Szantyr: 214; Kuryłowicz 1964: 171; Calboli 1963: 361; Hempel 1954: 218). Among the prepositions grammarians often distinguish 'proper' and 'improper' ('uneigentliche') prepositions (Kühner–Stegmann: I, 491; Szantyr: 218; 'semi-prepositions' in De Groot 1956b: 61). Examples of improper prepositions are *ergo* ('on account of'), *instar* ('like'), *causā* ('for the sake of'). They are of more recent date (Szantyr: 218) and were originally nominal case forms (Kühner–Stegmann: I, 491)[7].

Though, as far as I know, there are no grammarians who pretend that *all* prepositions were originally adverbs, most of them suggest at least that, formerly, prepositions did not exist. The only scholar I know to allow explicitly for original prepositions is Dietrich (1960: 10-1) on English: 'Damit soll sicher nicht gesagt sein, dass es nicht auch ursprüngliche Präpositionen gegeben haben könnte wie etwa 'till' und 'with'.' The words immediately following this quotation are worth citing as well: 'Einzuräumen ist freilich, dass heutigentags die Präposition sich durch elliptischen Gebrauch wieder ins Adverb zurückverwandeln kann'. Most grammarians do not point to a reverse development preposition → adverb. However, what Dietrich observes for 'today' might just as well have taken place in (prehistoric) Latin[8].

The idea that prepositions have to be traced back to adverbs is closely connected with the explanation of the fact that certain prepositions govern certain case forms. Two main positions are possible on this topic and can indeed be found (intermediary versions may be thought of, however).
(i)   The case form has to be explained as governed by the preposition and cannot be accounted for on the basis of the semantic and/or syntactic value of the case, though historically this may have been the source of its use.
(ii) the case form must be accounted for by the semantic value of the case. In fact all adherents of this theory assume a semantic value for each case. In this view prepositions are some sort of 'specifiers' of the particular semantic value of the case.

I will now discuss these two explanations. It will appear that only the

---

[7] Many scholars, on the other hand, consider adverbs as original case forms (p. 47) and then there is no essential difference between proper and improper prepositions as far as nominal origin is concerned. An excellent example of a development 'case form → adverb →preposition' is presented by *unā* ('at the same time', 'together') + ablative case, cf. *simul* + ablative. See Löfstedt (1936: 109-10).

[8] See Hand (1845: 543) on *praeter* ('except') for an exception among Latinists.

first explanation is feasible, since the latter creates more problems than it solves.

(i) Prepositions govern case forms. Position (i) can be conceived of in various ways. For example, just as most nouns are not morphologically marked for Gender, prepositions might be conceived has having an inherent functioning as their ATTRIBUTE of PREDICATIVE COMPLEMENT to be marked for Gender, prepositions might be conceived as having an inherent feature 'Case' and causing inflection for Case in nominal lexemes which they govern.

In this view it makes no difference whether one assumes a semantic value for each case or, as is preferable in my opinion, considers Case as a morphosyntactic category. Rubio (1969: 169) views Case as a morphosemantic category, but nonetheless he speaks about 'mechanical government' of the case, the semantic value of which is 'neutralized'[9].

Another version is presented by Kuryłowicz (1949: 131-2). *extra urbem* ('outside town') must be analyzed, in his opinion, as *extra/urb[em, extra* and *-em* (generally speaking: preposition and case element) being a discontinuous morpheme, comparable with the plural morpheme of German *Wälder* vs. singular *Wald* (morpheme ¨...*er*). In this way preposition + case can be compared with independent case.

(ii) Prepositions specify cases. Apart from the synchronic view Kuryłowicz (1964: 171) and, to my knowledge, all other linguists attribute the development of prepositions (and preverbs) from adverbs to syntactic shift.

(a)   adverb + verb → compound verb
(b)   (verb + adverb) + oblique case → verb + (adverb + oblique case)
Once the oblique case is attached to the adverb, the adverb becomes a preposition[10].

The historical development sketched in the preceding lines explains three phenomena according to Szantyr (: 215) and others: (i) so-called tmesis exemplified by (6); (ii) inversion of preposition and noun or pronoun (ex. 7); (iii) the fact that a number of words like *intra* ('inside') share

---

[9] What Rubio says here, as in other places, seems to derive from De Groot (1956a: 193), who discusses the 'category of semantically "governed" ablatives', in which 'category the noun in the ablative simply refers to the relatum of a relation that is already denoted, or implied, by the head of the group'. De Groot mentions in this connection the ablative with a preposition.

[10] Kuryłowicz (1964: 178) recognizes, of course, other origins of prepositions (e.g. *causā*), but he thinks that syntactic shift played a much more important role.

characteristics of both adverbs and prepositions and can be seen, therefore, as representatives of an intermediate stage (cf. 9.1.).

(6)   per te, ere, obsecro, deos immortales ('in name of the gods I beseech you'; Plt. *Bac.* 905-6).
(7)   nec demimus hilum tempore de mortis ('we deduct nothing from the time of death'; Lucr. 3, 1087).

Phenomena (i) and (ii) are both unproductive and highly stylistic (Szantyr: 216-7). In fact, the best examples come from Homer. In my opinion, inversion cannot be adduced as a proof of the development of prepositions from adverbs. It only illustrates that in prehistoric Latin, assuming that inversion was regular in that period, the term 'preposition' would have been inappropriate, 'prepositions' not being fixed to one definite, in this case preceding, position. Phenomenon (iii) has been discussed in 9.1. As far as a development is assumed it has to be proved, of course, that *intra*, etc. represent an intermediate stage of a development from adverb to preposition and not of a reverse development.

There are few grammarians who reject the view that, in historical Latin (in spite of phenomena like 'tmesis' mentioned in the preceding paragraph), prepositions govern case forms. Still, in many studies the 'specification hypothesis' plays a minor role. To the most outspoken adherents of the specification hypothesis belong Kühner–Stegmann (:I, 489), though their argument is ambiguous in some details[11].

They base their opinion on one empirical observation, viz. the fact that some prepositions occur with two cases, e.g. *in* with accusative case ('into') and ablative case ('(with)in'). The semantic aspect of the preposition coincides with the supposed semantic value of the cases, 'direction' or 'goal' for accusative and 'location' for (locative) ablative. In consequence, Kühner–Stegmann (:I, 490) do not recognize distinct semantic aspects of *in*, but consider the applicability of the different translations as determined by the context constituted by the accusative case form or the ablative case form.

The whole argument calls forth more problems than it solves. In the first place one must assume that cases do have a semantic value and do have, moreover, the specific semantic value which is assumed in the above argument. Secondly, it may be argued that only local prepositions can be

[11] They first explicitly point to the 'Unrichtigkeit der Vorstellung, dass der mit der Präposition verbundene *Kasus* von der Präposition *regiert* werde . . .'. A few lines later they remark: '. . . der Kasus ist *ursprünglich* durch sich selbst bedingt . . .'

explained along the lines set out by Kühner–Stegmann. The reality is, of course, that many prepositions have no local semantic aspect or at least have other semantic aspects as well. This problem can be solved only by the questionable assumption that the non-local semantic aspect is metaphorically derived from the local semantic aspect which has to be considered 'typical of all prepositions in Latin' (De Groot 1956b: 61). In fact, this is what Kühner–Stegmann do (: I, 488): 'Die räumlichen Beziehungen werden drittens auf die *Kausalität* und die *Art* und *Weise* übertragen, indem auch diese Verhältnisse auf sinnliche Weise als Raumverhältnisse angeschaut werden...'[12].

Thirdly, there are empirical observations. We find prepositions with a locative semantic aspect governing ablative case forms, e.g. *pro muro* ('before the wall'), beside other prepositions with the same semantic aspect governing accusative case forms, e.g. *ante murum* ('before the wall'). The reader will remember that with locative *in* ('(with)in') only the ablative case form is permitted, the accusative being reserved for directional *in* (Ernout–Thomas 1959: 10; Perrot 1966: 218). In addition, we find prepositions which may be used both in locative and directional expressions, without difference of case. In answer to a question *ubi est?* ('where is he?') we may say *intra urbem est* ('he is inside town') comparable with *in urbe est* ('he is in town'), accusative and ablative case, respectively. On the other hand we find, answering *quo venit?* ('where has he gone?'), *intra urbem venit* ('he has gone into town') — *intra* + accusative again — alongside *in urbem venit* ('he has gone into town') — *in* + accusative case. If the case were actually selected on account of its own particular value we ought to find (following this theory) **intra urbe est*, that is to say *intra* + ablative case. This objection is the more important in so far as *intra* is one of the words which have the characteristics of both adverbs and prepositions (9.1.) and were used to support the specification hypothesis (the third argument in the beginning of this section)[13].

---

[12] The history of the localistic theory which is at the back of this argument can best be found in Hjelmslev (1935: 39-42). A modern variety in modern terminology can be found in O'Brien (1965: 101): 'Lexically, nominal prepositions express refinements on a basically spatial matrix or frame of reference'. This author regards the ablative as 'positional', the accusative as 'directional' (1965: 187; 191).

[13] Kühner–Stegmann (:I, 490) refer to a certain deficiency ('Einen gewissen Mangel') of the Latin language which forces it to use the accusative case with locative prepositions. It is, of course, always easy to call a language deficient with respect to an ideal picture one has developed. The implication of such a remark is, of course, that the picture is wrong. Empirical observations of the above sort have been rejected explicitly by Casacci (1966: 8-9).

In view of the new difficulties which arise from the specification hypothesis it seems reasonable to accept the government hypothesis. This need not imply that, historically, the situation may not have been such that many prepositions were originally adverbs specifying as autonomous constituents the relations between verb and noun. There is, in my opinion, nothing that forces us to assume that all prepositions have developed from adverbs, implying that originally no prepositions existed and that cases alone expressed relations — incidentally supported by adverbs — which were expressed in historical Latin by prepositions governing case forms. A much more realistic picture of prehistoric Latin (and earlier stages) is one in which prepositions are present — though perhaps different from the ones in historical Latin — some of which were replaced by adverbs shifting to prepositions, and some of which survived, but became members of other categories. This picture would imply that cases functioned in a way which was perhaps more complex than in the historical period, but not essentially different[14].

Conclusion.   The synchronic relationship of adverbs and prepositions is not problematic, though words like *intra* need special attention. Prepositions are always constructed with case forms except in certain well-defined contexts (coordination patterns, for example). The relation between preposition and case form has to be described as one of government, and not as one of specification. In this part of the grammar, historical considerations have obscured the formation of a proper synchronic view of prepositions[15].

---

[14] To me it seems unattractive to set up a hypothetical language in which an important feature (e.g. prepositions) is lacking, which, however, occurs in all the languages supposed to be descended from this hypothetical language. See also ch. 11, n. 6. It would be interesting to know whether there are languages with case systems, but without prepositions.

[15] I have not been able to consult B. Moreux, 'Le rôle des cas dans les tours prépositionnels en attique et en latin classique'. *Canadian Journal of Linguistics* 14 (1968), 31-9.

10. ADVERBS AND CONNECTORS

This chapter will deal with the relationship between certain adverbs and a subclass of so-called coordinating conjunctions, which I call connectors[1]. These connectors are different from both coordinators (ch. 7) and subordinators, which will be dealt with in the next chapter.

Traditionally the category of conjunctions is divided into 'coordinating' and 'subordinating' conjunctions. German terminology as it appears in Kühner–Stegmann and Szantyr is rather confusing. The following scheme will perhaps help.

English	Kühner–Stegmann	Szantyr
conjunctions	Konjunktionen	Konjunktionen (= Bindewörter)
coordinating	Bindewörter	Partikel
subordinating	Fügewörter	Konjunktionen

The category of coordinating cónjunctions is usually subdivided in Latin grammars into four or five subcategories. They are

(i) copulative, e.g. *et* ('and'), *etiam* ('also'), *adhuc* ('yet')[2]
(ii) adversative, e.g. *sed* ('but'), *quidem* ('at least', 'certainly')[3], *tamen* ('still'), *ceterum* ('but', 'on the other hand')

---

[1] They are mutatis mutandis comparable with what Greenbaum (1969a: 25) calls *conjuncts* in English.
[2] The items given under these headings are, in fact, different in many respects. What I give is a selection from the grammars and does not imply agreement on my part.
[3] Marouzeau (1953: 77-8) assigns *quidem* and *equidem* to a distinct category of 'conjonctions assévératives', which stand apart from 'véritables adverbes' like *certe* ('surely'), *sane* ('indeed'), *profecto* ('actually'). The latter type are usually called 'modal adverbs'.

(iii)   disjunctive, e.g. *aut* ('or')
(iv)   causal, e.g. *nam, enim* ('for'), *tamen* ('still', 'yet') in Szantyr (p. 497)
(v)   consecutive (conclusive, illative), e.g. *ergo, igitur, itaque* ('thus', 'therefore')[4]

These subcategories are distinguished on semantic grounds. Syntactically, however, members of several different subcategories can be shown to behave in a comparable way. One subcategory of such semantically different but syntactically similar words is formed by what I call 'coordinators'. As such I recognized (7.3.2.) *et, atque, ac, -que, cum . . . tum, et . . . et, ut . . . ita* (copulative coordinators), *aut, vel, sive . . . sive, -ve* (alternative coordinators) and *at* and *sed* (adversative coordinators)[5]. It is clear that 'coordination' is meant here in a stricter sense than in the traditional term 'coordinating conjunction'. Traditionally, everything that is not subordination is called coordination.

By connectors I understand roughly all so-called coordinating conjunctions minus coordinators. I do by no means suggest that connectors have very much in common. I am aware, too, that since the term 'coordinating conjunction' is vague 'minus coordinators' is vague as well. I would certainly reckon among them *autem, nam, enim, ergo, igitur, itaque*. Characteristics of the latter three will be discussed below. So far the term 'connectors' is intended in the first place as a cover term for several subcategories that are themselves negatively defined. A rough definition might run as follows: connectors are those words which establish various semantic relations between paratactic sentences, are no coordinators, and can be shown not to be adverbs either.

The survey of items given above in the traditional subclassification of so-called coordinating conjunctions itself makes clear that words of varying syntactic characteristics are taken together. Words have been mentioned which are called adverbs elsewhere, e.g. *quidem* (in Kühner—Stegmann :I, 802). The borderline between coordinating conjunctions and certain adverbs seems not to be very clear. This is, in fact, explicitly formulated by Marouzeau (1953: 69): 'Les articulations de l'énoncé sont réalisées par des termes apparentés aux mots adverbiaux, qu'on appelle conjonctions'. He actually deals with both types together at various places, e.g., on p. 74-5,

---

[4] Kühner—Stegmann (:II, 112; 129) establish a bipartite division within one subcategory of causal conjunctions: causal in the strict sense and consecutive.
[5] I do not believe that Dik (1968: 278) is right in hypothetically proposing *ergo* as 'a genuine consecutive coordinator', in view of the observations which will be made below.

with *vero* (really') and *contra* ('on the contrary') being adverbs and a connector like *autem* ('but'). Criteria by which to assign a given word either to the category of adverbs or to the category of connectors — in particular, syntactic criteria — are not given. I give only one example. *vero* ('really') is mentioned by Kühner–Stegmann (:I, 798-9) as an affirmative modal adverb, but it is observed in the same paragraph that *vero* occurs also as an adversative coordinating conjunction. It is handled in the same way in II, 80-1 also, where the argument is entirely semantic and bears close resemblance to that in the first-mentioned section on modal adverbs. The only syntactic observation is that *vero* (conjunction) usually occupies the second place in the sentence or clause. This characteristic is mentioned, however, also for *vero* (modal adverb)[6].

I will now turn my attention to a number of semantically related words, which are usually (but not always) assigned to the category of what I call connectors on the one hand, and to the category of adverbs on the other, i.e. consecutive connectors and causal adverbs, respectively.

10.1. Consecutive connectors and causal adverbs

In particular, the category of what I call consecutive connectors (*ergo, itaque* and *igitur*) and so-called causal adverbs (*ideo, propterea*, etc. ('therefore')) are often mentioned together[7]. In fact, Priscian (16,1,5) assigns these latter words to the part of speech 'conjunction' (which contains coordinating and subordinating conjunctions), arguing, as he does throughout his chapter on conjunctions, from their common 'conjunctional meaning' (I borrow the term from Jacobson 1964: 25). Similarly, Kühner–Stegmann (:II, 145), in a chapter following the section about *ergo, itaque, igitur*, draw attention to the fact that 'Ausserdem wird die *Folge* oder *Folgerung* durch folgende *demonstrative* und *relative Adverbien* bezeichnet:' *eo, ideo, idcirco* ('therefore'), *quocirca* (relative 'therefore'), *propterea* ('therefore'), *hinc* ('in consequence of this'), etc. Szantyr (: 515) refers to these words as 'pronominale Adverbien u.ä. zur Bezeichnung der Folge'[8]. Adverbs like these are said to occur as what I call consecutive

---

[6] According to Marouzeau (1953: 75) we have to do with an 'affaiblissement du sens' in *vero* and *contra*.

[7] Adverbs and coordinating conjunctions are often seen in a wrong perspective. Take Marouzeau's remark on the coordinator *et* (1943: 61): 'une conjonction *et* est dite quelquefois adverbe conjonctif'.

[8] Strangely, this subcategory of adverbs is not mentioned by Kühner–Stegmann in their chapter on adverbs (:I, 792).

connectors. Notice the following expression taken from Kühner–Stegmann
(:II, 146): '*propterea* erscheint als Bindewort der *Folge*'[9]. Conversely,
itaque ('therefore'), which will appear to be a consecutive connector, is said
to be a particle which is used 'vi adverbii' in a number of instances (Thes.
s.v. 529,43ff.; Pasoli 1962: 100), along with its use 'vi conjunctionis
coordinantis' (ibidem). Thomsen (1930: 32, n. 1) calls *itaque* an adverb
straight off. Prinz, in his Thesaurus article on *ideo* (212, 29ff.), calls *ideo*
partially synonymous with *eo, itaque, ob id*. There is a priori no objection
to assigning one word to two distinct categories or to distinguish two
homophones (cf. 2.4.). There ought to be, however, well-defined criteria for
doing so. The fact is, that, as far as I know, no criteria are given. It seemed
to me to be useful, therefore, to compare on the one hand *itaque, igitur,
ergo* and on the other *eo, ideo, idcirco*, in order to establish a few syntactic
characteristics of both types. I used material from Thes. on these words[10].
    The following criteria show both types to be in contrast.

(i)   correlative pattern
eo, ideo, idcirco and other words belonging to the same subcategory such as
propterea, differ from *ergo, igitur, itaque* in that the former can be used
both alone and in a correlative pattern.

(1)   frater es. eo vereor. ('you are my brother. therefore I respect you';
       Cic. *Div.* 2,46).

eo is used anaphorically in order to refer to something said in the preceding
context.

(2)   sed ego eo nolo adesse quod aut sic mihi dicendum est aut . . . ('but
       that's why I don't want to be present: either I must speak in that
       strain or . . .'; Cic. *Att.* 9,18,1).

eo is used in a correlative pattern with an adverbial clause introduced by the

---

[9] Kühner–Stegmann express some criticism (note 5) on Reissinger (1897; 1900), who,
in their opinion, has not carefully distinguished between use as adverb and as
connector. This makes one curious about their own criteria, which are not given.
[10] Characteristics of other coordinating conjunctions, viz. coordinators, can be found
in the section on the coordination criterion (7.3.2.). The causal connectors *nam* and
enim have been the subject of a course at the University of Amsterdam (1969/70; syll.
p. 18-31). See also ch. 11, n. 14 below.

causal subordinator *quod*. These words may also be used in a correlative pattern with other subordinators, e.g. *ut*[11].

(3) quod ergo ideo in iudicium addi voluisti ut de eo tibi apud recuperatores dicere liceret ('you wanted this to be inserted in the sentence so as to be able to speak about it to the judges'; Cic. *Tul.* 39).

Causal and final clauses may both precede (final clauses rarely, however) the main clause.

Now, Kühner–Stegmann (:II, 145-6) draw attention to the fact that only when used anaphorically (as in sentence (1)), are *ideo, idcirco, eo* comparable with *igitur, itaque, ergo*. Still, the typical fact remains that *itaque*, etc. can only be used 'anaphorically'. The only classical example of so-called apodotic use is *ergo* in Lucr. 5, 258-60: *quoniam . . . ergo* ('because . . . therefore'; in 1,526 I follow Bailey's punctuation). Examples from later Latin can be found in Thes. s.v. *itaque* 531,75; *ergo* 766,83; *igitur* 261, 39[12]. Even in these examples, however, the correlation is always backwards, not forwards[13].

(ii)   occurrence in cur ('why? ') questions
Words *referring* to a 'cause' or 'purpose' (though not *denoting* these) could hardly be expected to occur in questions introduced by *cur* and *quare* ('why? ') and by *quin* ('why not? '). As a matter of fact, *ideo, eo, idcirco,* etc. do not occur in the list of expressions whose 'interrogative force is

---

[11] Other correlative patterns can be found in Thes. s.v. *ideo*. Causal and final clauses have much in common. Both may answer a question introduced by *cur* ('why? '). They can be coordinated (Cic. *Att.* 3,4).

[12] The examples in Thes., e.g. s.v. *ergo* 766,83ff. have to be selected. In a sequence *quia, ideo ergo* ('because . . . therefore then') the correlation is between *quia* and *ideo*. In the Thes. article on *igitur* 261,39ff. a few examples are mentioned of *si . . . igitur* and *si . . . ergo* ('if . . . therefore'). The authors observe, rightly in my opinion, that the examples are not much different from anacoloutha. So Plasberg in his Teubner edition of Cic. *N.D.* 3,30. See, however Kühner–Stegmann (:II, 138; 144) for the opposite view. Also Ströbel (1908: 37) on the apodotic use of *igitur* in Cic. *Inv.* 1,59 and elsewhere in Cicero.

[13] Only apparently exceptional is Cic. *Tusc.* 5,47 where *ergo* connects the whole sentence *honesta . . . quoniam laudabilis* with the preceding sentence. There is no correlation *ergo . . . quoniam.* The instance will be dealt with from a different point of view in note 20.
By 'late Latin' I understand roughly the period after 300 A.D.

'strengthened' — as it is called — by the addition of certain words, whereas
we do find *cur ergo* and *cur igitur* (Thes. s.v. *cur* 1443,35ff.).

(4)   cur igitur Lysias et Hyperides amatur . . . ('why then are L. and H.
       appreciated? '; Cic. *Brut.* 68).

(Cf. Cic. *Caecin.* 91.) *Itaque* does not collocate with *cur*, but this need not
worry us, since it is different from *ergo* and *igitur* in other respects as well:
(a) *itaque* can hardly be found in second position in the sentence[14]; (b)
itaque does not occur after a relative pronoun (Krebs—Schmalz 1905: 799).
These differences can be understood if we assume that, synchronically, the
complex structure of *itaque* (= *ita* + *que*) is still relevant. See also criterion
(iv) below.

(iii)   cooccurrence of consecutive connectors and causal adverbs
If *itaque, igitur, ergo* are different from *ideo, eo, idcirco*, that is to say, if
they belong to a different syntactic (and semantic) category, we might
expect that they cooccur with *ideo*, etc. (juxtaposition criterion — cf.
7.3.2.). Though there are not many examples, the results of an inquiry into
cooccurrence are clear enough. These results have been set out in the
following matrix, in which the words in the rows should be taken as
appearing sequentially before the words in the columns. An 'x' means 'is
attested'; 'l' means 'is attested in late Latin only'[15]. On the hypothesis of
categorial distinction we would expect the boxes top left and bottom right
to be empty. This is indeed the case apart from some minor problems.

---

[14] A notable exception is Lucretius, with all (11) instances of *itaque* in second
position. More details can be found in Thes. s.v. *ergo* 760-1.
[15] My observations on cooccurrence have been taken from Thes. s.v. *ergo* 774,68;
idcirco 177,57; *ideo* 220,11; *itaque* 530,18ff.

	itaque	igitur	ergo	eo	ideo	idcirco	propterea, etc.
itaque			x		x[16]	x[17]	x
igitur						x	
ergo		x			x	x[18]	x
eo							
ideo			1				
idcirco	1	1	1				
propterea		1	1				
etc.							

That we have to do with minor difficulties will be clear if we realize that the 'exceptions' top left are also remarkable in that they are used in relatively large number by particular authors: *itaque ergo* 5 times in Livy[19], *ergo igitur* twice in Plautus (*Mos.* 847, *Trin.* 756) and 17 times in Apuleius, only in his Metamorphoses (Koziol 1872: 145-6).

The matrix allows for another observation. It is strange that in the bottom left box only '1's can be found. Why can only *igitur idcirco* be found in classical Latin and why does *idcirco igitur* not appear before late Latin? One explanation might run along these lines: in classical Latin *igitur* establishes a backward relation to the preceding sentence, whereas *idcirco, ideo, eo* introduce a new cause; in late Latin the distinction between the two types was blurred. There are indeed examples of *itaque ideo* + final or causal clause (e.g. Cic. *Balb.* 19; cf. Landgraf's comment on Cic. *S. Rosc. Am.* 112); but there are also cases which are in conflict with this explanation (e.g. Varro *L.* 5,24).

It is then better to say that in late Latin *igitur*, etc. have acquired a

---

[16] On *itaque ideo* see Löfstedt (1933: II, 221).

[17] Cic. *Balb.* 19.

[18] Cic. *S. Rosc. Am.* 112.

[19] Thes. s.v. *ergo* 775,9. The example Ter. *Eun.* 317 does not belong here, since it has to be analyzed = *et ita* ('and so'). At any rate it can be analyzed that way. Methodologically it is unattractive, if two alternatives are available – one of which is in agreement with the rules as far as these can be set up with regard to other criteria, the other not in agreement – to choose the disagreeing alternative.

Krebs–Schmalz (1905: 799) consider *itaque ergo* 'not un-Latin' (= 'daher also'). This may be correct if *itaque* and *ergo* have different semantic and syntactic characteristics, as has been suggested under (ii), as well as certain similarities. The correctness of the cooccurrence cannot be proved, however, by pointing to examples like *itaque ideo*, as they do. A similar mistake is made by Kühner–Stegmann (: II, 145) on *ergo propterea* (Ter. *Hec.* 63).

number of characteristics which were typical of *idcirco*, etc., as appeared already from the paragraph on occurrence in correlative patterns (i). Whereas, in classical Latin, *igitur*, etc. were sentence connectors having their place at the beginning of the sentence, *idcirco*, etc. did not so much connect sentences, but referred to a specific goal, reason, etc. and had a freeer position in the sentence. It may be possible that *idcirco*, etc. took on some of the characteristics of sentence connectors in late Latin.

Cooccurrences as shown in the matrix are usually regarded as instances of redundancy. In view of the observations given here it is questionable whether an expression like 'Abundante konjunktionale Verbindungen' (Szantyr: 525) is correct. The expression could at its best be used with regard to cooccurrences like *itaque ergo*, but here, too, subtle differences between *itaque* and *ergo* may be present. At any rate, it seems to be out of place in cases like *itaque ideo*.

(iv)   occurrence in clauses which follow another (main) clause
Whereas *idcirco* and *ideo* occur in relative and so-called adverbial clauses which *follow* the main clause, *ergo, igitur* and *itaque* cannot be found so. An example with *idcirco* is (5).

(5)   philosophi, qui . . . nec idcirco minus quaecumque res proposita est suscipiunt ('philosophers who nonetheless undertake to discuss whatever subject is laid before them'; Cic. *de Orat.* 2,151).

An example with *ideo* is Varro *L.* 6,14.

This circumstance once again makes it clear that *ergo, igitur, itaque* connect sentences, whereas *idcirco* and *ideo* refer to a particular cause. The position of *ergo*, etc. at the beginning of the sentence is probably connected with this semantic fact.

As far as position in complex sentences is concerned, there exist three possibilities. I illustrate these with shortened examples of causal clauses.

(6)   (i)   ergo, id quia poterat fieri . . ., idcirco non satis habitum est . . . ('therefore, since this could happen, it has not, for that reason, been considered sufficient . . .'; Cic. *Tul.* 27).
      (ii)   quoniam igitur . . ., idcirco ('since then . . . therefore'; cf. Cic. *Font.* 15).
      (iii) itaque idcirco . . ., quoniam ('therefore then . . . since'; cf. Cic. *Balb.* 19).

(i)–(iii) demonstrate enclosed, preceding and following causal clause, respectively. In (ii) *igitur* is placed within the causal clause. It is not a constituent of it, however, but pertains to the sentence as a whole, including both causal clause and main clause.

(v)   occurrence in the second member of a coordination pattern
Another difference between *itaque*, etc. and *idcirco*, etc. is that *itaque*, *igitur* and *ergo* cannot occur in the second or following member of a coordination pattern which consists of two or more coordinated clauses. *idcirco*, *eo*, *ideo* can.

(7)   est enim hiberna navigatio odiosa, eoque ex te quaesieram mys-
teriorum diem ('a winter voyage is disagreeable, and that is why I
asked you the date of the mysteries'; Cic. *Att.* 15,25).

The following patterns actually do exist:

(8)   (i)   clause A   &   *ideo* clause B
        (ii)   sentence A.   *ideo* sentence B
        (iii)   sentence A.   *igitur* sentence B

We do not find, however,

        (iv)   *clause A   &   *igitur* clause B[20]

---

[20]   Cf. Krebs–Schmalz (1905: I, 799).

An apparent counterexample is Cic. *Tusc.* 5,47: *adfectus autem animi in bono viro laudabilis et vita igitur laudabilis boni viri et honesta quoniam laudabilis* ('the disposition of the soul in a good man is praiseworthy. The life of a good man is therefore praiseworthy, too, and right, since it is praiseworthy').

Thes. s.v. *et* 908,81 and already long before Hand (1832: II, 506) range *et* before *vita* under *et* = *etiam* ('also'), rightly in my opinion. In this way the contrast between *adfectus* and *vita* comes out clearly. I would suggest the same for Colum. 4,4,1 and the other example cited by Thes. s.v. *igitur* Plin. *Nat.* 18,227. I have not checked the other examples that exist according to Thes. (indicated by 'al.').

Those who are sceptical about the reality of *et* = *etiam*, i.e. non-coordinating *et* may consider the fact that *et* may be preceded by genuine coordinators (*sed, et, aut, atque*). See Thes. s.v. *et* 910,31ff. For this criterion see Dik (1968: 34).

In *omnia profluenter, absolute, prospere, igitur beate* ('everything goes abundantly, perfectly, succesfully, therefore happily'; Cic. *Tusc.* 5,53) we might perhaps speak of asyndetic coordination, with *igitur* belonging to the last member. The whole passage is written in a terse style, so that it is doubtful whether examples like these should be given much attention.

There might arise dispute about punctuation in (8i) and (iii). Even if it is not accepted that these are distinct sentences, the difference between (8i) and (iv) remains intact.

Sequences & *itaque/igitur/ergo* do occur in late Latin. This is in conformance with observations under (i) and (iii) above[21].

(vi)   cooccurrence with other sentence connectors
Igitur, itaque and *ergo* connect sentences and indicate the semantic
relationship between them. Their semantic aspect is different from that of
e.g. *autem*, with which they are comparable in some syntactic respects.
Therefore, they might be expected to be mutually exclusive. On the other
hand *ideo*, etc., not being sentence connectors, might be expected to occur
with *autem*. I cannot be very confident in my affirmation of this
hypothesis. The Thes. article on *autem* (1592, 82ff.) is not as clearly
arranged as articles in later volumes, but I have no reason to believe that the
few findings I can present are mere coincidences. An example with *idcirco* is

(9)   ita fit ut adsint propterea quod officium sequuntur, taceant autem
        idcirco quia periculum vitant ('hence it is that they are present in
        fulfilment of a duty, but remain silent because they want to avoid
        danger'; Cic. *S.Rosc. A.* 1; cf. Cic. *Div.* 2,25; for *propterea* Caes. *Gal.*
        1,16).

My suggestion is that **igitur autem* and the like are ungrammatical.

(vii)   other criteria which do not work
The following tests proved unsuccessful, since I did not find those
expressions which seemed grammatical to me, actually attested. In the first
place I expected that *ideo*, etc. just like other adverbs might be emphasized
by having *quidem* put behind it. On the other hand I did not expect
expressions like *igitur quidem*, etc. (and did not find them either).
        Secondly, I expected that *ideo*, etc. could be the 'focus' (term borrowed
from Greenbaum 1969a: 20) of a negation. A suitable test for determining
whether a word or phrase is actually negated has been used by Greenbaum.
We may say

(10)   homo non bonus est sed malus ('the man is not good but bad').

---

[21] In (8i) we need not necessarily have two coordinated so-called main clauses.
Clauses A and B may be constituents of another (relative, adverbial, or main) clause.
E.g. Varro *L.* 5,95: *si cui ovi mari testiculi dempti et ideo vi natura versa* ('if the testicles
are removed from a male sheep and its nature is therefore forcibly altered'). Examples
with *idcirco* in Thes. s.v. 177, 65ff.

In this way *bonus* appears to be the focus of negation. Now I searched in vain for an example of the following type (*ideo* pointing back).

(11) Brutus Caesarem necavit quia regni cupidus erat :: non ideo fecit sed quia patriam servare voluit ('B. killed Caesar because he was greedy for absolute power :: he did not kill him for that reason, but because he wanted to save his country').

Igitur I supposed not to occur as focus of negation, which would exclude it from replacing[22] *ideo* in (11). There are, of course, numerous examples like

(12) quos ego non idcirco esse arbitror in integrum restitutos, quod planum fecerint illos ... pecuniam accepisse, sed quod ... ('I hold that they were not restored to their full rights because they had revealed that they had taken a bribe, but because ...'; Cic. *Cluent.* 98).

However, these examples constitute a different type[23].

The third unsuccessful test concerned the possibility of *idcirco*, etc. occurring in one-word-sentences, versus the non-occurrence of *igitur*, etc. I did not find an example of *idcirco*, etc. (e.g. in answer to a *cur* ('why') question). Still, the hypothesis seems right. *Idcirco*, etc. occur in a correlative pattern with causal and other clauses, cf. (i). These clauses may be used in answer to a *cur* question by themselves.

---

[22] In the end this is the same, of course, as not being coordinatable with *ideo*. Heuristically it is another useful method for reaching the same goal.

[23] This test uses the *non . . . sed* pattern, which is, of course, closely related to other coordination patterns. Among these there is another contrastive pattern, with *aut . . . aut* ('either . . . or'). I have found one relevant example. Cic. *N.D.* 3,21: *idcirco* (pointing back) *aut idcirco, quoniam . . .*

Additional note (23 continued):

See, however, E. Laughton (1951, 'The prose of Ennius'. *Eranos* 49, 35-49), who draws attention to an instance of coordination *idcirco . . . et quod videbat . . .* in Ennius' *Euhemerus*, fr. III (p. 223V.).

(13) cur me verberas? :: quia vivis ('what are you hitting me for? :: for living'; Plt. *Mos.* 10-1)[24].

Conclusion. There are a number of syntactic differences between consecutive connectors and causal adverbs. Semantically the two types are related, but not identical. It has been the 'conjunctional semantic aspect' especially which induced Kühner–Stegmann and others to say that causal adverbs can be used as consecutive connectors. Actually, in these cases the antecedent of the causal adverb is difficult to establish. It is often the entire content of the preceding sentence. In these circumstances they do semantically resemble consecutive connectors, which indicate the semantic relationship between the content of the sentence in which they occur and the preceding sentence.

[24] A situation in which *idcirco*, etc. alone might be used would rarely occur. In slapstick comedies, however, such a situation seems not unlikely, where one answers *idcirco* alone, in order to avoid any meaningful answer. (In Dutch, for example, one may answer 'Why did you do that? ' with 'That's why', implying that someone does not want to give a direct answer to the question.)

11. ADVERBS AND SUBORDINATORS

This chapter has to be viewed on the one hand as a supplement to what has been said about connectors (ch. 10), intended to bring this class of words out in full relief. On the other hand, I will contend at the end of this chapter that at least some so-called subordinating conjunctions resemble adverbs, and could be described as relative adverbs, having a function within the clause that is comparable with the function of other adverbs elsewhere. I will use the term 'subordinator' instead of 'subordinating conjunction' throughout.

As far as connectors are concerned, I have tried to show in ch. 10 that syntactic distinctions between connectors and adverbs have been neglected in favour of semantic similarities. This is done even more so with respect to the relationship between connectors and subordinators. Subordinators, coordinators and connectors have been regarded as one part of speech from antiquity onwards (cf. 3.2.; Kühner–Holzweissig 1912: 254; Blatt 1952: 33) in spite of the obvious syntactic fact that subordinators can be used in hypotactic constructions only.

Their, in many respects, identical treatment was (and is) believed — with more or less reservation — to find support in two connected considerations, which are both open to criticism and comment: (i) the historical relationship between adverbs, connectors and subordinators; (ii) the supposed comparatively recent emergence of the complex sentence, especially the hypotactic type. It is problably due to the diachronic preoccupation of Latin grammars that the precise relationship between parataxis and hypotaxis has not been clearly realized. I now want first to give a survey of the various types of relationships that are possible between sentences and between clauses, next discuss the position of most Latin grammars with respect to these facts and, thirdly, add a few remarks of my own about hypotaxis and subordinators.

11.1. Types of connection between sentences and clauses

I will first briefly deal with the semantic relationship between (the content of) sentences. Clauses will be discussed in the next paragraph[1]. The semantic relationship between sentences may become clear in three ways, either implicitly from the intrinsic relationship of two or more sentences without connecting words and phrases (1) or explicitly by means of demonstrative (deictic) words (2) or connectors (3). Since the problem does not concern specifically Latin alone, I give English examples. For the explicit connecting devices I will add Latin translations.

First the case that no overt expression is present.

(1)   The house burnt down. John's thesis was destroyed.

Judging by means of our knowledge of the world, our knowledge of context and situation and the content of both sentences we may well interpret these two sentences together to the effect that the fire caused John's thesis to be destroyed, or, conversely, that the destruction of John's thesis followed as a consequence of the fire. Yet, there is no overt expression of the cause or consequence relation between these two sentences. Notice that instead of two sentences we might equally have had two clauses coordinated by *and* (*et, atque, -que*), with the same interpretations. *And* or its Latin equivalents need not be regarded as genuinely being 'and consequently' or the like. They merely connect the two clauses (Dik 1968: 271-4; Kühner—Stegmann: II, 28-9).

Now, let us examine a few cases with overt expression of the semantic relationship.

(2)   The house burnt down. *As a result of this* John's thesis was destroyed (*ideo, hinc*).

The consecutive relationship is overtly expressed by *as a result of this*, which by its deictic semantic aspect points back to the content of the preceding sentence. (Example of a connecting preposition phrase in English, adverb in Latin.)

(3)   The house burnt down. *Therefore* John's thesis was lost (*itaque*).

---

[1]   Cf. Karlsen (1959) on English.

Here, too, the semantic relationship of the two sentences is overtly expressed, but by a different type of word (connector).

As far as clauses[2] are concerned, the relation can be overtly expressed with either coordinators or subordinators. Examples of the latter type are

(4) (i)   The house burnt down *so*[3] John's thesis was destroyed (*ut*).
     (ii) Because the house burnt down John's thesis was destroyed (*quia*).

These clauses are presented as related by consequence or cause, respectively. As an example of coordinated clauses I give a slightly different version, with *but* (*sed*) as an overt indicator of the semantic relationship.

(5) The house burnt down, *but* John's thesis was not destroyed (*sed*).

Comparison with

(6) *Though* the house burnt down, John's thesis was not destroyed (*quamquam*),

shows that nearly the same semantic relationship between two clauses may be expressed by a coordinator and a subordinator, respectively. In this way it becomes understandable why coordinators and subordinators could be assigned to one category of 'conjunctions'[4].

11.2.   The traditional description

The usual view about the sentences and clauses in 11.1. is that there is a historical development from one type to the other. Hypotaxis, in this view, has developed from parataxis and, in addition, parataxis with connectors has developed from parataxis with connecting adverbs. The development would proceed, accordingly, from sentence type (1) to (4). Coordination (5) is

---

[2] Cf. Longacre (1964: 35): 'Definition of clause: a class of syntagmemes of a median hierarchical order ranking above such syntagmemes as the phrase and word and below such syntagmemes as the sentence and discourse'.
[3] The status of *so* is problematic. See Greenbaum (1969a: 25-7).
[4] *and* instead of *but* would have been less clear, since, as I said, *and* merely connects clauses. Its semantic aspect (addition) is not as clear as that of *but*. Coordinators connect sentences as well, of course. See Thes. s.v. *et* 890, 14ff.

explained as originating in a construction of the kind of type (3).

What is assumed for the development of these types of connecting sentences and clauses is assumed also for the words and phrases through which the relationships are expressed. Two examples: Ernout–Thomas (1959: 291) and Kühner–Stegmann (:II, 172) say that subordinators are former adverbs or former particles (i.e., probably, 'coordinating conjunctions' – cf. ch. 8, n. 2); many a chapter on a so-called coordinating conjunction starts with a remark about the adverbial origin of the word, e.g. Kühner–Stegmann (:II, 91) on the connector *autem* ('however').

Two things have to be distinguished carefully: there may be types of hypotaxis that have developed from parataxis and, accordingly, there may be subordinators that developed from connectors and from adverbs[5]; this should not be taken to imply, however, that all types of hypotaxis have developed from parataxis, nor that subordinators did not originally exist. One quotation may suffice, however, to demonstrate that the latter view is actually held. Szantyr (: 526) remarks: 'In der ältesten idg. Zeit gab es keine 'Nebensätze', sie sind in allen Sprachen aus der Beiordnung hervorgegangen'. For further literature see Calboli (1966: 308-14) and Pinkster (1971: 385-6).

This hypothesis is probably motivated by speculations about the development of man's faculty of speech (Kühner–Stegmann: II, 1) and is supposed to find support in the development of infant speech. It has serious consequences. R. Lakoff (1968: 4-6) has rightly pointed to the fact that the hypothesized protolanguage would, on this hypothesis, differ in at least one essential trait from all known human languages. All these have recursion patterns similar to coordination, relativization and embedding[6].

With respect to subordinators, Meillet, as early as 1915 (in an article reprinted as 1948: 159-74) drew attention to the danger of arguing ex silentio. The fact that we do not know what 'conjunctions' there were in the protolanguage does not necessarily imply that no conjunctions existed and that only parataxis existed. We have, for example, no traces of *sed* and *nam*,

---

[5] We do have indications for such developments, e.g. there are some examples of adverb *dum* ('a while') beside usual subordinator *dum* ('while', 'until'; Hahn 1956).

[6] If one prefers to stick to the idea that the protolanguage is an hypothetical abstract construct reflecting similarities shown by all, or most, so-called daughter-languages (Robins 1964: 319-20), it would seem therefore incorrect to omit what is an essential feature of all these languages. Surely, for example, it would be ridiculous to reject inflection for the I.E. protolanguage. It is strange that Palmer (1966: 210), who is well aware of the abstract status of reconstruction should, however, remark (p. 329): 'The complex sentence is a comparatively recent growth in linguistic history'.

and no traces of the subordinators *ut* ('that') and *cum* ('when') in the Romance languages. Nevertheless they existed in Latin, and not only in literary Latin. Suppose Latin had been lost and become as unknown to us as is Proto-Indo-European. We would never be able to reconstruct them (Meillet 1948: 162-3). It would seem better, therefore, to leave historical speculation aside in a case where we do not possess any definite evidence and to concentrate on the synchronic difference between hypotaxis and parataxis and the nature of subordinators.

11.3.   The role of the subordinate clause in the sentence

The effect of hypotaxis is, in Kühner—Stegmann's opinion (:II, 2) that a thought is made part of another thought ('Gedanke'), with respect to which it is less important. Along the same lines Szantyr (: 85*) defines subordinate clauses as deficient in meaning ('Bedeutungsfülle') with respect to so-called main clauses. It is not clear what observations this claim is based on, perhaps on pseudo-logical arguments like the following one: one sentence (defined as SUBJECT + PREDICATOR constituents + complements) embedded in another sentence (similarly defined) must be less important by its very lack of autonomy. Why, actually, should it be less important? At any rate the claim results in problems.

For a start, there are sentences of the following type

(7)   scribebam epistulam cum pater intravit ('I was writing a letter when my father came in'),

which is almost equivalent to

(8)   pater intravit cum epistulam scriberem ('my father came in when I was writing a letter').

(7) is an example of so-called *cum*-inversum. The difference between the two sentences is that in (7) the father's coming in is presented as something unexpected. In both sentences the father's coming in is the incident which occurs in a certain situation (of writing)[7].

Arguing from Szantyr's point of view, (8) should be considered normal, whereas (7) would have to be considered abnormal, since in this sentence what is most important (father's coming in) is expressed in a subordinate

---

[7]   The relation 'incident' vs. 'state' appears from the tenses (perfect:imperfect) as well.

clause. The expression '*cum*-inversum' may be due to such a reasoning. Examples like (7) should make clear that the claim (subordinate clause less important) is incorrect. However, Szantyr (l.c.) maintains the claim. In his opinion we should leave examples of this sort, which are of a more recent date, out of account: 'Für die Begriffsbestimmung des Nebensatzes ist nicht von jungen, weiterentwickelten Typen wie *cum* 'inversum' . . . auszugehen, sondern von den regelmässigen Gestaltungen'[8].

The essential flaw in the argument is, I think, that subordinate clauses, which constitute a syntactic category, are defined in terms of *semantics*. Actually, there is no need to suppose that there is a one-to-one correspondence such that syntactically subordinate clauses are also, so to speak, semantically subordinate.

The defining characteristic of subordinate clauses is, of course, that they are constituents within a sentence and resemble other constituents, words or phrases, as to their function in the sentence. They may be substituted for these without changing the construction of the sentence as a whole. A simple test for determining this is to see whether a clause can be given as an answer to a particular question word. An example is

(9)   cur me verberas? :: quia vivis ('what are you hitting me for? :: because you live'; Plt. *Mos.* 10-1).

quia vivis behaves in no way differently from a single word such as e.g. *inopia* (ablative case of a noun: so-called ablativus causae) in

(10)   si me arbitrabare isto pacto ut praedicas cur conducebas? :: inopia. alius non erat ('if you thought me the kind of person you say, why did you hire me? :: a shortage. No one else to be had'; Plt. *Ps.* 798-9)[9].

Another test is, once again, coordination (7.3.; Dik 1968: 36): subordinate clauses may be coordinated with constituents belonging to other categories, e.g. a causal clause on a level with an ablative case form of a noun in (11).

(11)   irritati animi et consanguinitate et . . . quod ipsa propinquitas loci . . . stimulabat ('their anger was aroused by their kinship and because the

---

[8] How do we know that this type is of more recent date?
[9] Sentences like these prove the necessity of recognizing suprasentential units. This particular sentence would have been uninterpretable if a question did not precede it whose pattern it fitted into (Dik 1968: 164-7).

v.ery proximity of the place intensified (their hostility)'; Liv. 1,15,1).

The fact that subordinate clauses are constituents within a sentence is clearly expressed by Kühner—Stegmann (:II, 172), who say that subordinate clauses 'in a sense only express individual concepts in the form of propositions' (my translation). It is remarkable that they have also the historical hypothesis about the origin of hypotaxis and the quasi-logical description of main[10] and subordinate clauses in terms of importance. Their exposition of the constituent charaċter of subordinate clauses is made from the synchronic point of view, in their own words (:II, 172) : 'der Standpunkt der gewordenen Sprache nach logischen Gesichtspunkten'.

As for the characteristics of subordinators they mark the function and semantic role of the subordinate clause within the sentence as a whole. For example, *quia* ('because') in

(12) te verbero quia vivis ('I hit you because you live'),

indicates the causal role of the subordinate clause to which it belongs (*quia vivis*) in the sentence (*te verbero quia vivis*). The subordinate clause functions as an ADJUNCT.

11.4. Subordinators

In section 11.3. I discussed the subordinate clause as a constituent within the sentence. In this section the status of subordinators within the clause will be examined.

Subordinators belong to the subordinate clause. This is clear from the fact that in (9) *quia* is present in the answer. In addition, if subordinate clause and 'main' clause can be permuted, the subordinator remains with the subordinate clause:

(13) (i)   sol efficit ut omnia floreant ('the sun makes that all things flower').
      (ii)   ut omnia floreant sol efficit.

(Example from Kühner—Stegmann : II, 626; cf. Dik 1968: 37.) In this

---

[10] 'Main' clause becomes a meaningless expression in the explanation of subordinate clauses as constituents of sentences.

respect they differ from coordinators, which do not belong to the constituents they coordinate and keep their position between the members of a coordination (Swüste 1963: 113; Dik 1968: 52-5).

(13) (iii) Cicero erat eloquens et Atticus erat urbanus ('Cicero was eloquent and Atticus was elegant').

    (iv) Atticus erat urbanus et Cicero erat eloquens ('Atticus was elegant and Cicero was eloquent').

This can also be illustrated from a different angle. Given (14)

(14) Cicero erat eloquens atque urbanus ('Cicero was eloquent and elegant'),

we might ask
(14)' qualis erat Cicero? ('what was Cicero like? ').

Both the answers

(14)" Cicero erat eloquens ('Cicero was eloquent'),

and

(14)" Cicero erat urbanus ('Cicero was elegant'),

would correctly inform us about Cicero's qualities, though neither of them would do so completely. On the other hand it would be incorrect to answer

(14)''' *Cicero erat eloquens atque
     *Cicero erat atque urbanus[11].

Another proof of the fact that coordinators do not belong to the constituents they coordinate lies in the behaviour of *cum . . . tum* ('both . . . and'), e.g. in (15)

(15) dulce . . . nomen est pacis, res vero ipsa cum iucunda tum salutaris ('the name of peace is pleasant, while peace itself brings not only delight but safety'; Cic. *Phil.* 13,1)

---

[11] I take *atque* on purpose. Of course, *et urbanus* would be correct, but grammatically and semantically different from what is intended, *et* being an adverb ('also').

iucunda and *salutaris* may be interchanged. *cum iucunda* and *tum salutaris* cannot.

In being a constituent of the subordinate clause subordinators resemble prepositions which form a unit together with the noun phrase they govern. Kühner–Stegmann (:II, 172) observe that 'subordinators are in a sense prepositions of sentences'. In tagmemic grammar the resemblance is expressed in the terminology: 'relator-axis clauses' vs. 'relator-axis phrases' (Longacre 1964: 37)[12]. There are also similarities like

(16) (i)   He waited until dark.
     (ii) He waited until it became dark.

Just as there is a relation between the semantic aspect of the preposition and the semantic role of the preposition phrase (Steinitz 1969: 68-9), there is a relation between the semantic aspect of the subordinator (if there is one – see below) and the semantic role of the subordinate clause within the entire sentence[13].

The difference between subordinators and connectors becomes clear if one tries to substitute a connector for a subordinator. The resulting sentence usually becomes ungrammatical, not to say nonsensical. In (12) none of the connectors would fit. In (9) substitution of *enim* ('for') for *quia* is possible[14], but it should be kept in mind that (9) is a specific type of subordinate clause (cf. n. 9). We could perfectly well say instead of (9)

(17) cur me verberas? :: vivis enim ('why do you hit me? :: you live don't you').

The following example makes clear that *vivis enim* can be compared with

---

[12] Cf. Becker (1967b: 141) and O'Brien (1965: 101-7), who distinguishes verbal prepositions and nominal prepositions.
[13] In ch. 9 I have stated that, in my view, prepositions ought to be described as governing case forms. Subordinators might be described as governing subordinate clauses if one puts the emphasis on government of mood by subordinators, e.g. in *hortor ut venias* (lit.: 'I urge that you come'). On the other hand this may be pressing the resemblance too far.
[14] There are no equivalents of *enim* (and *nam*) in English. 'For' is not always suitable and differs syntactically (see Greenbaum 1969a: 28-9 on *for*), nor can 'because' always be used. In my opinion *enim* appeals to the knowledge the speaker/hearer has, or rather is supposed to have, either on the basis of the accompanying context and situation or on the basis of his general knowledge. It does not really establish a causal relation. *nam*, on the contrary, does.

vivis alone and not with *quia vivis*. *vivis* would have sufficed to get the point across. Alongside *quia vivis* stands *quia vivis enim* ('because you live, of course'). Cf. Plt. *Mer.* 648. The very occurrence of *enim* in the subordinate clause along with *quia . . . vivis* proves that *enim* is firstly different from *quia*; and secondly, given the knowledge that *quia* is a subordinator, certainly not itself a subordinator: two subordinators cannot follow each other unless the second one marks a subordinate clause which is embedded within the subordinate clause marked by the first subordinator[15].

I come now to the relationship between adverbs and subordinators[16]. At first sight there is no resemblance whatsoever, given the ,description of subordinators so far. In fact, what has been pointed out is that the subordinate clause as a whole can fulfil functions which words or phrases belonging to other categories can fulfil as well. More specifically, certain subordinate clauses resemble adverbs in that they may function as ADJUNCT in the sentence. This similarity of syntactic behaviour is reflected in common terminology in which substantival, adjectival and adverbial subordinate clauses are distinguished (e.g. in Kühner–Stegmann: II, 171). From a less categorial point of view (cf. 3.3.) we might say that particular subordinate clauses may function as SUBJECT or OBJECT, as ATTRIBUTE or as ADJUNCT. I illustrate this with three examples – (18 i)-(iii) – from Kühner–Stegmann (:II, 171).

(18)   (i)   sol efficit *ut arbores floreant* ('the sun causes the flowering of
              the trees') – OBJECT.
       (ii)   deus *qui universum mundum regit* ('the god who reigns the
              whole world') – ATTRIBUTE.
       (iii) *cum advesperasceret* milites profecti sunt ('when evening fell the
              soldiers left') – ADJUNCT.
       (iv)   *cum advesperasceret* tum milites profecti sunt ('when evening
              fell the soldiers left') – ATTRIBUTE.

As to (18i), the subordinate clause *ut arbores floreant* may be analysed (*ut*)

---

[15] There are, of course, examples of so-called pleonastic use of subordinators. They have to be considered as ungrammatical, though the text, as we have it, may be correct. An example is *nam c u m inter Ateguam et Ucubim . . . Pompeius ut habuit castra constituta* ('for when Pompey had his camp established between Ategua and Ucubi'; *B. Hisp.* 8,6). See Baehrens (1912: 415ff.); Löfstedt (1933: II, 224ff.); Herman (1963: 112-6).

[16] For the following discussion compare Ruijgh (1971: 154-6; 335-7) on Greek and Swüste (1963: 136-9). Their treatment is different in several respects.

(*arbores floreant*). *ut* has no function of its own in the clause, but merely establishes a link between *arbores floreant* and the whole sentence. It might be described as a simple marker of subordination. It has no semantic aspect, apart from its being in contrast with *ne* ('that not')[17].

(18ii) is different. *qui universum mundum regit* cannot be analyzed in (*qui*) (*universum mundum regit*). The relative pronoun *qui* does, it is true, relate the subordinate clause to its antecedent (*deus*), but also functions as SUBJECT in the subordinate clause (which explains the nominative case). Apart from its relational characteristic *qui* can be described in very much the same way as *is* (anaphoric pronoun) and *quis* (interrogative pronoun).

In (18iii) the status of *cum* in *cum advesperasceret* is difficult to explain. The explanation in Kühner–Stegmann (:II, 327) runs to the effect that *cum* is a 'relative conjunction', which corresponds to a demonstrative adverb in the 'main' clause, whether this is actually present or must be understood ('entweder wirklich ausgedrückte oder gedachte demonstrative Adverbien'), (18iii), for example, is handled identically to (18iv). The subordinate clause is temporal because *tum* ('then') is a temporal adverb[18]. Similarly in

(19)   qui deum amat virtutem amat ('who loves God loves virtue'),

qui deum amat could be considered an ATTRIBUTE of an unexpressed *is* ('he'). The advantage of this treatment is the semantic equivalence of (18iii) and (iv). A disadvantage is that little attention is given to the fact that, in (18iii), an antecedent is missing. A decision depends on the degree to which one wants to express similarities or differences. I prefer the latter course, in opposition to Kühner–Stegmann, who think that most subordinate clauses should be dealt with along the lines of the first solution. Exceptions are, according to them, clauses introduced by *dum* ('while'), *si* ('if') and a few others.

The problem is whether *cum* should be considered a relative adverb, having a function within the clause, comparable in certain respects with *tum* ('then') and *quando* ('when? '), or should be dealt with like *ut* in (18i), i.e. as a meaningless complementizer. The second solution would not account for the fact that *cum advesperasceret* is in contrast with e.g. *ut advesperasceret* ('in order that the evening fell' – pretty nonsensical in this

---

[17] In transformational grammar *ut* in example (18i) would be considered a meaningless complementizer, which 'is not generated in the deep structure, but rather inserted by a transformational rule' (R. Lakoff 1968: 20).

[18] This sounds as if in this view *cum* has no semantic aspect of its own.

particular example, but in itself correct). The contrast can best be accounted for by attributing the semantic (and syntactic) difference to the subordinator. That certain subordinators, in opposition to *ut* in (18i), have a semantic aspect of their own is apparent also from the fact that some are incompatible with the semantic aspect of certain other constituents in the clause. For example, *postquam* ('after') is incompatible with a future I tense form.

(20) (i)   *postquam veniet punietur ('after coming he will be punished').
     (ii)   postquam venerit punietur.

Following the first explanation *cum* should be analyzed as a relative temporal adverb functioning as ADJUNCT$_{TEMP}$ in the subordinate clause. The subordinate clause would be dealt with as a temporal subordinate clause functioning as ADJUNCT$_{TEMP}$ in the sentence (18iii), as an ATTRIBUTE with *tum* in (18iv).

There are a number of considerations that suggest that such an analysis is correct. Firstly, a number of subordinators can be replaced by relative noun phrases, consisting of a relative adjective and a noun (phrase), e.g.

(21) (i)   quo tempore Hannibal in Italia erat ('at which time H. was in Italy').
     (ii)   cum Hannibal in Italia esset ('when H. was in Italy').

quo tempore could not possibly be described in any other way than as a noun phrase functioning as ADJUNCT$_{TEMP}$ within the clause, just as deictic *eo tempore* would be described as an ADJUNCT$_{TEMP}$ in

(22) (i)   eo tempore Hannibal in Italia erat ('at that time H. was in Italy').

Compare

     (ii)   tum Hannibal in Italia erat ('then H. was in Italy').

Another consideration is that relations hold between verbs and subordinators, which are also valid for these verbs and related deictic adverbs. Take, for example, *habitare* with which (if intransitive) an ADJUNCT$_{LOC}$ is obligatory (6.1.2.2.).

(23) (i)   in ea villa habitat   ('he lives in that villa').
    (ii) ibi habitat   ('he lives there').
(24) (i)   in qua villa habitat   ('in which villa he lives').
    (ii) ubi habitat   ('where he lives').
    (iii) villa ubi habitat   ('the villa where he lives').

These two considerations suggest that *cum* and *ubi* ought to be taken as relative adverbs. For *si* there are no such facts. It might be sensible therefore not to generalize the equation with relative adverbs. On the other hand, *si, dum* and other subordinators have a definite semantic aspect such that they cannot be handled like *ut* in (18i). There are three more arguments for regarding at least some subordinators as relative adverbs.

Within the class of adverbs not only interrogative adverbs, but also relative adverbs would be accepted. The following correlations could then be accounted for.

(25) tum   quando cum   ('then, when?, when')
    ideo   cur   quia   ('therefore, why?, because')
    ideo   cur   ut   ('therefore, why?, in order that')
    ibi   ubi   ubi   ('there, where?, where')
    ita   ut   ut   ('so, how?, as')

Correlative patterns are not as clear with other words like *si* and *dum*, but perhaps this need not worry us with respect to the words in (25).

A clear distinction is made between (18i) and (18iii). As a matter of fact, we often encounter outwardly the same forms in both types. We should have to speak of homophones, if this explanation is accepted, instead of homonyms. For example, *ut* ('that') and *ut* ('in order that') have to be described differently anyway, since subordinate clauses introduced by them occur in the same sentence, e.g.

(26) intellexi . . . nihil mihi optatius cadere posse quam ut tu me quam primum consequare ut . . . tuo . . . praesidio uteremur ('I see that nothing could be more desirable for me than that you should overtake me as soon as possible so that I may have your protection'; Cic. *Att.* 3,1).

ut consequare is SUBJECT of *cadere* on the same level as *nihil*, whereas *ut uteremur* is an ADJUNCT$_{PURPOSE}$.

The synchronic relationship assumed above could explain the development of some subordinators from relative and, furthermore, interrogative adverbs[19].

Conclusion. We have seen that subordinators are not clearly set apart from connectors and coordinators due to too much attention being paid to semantic characteristics. Moreover the distinctions are not emphasized since a historical relation is assumed between them. This assumption is based to some extent on the idea that all hypotaxis has developed from parataxis, which is improbable.

Subordinators belong to the clause they introduce. They differ from coordinators in this respect. They mark a hypotactic relation and differ in this from both coordinators and connectors. There are a number of arguments for distinguishing within the class of subordinators. On the one hand we have meaningless complementizers introducing SUBJECT and OBJECT clauses and on the other hand we have relative adverbs introducing ADJUNCT clauses. It is not clear whether an intermediate type (*si*) has to be assumed.

---

[19] For example, *cur* ('why') = 'because' in Hier. *Epist.* 52,6,1: *doleo cur* ... ('I deplore that ...').

BIBLIOGRAPHY

For abbreviations consult Marouzeau, *L'Année Philologique*. Paris, Belles Lettres.

Folia Ling.	=	*Folia Linguistica*
FoL	=	*Foundations of Language*
JoL	=	*Journal of Linguistics*
Ling. Inq.	=	*Linguistic Inquiry*

Ahlman, E.
    1938   'Über Adverbien'. *Studia Fennica* III, 3,19-44.
Allen, W.S.
    1965   *Vox Latina*. Cambridge, U.P.
Austin, R.G.
    1964   *Commentary on Verg. A. II*. Oxford, U.P.

Bach, E.
    1964   *An introduction to transformational grammars*. New York, Holt, Rinehart & Winston.
    1968   'Nouns and noun phrases'. In: Bach–Harms (eds.) 1968, 91-122.
Bach, E. & R.T. Harms (eds.)
    1968   *Universals in linguistic theory*. New York, Holt, Rinehart & Winston.
Baehrens, W.A.
    1912   *Beiträge zur lateinischen Syntax. Phil. Suppl.* 12,2.
Bally, Ch.
    1965[4]   *Linguistique générale et linguistique française*. Bern, Francke.
Barwick, K.
    1922   *Remmius Palaemon und die römische Grammatik*. Leipzig (repr. Hildesheim, Olms, 1967).
Bazell, C.E.
    1952   'The correspondence fallacy in structural linguistics'. In: *Studies by members of the English department*, Istanbul University, 3, 1-41.

179

Becker, A.L.
    1967a   'Conjoining in a tagmemic grammar of English'. *Georgetown Mono-
             graphs on Languages and Linguistics* 20, 109-21.
    1967b   *A generative description of the English subject tagmemes.* Ann Arbor
             (unpubl. diss. Michigan 67-17,725).
Bergsland, K.
    1940   'Les formations dites adverbiales en *-tim, -atim* et *-im* du Latin
             républicain'. *SO* 20, 52-85.
Blatt, F.
    1952   *Précis de syntaxe latine.* Lyon-Paris, I.A.C.
Bloomfield, L.
    1935   *Language.* London, Allen & Unwin.
Booth, B.E.
    1923   *The collocation of the adverb of degree in Latin comedy and Cato.*
             Diss. Chicago.
Bos, G.F.
    1967   'L'adverbe en Latin. Tentative de classification structurale'. *B.S.L.* 62,
             106-22.
Brinkmann, H.
    1950-1   'Die Wortarten im Deutschen. Zur Lehre von den einfachen Formen
             der Sprache'. *Wirkendes Wort* 1, 65-79 (repr. in: Moser (ed.) 1965:
             101-27).

Calboli, G.
    1963   'Osservazioni grammaticali'. In: *Il Liceo 'Torricelli' nel primo
             centenario della sua fondazione* (1860/1-1960/1), Faenza, 349-79.
    1966-8   'I modi del verbo greco e latino'. *Lustrum* 11, 173-349; 13, 405-511.
    1967   Rev. of Cupaiuolo (1967). *Lingua e Stile* 2, 404-6.
    1971   'Due questioni filologiche' *Maia* N.S. 23, 115-28.
Carvelland, H.T. & J. Svartvik
    1969   *Computational experiments in grammatical classification.* The Hague,
             Mouton.
Casacci, A.
    1966   *Pro lingua latina.* Padova, Liviana Editrice.
Chomsky, N.
    1957   *Syntactic structures.* The Hague, Mouton.
    1965   *Aspects of the theory of syntax.* Cambridge (Mass.), MIT.
Crystal, D.
    1967   'English'. *Lingua* 17, 24-56.
Cupaiuolo, F.
    1967   *La formazione degli avverbi in Latino.* Napoli, Libreria Scientifica.

Dahlmann, H.
    1940   *Varro, De Lingua Latina l. VIII* (comm.). Berlin, Weidmann (repr.
             1965).

De Groot, A.W.
  1948 'Structural linguistics and word-classes'. *Lingua* 1, 427-500.
  1956a 'Classification of cases and uses of cases'. In: *For Roman Jakobson*, The Hague, Mouton, 187-94.
  1956b 'Classification of the uses of a case illustrated on the genitive in Latin'. *Lingua* 6, 8-66.
  1964[2] *Inleiding tot de algemene taalwetenschap.* Groningen, Wolters.
De Man, A.G.
  1965[3] *Ars Grammatica.* Groningen, Wolters.
Dietrich, G.
  1960 *Adverb oder Präposition. Zu einen klärungsbedürftigen Kapitel der englischen Grammatik.* Halle.
Dik, S.C.
  1968 *Coordination. Its implications for the theory of general linguistics.* Amsterdam, North-Holland.
  1970 *Semantische strukturen X* (unpubl.).
Dressler, W.
  1970 'Comment décrire la syntaxe des cas en Latin'. *R.Ph.* 44, 25-36.

Eklund, S.
  1970 *The periphrastic, completive and finite use of the present participle in Latin.* Uppsala, Almqvist & Wiksells.
Ernout, A. & F. Thomas
  1959[2] *Syntaxe latine.* Paris, Klincksieck.

Fillmore, Ch. J.
  1968 'The case for case'. In: Bach–Harms (eds.) 1968, 1-89.
  1969 'Types of lexical information'. In: Kiefer (ed.) 1969, 109-37.
Fries, C.C.
  1957 *The structure of English.* London, Longmans.

Garvin, P.L.
  1958 'Syntactic units and operations'. *Proc. VIIIth. Intern. Congress of linguists at Oslo*, 626-32 (quoted from *On linguistic method.* The Hague, Mouton, 1964, 56-62).
Gleason, H.A.
  1965 *Linguistics and English grammar.* New York, Holt, Rinehart & Winston.
Greenbaum, S.
  1969a *Studies in English adverbial usage.* London, Longmans.
  1969b 'The question of but'. *Folia Ling.* 3, 245-54.
Greenberg, J.H.
  1963 *Essays in linguistics.* Chicago, U.P.
  1966 'Some universals of grammar'. In: Greenberg (ed.) 1966, 73-113.
Greenberg, J.H. (ed.)
  1966[2] *Universals of language.* Cambridge (Mass.), MIT.

Hache, F.
  1907 *Quaestiones archaicae.* Diss. Breslau.

182   *Bibliography*

Hahn, E.A.
1922   'Hendiadys. Is there such a thing? '. *Cl. W.* 15, 193-7.
1930   *Coordination of non-coordinate elements in Vergil.* Diss. New York.
1956   '*Dum* in main clauses'. In: *Mél. Niedermann*, Bruxelles, 140-58.
Halliday, M.A.K.
1970   'Language structure and language function'. In: Lyons (ed.) 1970, 140-65.
Hand, F.H.
1829-45 *Tursellinus seu de particulis latinis commentarii.* 4 vls. Leipzig (repr. Amsterdam, Hakkert, 1968).
Happ, H.
1967   'Die lateinische Umgangssprache und die Kunstsprache des Plautus'. *Glotta* 45, 60-104.
Harris, Z.S.
1966[7] *Structural linguistics.* Chicago, U.P.
Hatz, G.
1886   *Beiträge zur lateinischen Stilistik (Hendiadys in Ciceros Reden).* Progr. Schweinfurt.
Helbig, G. & W. Schenkel
1969   *Wörterbuch zur Valenz und Distribution deutscher Verben.* Leipzig, V.E.B. Bibliographisches Institut.
Hempel, C.G.
1965   'Fundamentals of taxonomy'. In: *Aspects of scientific explanation. And other essays in the philosophy of science.* New York, The Free Press, 137-54.
Hempel, H.
1954   'Wortklassen und Bedeutungsweisen'. In: *Festschrift E. Öhmann*, 531-68 (repr. in: Moser (ed.) 1965, 217-54).
Herman, J.
1963   *La formation du système roman des conjonctions de subordination.* Berlin, Akademie Verlag.
Hermann, E.
1928   'Die Wortarten'. *NGG*, 1-44.
Hermes, E.
1968   'Linguistische Analyse von Übersetzungsfehlern im Latein-Unterricht'. *Folia Ling.* 1, 96-109.
Hill, A.A.
1961   'Grammaticality'. *Word* 17, 1-10.
Hjelmslev, L.
1935   *La catégorie des cas I.* Aarhus, Universitetsforlaget.
1939   'La notion de rection'. *A.L.* 1, 10-23 (quoted from Hjelmslev 1959, 139-51).
1959   *Essays linguistiques.* Copenhague, Nordisk Sprog og Kulturforlag (= *TCLC* 12).
Hockett, C.F.
1958   *A course in modern linguistics.* New York, Macmillan.
Hofmann, J.B.
1963   *Lateinische Umgangssprache.* Heidelberg, Winter (= 1951[3] + indices).

Householder, F.W.
    1967   'Ancient Greek'. *Lingua* 17, 103-28.
Huddleston, R.
    1970   'Some remarks on case-grammar'. *Ling. Inq.* 1, 501-11.

Isenberg, H.
    1965   'Diachronische Syntax und die logische Struktur einer Theorie des Sprachwandels'. In: *Studia Grammatica* V. Berlin, Akademie Verlag, 133-68.

Jacobson, S.
    1964   *Adverbial positions in English.* Stockholm, Ab Studentbok.
Jakobson, R.
    1959   'Boas' view of grammatical meaning'. *American Anthropologist* 61, 139-45.
Jeep, L.
    1893   *Zur Geschichte der Lehre von den Redeteilen bei den lateinischen Grammatikern.* Leipzig, Teubner.
Jensen, H.
    1949   'Das Problem der Wortarten'. *Zeitschrift f. Phonetik und allgemeine Sprachwissenschaft* 3, 150-5.
Jespersen, O.
    1933   *The system of grammar.* London, Allen & Unwin.
Juilland, A & H.H. Lieb
    1968   *'Klasse' und Klassifikation in der Sprachwissenschaft.* The Hague, Mouton.

Karlsen, R.
    1959   *Studies in the connection of clauses in current English.* Bergen, Eides.
Karçevsky, S.
    1936   'Sur la nature de l'adverbe'. *TCLP* 6, 107-11.
Kiefer, F. (ed.)
    1969   *Studies in syntax and semantics.* Dordrecht, Reidel.
Kiparsky, P.
    1968   'Linguistic universals and linguistic change'. In: Bach-Harms (eds.) 1968, 171-202.
Klum, A.
    1961   *Verbe et adverbe.* Uppsala, Almqvist & Wiksells.
Koestermann, E.
    1963   *Kommentar zu Tac. Ann. 1-3.* Heidelberg, Winter.
Kooij, J.G.
    1971   *Ambiguity in natural language.* Amsterdam, North-Holland.
Koziol, H.
    1872   *Der Stil des L. Apuleius.* Wien.
Kratochvil, P.
    1967   'Modern Standard Chinese'. *Lingua* 17, 129-52.
Krebs, J.P. & J.H. Schmalz
    1905[7]   *Antibarbarus der lateinischen Sprache.* 2 vls. Basel (repr. Darmstadt, Wissenschaftliche Buchgesellschaft, 1962).

Kuryłowicz, J.
1936   'Dérivation lexicale et dérivation syntaxique (contribution à la théorie des parties du discours)'. *B.S.L.* 37, 79-92 (repr. 1960, 41-50).
1949   'Le problème du classement des cas'. *Biuletyn Polskiego Towarzystwa Jezykoznarnezego* 9, 20-43 (quoted from 1960: 131-50).
1954   'Remarques sur le comparatif'. In: *Festschrift Debrunner*, 251-7 (quoted from 1960: 164-71).
1960   *Esquisses linguistiques.* Wroclaw, Polish Academy.
1964   *The inflectional categories of Indo-European.* Heidelberg, Winter.
Kühner, R. & F. Holzweissig
1912²   *Ausführliche Grammatik der lateinischen Sprache I. Elementar-, Formen- und Wortlehre.* Hannover (repr. Wissenschaftliche Buchgesellschaft, Darmstadt, 1966).
Kühner, R. & C. Stegmann
1912²   *Ausführliche Grammatik der lateinischen Sprache II. Satzlehre.* Hannover (abbrev.: Kühner–Stegmann; repr. Darmstadt, Wissenschaftliche Buchgesellschaft, 1962).

Lakoff, G.
1968   'Instrumental adverbs and the concept of deep structure'. *FoL* 4, 4-29.
Lakoff, G. & J.R. Ross
1966   'Criterion for Verb Phrase constituency'. *Mathematical Linguistics and Automatic Translation* Report No NSF-17. Computational Laboratory of Harvard University.
Lakoff, R.T.
1968   *Abstract syntax and Latin complementation.* Cambridge (Mass.), MIT.
Landgraf, G.
1914²   *Cic. Pro Sex. Roscio Amerino* (comm.). Leipzig, Teubner (repr. Hildesheim, Olms, 1966).
Lausberg, H.
1960   *Handbuch der literarischen Rhetorik.* 2 vls. München, Hueber.
Leumann, M.
1926-8 *Lateinische Grammatik I. Laut- und Formenlehre.* München, Beck (repr. 1965).
Lewis, C.T. & C. Short
1879   *Latin Dictionary.* Oxford, U.P.
Lodge, G.
1904-24 *Lexicon Plautinum.* Leipzig, Teubner (repr. Hildesheim, Olms, 1967).
Löfstedt, B.
1967   'Bemerkungen zum Adverb im Lateinischen'. *IF* 72, 79-109.
Löfstedt, E.
1936   *Vermischte Studien zur lateinischen Sprachkunde und Syntax.* Lund, Gleerup.
1942²   *Syntactica* I. Lund, Gleerup (repr. 1956).
1933   *Syntactica* II. Lund, Gleerup (repr. 1956).
Longacre, R.E.
1964   *Grammar discovery procedures.* The Hague, Mouton.

Lundström, S.
1961   *Abhinc und ante.* Lund, Gleerup.
Lussky, E.A.
1953   'Misapplication of the term 'zeugma''. *Cl. J.* 48, 285-90.
Lyons, J.
1966   'Towards a 'notional' theory of the 'parts of speech''. *JoL* 2, 209-36.
1968   *Introduction to theoretical linguistics.* Cambridge, U.P.
Lyons, J. (ed.)
1970   *New horizons in linguistics.* Harmondsworth, Pelicanbooks.

Madvig, J.N.
1876   *Cicero de Finibus bonorum et malorum libri V* (comm.). Copenhague
        (repr. Hildesheim, Olms, 1965).
Marouzeau, J.
1943²   *Lexique de la terminologie linguistique.* Paris, Paul Geuther.
1949   *L'ordre des mots dans la phrase latine III. Les articulations de
        l'énoncé.* Paris, Belles Lettres.
1953   *L'ordre des mots dans la phrase latine. Vol. complémentaire.* Paris,
        Belles Lettres.
Matthews, P.H.
1965   'The inflectional component of a word-and-paradigm grammar'. *JoL*
        1, 139-71.
1967   'Latin'. *Lingua* 17, 153-81.
1970   'Recent developments in morphology'. In: Lyons (ed.) 1970, 96-114.
Meillet, A.
1948   *Linguistique historique et linguistique générale I.* Paris, Honoré
        Champion.
Meillet, A. & J. Vendryes
1960³   *Traité de grammaire comparée des langues classiques.* Paris, Honoré
        Champion.
Merten, G.
1893   *De particularum copulativarum apud veteres Romanorum scriptores
        usu.* Diss. Marburg.
Michelson, D.
1969   'An examination of Lakoff and Ross' criterion for verb phrase
        constituency'. *Glossa* 3, 146-64.
Moser, H. (ed.)
1965   *Das Ringen um eine neue deutsche Grammatik.* Darmstadt, Wissen-
        schaftliche Buchgesellschaft.
Müller, C.F.W.
1895   'Zu Caesars Bellum Civile'. In: *Festschrift L. Friedländer*, Leipzig,
        Hirzel, 543-54.
Nisbet, R.G.M.
1961   *Commentary on Cicero's in Pisonem.* Oxford, U.P.
Nisbet, R.G.M. & M. Hubbard
1970   *A commentary on Horace: Odes book I.* Oxford, U.P.

O'Brien, R.J.
    1965   *A descriptive grammar of ecclesiastical Latin based on modern structural analysis.* Chicago, Loyola U.P.
Oller, J.W. & B.D. Sales
.. 1969   'Conceptual restrictions of English'. *Lingua* 23, 209-32.
Onnerfors, A.
    1956   *Pliniana.* Uppsala, Almqvist & Wiksells.
Otto, E.
    1928   'Die Wortarten'. *Germ. Rom. Monatschrift* 16, 417-24.
Oxford Latin Dictionary (New . . .).
    1968   Oxford, U.P.

Palmer, L.R.
    1966[5]   *The Latin language.* London, Faber & Faber.
Pasoli, E.
    1962   'De quodam particulae *itaque* usu particulari'. *Latinitas* 10, 100-6.
Paul, H.
    1920[5]   *Prinzipien der Sprachgeschichte.* Tübingen (repr. Darmstadt, Wissenschaftliche Buchgesellschaft, 1960).
Perrot, J.
    1966   'Le fonctionnement du système des cas en Latin'. *R.Ph.* 40, 217-27.
Pike, K.L.
    1967   *Language in relation to a unified theory of the structure of human behaviour.* The Hague, Mouton.
Pinkster, H.
    1969   Rev. of Grassi, C. *Problemi di sintassi latina.* Lingua 24, 33-45.
    1971   Rev. of Lakoff, R. (1968). *Lingua* 26, 383-421.
Pottier, B.
    1962   *Systématique des éléments de relations. Études de morphosyntaxe structurale romane.* Paris, Klincksieck.
Priess, H.
    1909   *Usum adverbii quatenus fugerint poetae latini quidam dactylici.* diss. Marburg.

Quirk, R. & J. Svartvik
    1966   *Investigating linguistic acceptability.* The Hague, Mouton.

Reichling, A.
    1969[5]   *Verzamelde Studies.* Zwolle, Tjeenk Willink.
Reissinger, K.
    1897, 1900   *Über Bedeutung und Verwendung der Präpositionen ob und propter.* I, diss. Erlangen; II, Progr. Speyer.
Richter, E.L.
    1856   *De supinis linguae latinae I.* Progr. Königsberg.
Riemann, O.
    1879   *Études sur la langue et la grammaire de Tite-Live.* Paris.
Ries, J.
    1928   *Zur Wortgruppenlehre.* Prag, Taussig & Taussig.

Robins, R.H.
1951   *Ancient and mediaeval grammatical theory in Europe.* London, Bell & Sons.
1959   'In defence of WP'. *TPS*, 116-44.
1964   *General linguistics. An introductory survey.* London, Longmans.
1966   'The development of the word class system of the European grammatical tradition'. *FoL* 2, 3-19.
1967a   *A short history of linguistics.* London, Longmans.
1967b   'Yurok'. *Lingua* 17, 210-29.
Roose, H.
1964   *Het probleem van de woordsoorten, in het bijzonder van het bijwoord in het Nederlands.* The Hague, Mouton.
Rubio, L.
1966   *Introducción a la sintaxis estructural del latín. I Casos y preposiciones.* Barcelona, Ariel.
Ruwet, N.
1968   *Introduction à la grammaire générative.* Paris, Plon.
Ruijgh, C.J.
1971   *Autours de te épique.* Amsterdam, Hakkert.

Sanctius, F.
1704[3]   *Minerva seu de causis linguae latinae* (ed. by G. Scioppius & J. Perizonius) Amsterdam.
Sandmann, M.
1939   'Substantiv, Adjektiv-Adverb und Verb als sprachliche Formen. Bemerkungen zur Theorie der Wortarten'. *IF* 57, 81-112.
Scaliger, J.C.
1540   *De causis linguae latinae libri XIII.* Leyden.
Schopf, A.
1963-4   'Grammatische Kategorie und Satz in traditioneller und strukturalistischer Sicht (Jespersen und Fries)'. *Beiträge zur Sprachkunde und Informationsverarbeitung* 2, 62-80; 3, 19-40.
Schreiber, P.A.
1971   'Some constraints on the formation of English sentence adverbs'. *Ling. Inq.* 2, 83-101.
Seel, O.
1960   'Zur Kritik des Textes von Caesars Bellum Gallicum'. In: *Studi in Onore di L. Castiglioni*, Firenze, Sansoni, 896-968.
Seiler, H.J.
1968   'Probleme der Verb-Subkategorisierung mit Bezug auf Bestimmungen des Ortes und der Zeit'. *Lingua* 20, 337-67.
Seyffert, M. & C.F.W. Müller
1876   *Cicero Laelius* (comm.). Leipzig (repr. Hildesheim, Olms, 1956).
Shackleton Bailey, D.R.
1965-70 *Cicero's letters to Atticus* (transl. + comm.). 7 vls. Cambridge, U.P.
Sievers, G.
1907   *De zeugmatis quod dicitur usu Horatiano.* Diss. Jena.

Slotty, F.
    1929a   'Das Wesen der Wortart'. In: *Donum Natalicum Schrijnen*, Nijmegen,
            Dekker & V.d. Vegt, 130-41.
    1929b   'Wortart und Wortsinn'. *TCLP* 1, 93-106.
Steinitz, R.
    1969   *Adverbialsyntax* (= *Studia Grammatica* X). Berlin, Akademieverlag.
Steinthal, H.
    1890²   *Geschichte der Sprachwissenschaft bei den Griechen und Römern.*
            Berlin (repr. Hildesheim, Olms, 1960).
Ströbel, E.
    1908   *Tulliana.* Progr. München.
Swüste, H.A.A.
    1963   *De structuur van de Latijnse zin.* Groningen, Wolters.
Szantyr, A.
    1965   *Lateinische . Grammatik II. Syntax und Stilistik.* München, Beck
            (continues J.B. Hofmann's 1928 edition; abbrev.: Szantyr).

Tesnière, L.
    1959   *Éléments de syntaxe structurale.* Paris, Klincksieck.
Thesaurus Linguae Latinae
    in progress. Leipzig, Teubner (abbrev. Thes.).
Thesleff, H.
    1960   *Yes and no in Plautus and Terence.* Helsingfors, Societas Scientiarum
            Fennica.
Thomsen, H.
    1930   *Der Pleonasmus bei Plautus und Terenz.* I. Uppsala, Almqvist &
            Wiksells.

Van der Heyde, K.
    1930   'Plus, minus, amplius, longius'. *Mnem.* N.S. 58, 121-33; 385-401.
Van Wijk, E.B.
    1967   'Northern Sotho'. *Lingua* 17, 129-52.
Von Nägelsbach, K.F. & I. Müller
    1905⁹   *Lateinische Stilistik.* Nürnberg (repr. Darmstadt, Wissenschaftliche
            Buchgesellschaft, 1967).
Vossius, G.J.
    1662²   *Aristarchus sive de arte grammatica VII.* Amsterdam.

Watt, W.S.
    1964   'Notes on Cicero, *ad Att.*, book IV'. *Hermes* 92, 395-407.
West, D.
    1969   *The imagery and poetry of Lucretius.* Edinburgh, U.P.
Wheatley, J.
    1970   *Language and rules.* The Hague, Mouton.
Williams, R.D.
    1960   *P. Vergili Maronis Aeneidos Liber V.* (comm.). Oxford, U.P.
Woelfflin, E.
    1885   'Das adverbielle cetera, alia, omnia'. *ALL* 2, 90-9.

INDEX RERUM

INDEX LOCORUM

INDEX AUCTORUM